ISBN 978-3-11-125771-6
e-ISBN (PDF) 978-3-11-065956-6
e-ISBN (EPUB) 978-3-11-065573-5

Library of Congress Control Number: 2021935148

Bibliographic information published by the Deutsche Nationalbibliothek
The Deutsche Nationalbibliothek lists this publication in the Deutsche Nationalbibliografie;
detailed bibliographic data are available on the Internet at http://dnb.dnb.de.

www.degruyter.com

Ethical Approaches to Marketing

—

Positive Contributions to Society

Edited by
Carolyn Strong

DE GRUYTER

Foreword: Ethical Approaches to Marketing – Positive Contributions to Society

If you put the words 'ethical' and 'marketing' together in the same sentence, it's a fair bet that someone will play the oxymoron card. Marketing has always struggled to shake off an early bad reputation, as highlighted by Richard Farmer in a 1967 *Journal of Marketing* provocation with the (somewhat sexist) title of 'Would you want your daughter to marry a marketing man?'. Farmer argues that '[f]or the past 6,000 years the field of marketing has been thought of as made up of fast-buck artists, con-men, wheeler-dealers, and shoddy-goods distributors. Too many of us have been "taken" by the tout or con-man; and all of us at times have been prodded into buying all sorts of "things" we really did not need, and which we found later on we did not even want.'[1] His conclusion is that the marketing practice in vogue at the end of the *Mad Men* era was neither relevant nor ethical, yet had the potential to be both. The problems he perceived were largely due to marketing in America being highly promotion orientated and obsessed with persuading those already consuming the most on a global scale to consume even more, whilst avoiding pressing problems linked to poverty, racial discrimination and urban redevelopment. Now, on the one hand you could argue that with the marketing philosophy, customer relationship management, marketing analytics and online marketing the field has come a long way since then. On the other hand, you could focus on those problems and wonder whether much has really changed.

Two years after Farmer's piece, another *Journal of Marketing* paper, this time from Philip Kotler and Sidney Levy, entitled 'Broadening the concept of marketing', provided something of a riposte. It argued that commercial marketing techniques had the power and potential to make a positive impact beyond the normal realm of buying and selling within markets, and that organisations other than companies already engaged in activities that looked very like marketing. It was a further two years before Kotler, with Gerald Zaltman, coined the term 'social marketing' to recognise a growing set of practices applied in various social settings as 'marketing' and launch a new and distinctive marketing sub-discipline. This sense of moving the marketing discipline towards positive social good was complemented a year later by Kotler's *Harvard Business Review* article 'What Consumerism Means For Marketers' introducing the concept of '*societal marketing*' (developing ideas previously presented in his book *Marketing Management*). This vision of marketing saw the pursuit of profit via customer satisfaction balanced by a concern for human welfare and any impacts on wider society.

---

1 Farmer, R. N., (1967). Would You Want Your Daughter to Marry a Marketing Man? Journal of Marketing. 31(1), 1–3.

https://doi.org/10.1515/9783110659566-202

The synchronous emergence of these two conceptions of 'marketing for good' with similar names created the potential for confusion, something which social marketing expert Alan Andreasen has noted afflicted his field for decades afterwards. This confusion was later exacerbated by the emergence of 'social media marketing', generating a steady stream of student essay corrections and redirected enquiries for those working in social marketing. It is perhaps the potential for confusion between social marketing and societal marketing that led to the differences between them being emphasised for much of the next 40 years. Social marketing was seen as operating in the public sector, using marketing approaches to achieve pro-social and/or pro-environmental behaviour change amongst their target audiences (and those who might influence them). Societal marketing was the preserve of private companies, and was largely focused on harm reduction in terms of the consequences of the production, consumption and disposal of products.

OK, so why the potted marketing history lesson? Because it contains all the threads that make this collection timely and valuable, threads relating to controversy, power, boundaries and responsibility. The chapter from Gerard Hastings shares some DNA with Farmer's original provocation, but updated with new knowledge about marketing's socio-environmental consequences and the need for more sustainable consumption and production behaviours within societies. That means not just the harm reduction that societal marketing pursues, and not just consuming differently, but ultimately acknowledging the need to market and consume less (at least in richer countries). This is an argument I've been making for decades, to businesses, conference audiences, politicians and students. It is an argument that is frequently met with disbelief – 'you have to have growth!', 'what about jobs?', 'what about poor countries?' – are typical reactions. However, one thing the Covid pandemic has revealed is how much our previous way of living and consuming was a matter of choices and priorities. Even once released from lockdowns, many of us chose not to go out and behave and consume as usual because we prioritised our health and the lives of our loved ones more highly. Covid illustrated through a 'fast' crisis exactly the same issues we face through the more slowly unfolding crisis of the climate emergency. Do we return to producing and consuming at levels the science makes clear are unsustainable, or do we change to protect the wellbeing and prospects of future generations and those living in vulnerable locations now?

This last theme is picked up in the chapter from Mike Marinetto, who considers ethical consumerism and the potential of the 'citizen consumer' to achieve change by boycotting or supporting products, companies or technologies on the basis of their socio-environmental consequences. It is, after all, the potential willingness of consumers to reward 'good' companies that forms a key plank in the 'business case' behind societal marketing and the push to persuade companies to embrace sustainability. However, this chapter suggests that the prospects for post-Covid progress towards sustainability are limited unless consumers start to boycott, not just individual companies or products, but the whole notion of well-being through ever-growing material prosperity and consumption. This will involve a challenge to people's fundamental sense of identity to think, not just as consumers or even as citizen-consumers, but as members of a global community, and as part of an interconnected ecological system on which we all depend.

Concerns about sustainability and the rise of the citizen consumer have contributed to a blurring of the perceived boundaries between societal and social marketing, a theme considered in the chapter on Fairtrade Towns contributed by Anthony Samuel and myself. Fairtrade consumption seems to exist within a conventional world of societal marketing in which ethically superior products are purchased by consumers on the basis of socio-environmental credentials. The closer you look at it however, the more it is clear that the Fairtrade consumer is not buying a product like a coffee so much as buying into an idea of a fairer world, and what emerges is a hybrid form of marketing sharing many characteristics of social marketing. With the growth of social enterprise and the third sector, and the rise of partnerships between ethically-orientated businesses and public sector social marketing campaigns, the boundary between social and societal marketing is becoming increasingly porous and indistinct.

One perceived difference in emphasis between the social and societal versions of marketing is challenged in Ekant Veer and Kseniia Zahrai's chapter on the ethicality of social marketing programmes. People often tend to think of social marketing from the perspective of ends (the social good the marketing effort does) whilst societal marketing is more about means (reducing any harm caused by products or their consumption). This can give social marketers a sense of 'being on the side of the angels', making them perhaps less critical when thinking about the means they employ in pursuit of socially beneficial ends. The chapter highlights that social marketing efforts face important questions about harmful unintended consequences and who holds the power to assign priorities, labels and resources in pursuit of particular social goals.

A further benefit of considering both social and societal marketing is that it can take you beyond the 'usual suspects' of marketing discourse geographically, demographically and conceptually. Farmer's original complaint that marketing is over-obsessed with how to sell more products to already materially wealthy Americans still seems relevant. You could also argue that the worlds of marketing and advertising have always been over-obsessed with youth in ways that don't reflect cultural and demographic realities. An interesting clue to the continuing over-emphasis on the 'Young Americans' that David Bowie once sang about, is revealed in a startling statistic from a review by Arnett[2] of five years of the experimental psychology literature (a keystone in the house of marketing). This found that 96% of subjects enlisted

---

2 Arnett, J. (2008). The neglected 95%: Why American psychology needs to become less American. *American Psychologist*, 63, 602–614.

in the research came from North America, Northern Europe, Israel or Australia, while in the leading social psychology journal, 67% of the American samples were composed entirely of psychology undergraduates. Three of the chapters here move beyond the typical boundaries of geo-demographics when considering marketing and its potential contribution to social wellbeing. The chapter from Maedeh Ghordanian et al. considers marketing to elderly consumers across three countries that rarely feature in the marketing literature despite a combined population of over 170 million: Iran, Turkey and Azerbaijan. The chapters by Amy Yau and by Lukas Parker et al. shift the marketing telescope to consider both social and sustainability marketing in the context of Asian countries which, given their economic, demographic and cultural significance, are going to be vital in determining the future of the planet and its population. These chapters all highlight the importance of ensuring that campaigns are appropriately suited to the cultural contexts in which they operate. This can require careful adaptations of marketing theories and initiatives that have usually been developed in Western contexts, to maximise their chances of delivering positive contributions to wellbeing and development in practice.

The chapter on societal marketing in relation to elderly consumers, and the chapter by Erin Hurley et al. on the use of social marketing to tackle teenage drinking (which is also a challenging societal marketing issue), highlight a further interesting set of issues relating to responsibility. The conventional marketing vision of consumer sovereignty gives each and every consumer divine and absolute power, with the marketer's role (at least in theory) that of the genie of wish fulfilment. However, what happens if a monarch becomes too old and infirm, or is too young, to understand and articulate their own best self-interest? It has always puzzled me that people who insist on the principle of consumer sovereignty, and who view any attempts to influence consumers for their own good as patronising and misguided, seem to overlook a range of markets from dental services, to car repairs, to computer purchases where we often need someone to take some responsibility for our best interests and help us to decide what we need. This sense of marketing as something that can help people to make difficult and often very personal decisions is illustrated by the social marketing intervention in the chapter from Erin Hurley et al. which sought to shape the behaviour of parents, and their interactions with their children, in order to reduce the latter's risk from alcohol. Similarly, the chapter by Amani Alsalem et al. adopts a social marketing perspective to consider organ donation, a "behaviour" that requires people to confront scenarios and issues that they'd really prefer not to think about. My own personal experience has brought me closer to the tragedies linked to organ donation than I would have wished, but also closer to the good that it can do than I would have expected. The importance of the issue makes me convinced that it is an important arena in which social marketing can make a contribution, but that it will also require sensitive and responsible marketing behaviour of the highest order to avoid causing unintended distress or harm. Organ donation and alcohol also feature in the vignettes presented in Giuseppe

Fattori's chapter on the potential of social media to be used in health-based social marketing applications. As well as demonstrating the power of social media to influence behaviour, and the importance of wielding that power responsibly, this chapter will also (I hope) contribute to reducing the problem of people confusing social media and social marketing.

Responsibility and identity are the themes with which I'd like to conclude this foreword. Corporate social responsibility has become a widely accepted concept in recent decades, and the importance of communicating effectively about it to consumers and other stakeholders is explored in the chapter by S Sreejesh. It has therefore always struck me as strange that a matching principle of consumer social responsibility is missing in action from most marketing text books and discussions. As sovereign consumers we seem to have (at least in theory) been granted absolute power, but no responsibilities to go with it. This situation gradually seems to be changing, with emerging concepts like the citizen consumer, and survey data indicating that consumers are willing to accept some of the responsibility for problems like climate change. For marketing to make the positive social contribution it seems capable of, a more mutual and mutually reinforcing sense of responsibility will be required. For the marketer (both social and commercial) this will mean taking ever-more responsibility for the overall impacts of our activities for all stakeholders, not just the generation of satisfaction for, or behaviour change within, our target market. For the consumer, it means accepting some responsibility for the consequences of production and consumption, and for the well-being of the people and places from which the goods we consume come. As consumers we've been taught for decades to ask 'How much does this cost?' in monetary terms, when trying to judge the value of a purchase. With what we now know about sustainability, we need to reframe that question as 'How much did this cost?' in social and environmental terms, to make more responsible choices and to challenge the dominant paradigm in which it is consumption that defines our senses of wellbeing, identity and progress.

To a large extent this means challenging our own sense of identity and how we see ourselves, which is the theme of the chapter by McGowan and Hassan. Years ago, I was puzzled within a project aiming to promote domestic composting why so many people who were enthusiastic about recycling were so reluctant to compost (even when they had a suitable garden). The bottom line was a question of identity; these people saw themselves as recyclers but couldn't envisage themselves as composters (who were seen, as one respondent put it, as 'probably an old bloke on an allotment, in a hat'). It's the same reason that I, and many others I know, get in an emotional tangle at the prospect of flying. We see ourselves, and want others to see us, as environmentally responsible types, but we also want to appear well-travelled, cultured and successful – all traits associated with international travel. For social marketers perhaps their ultimate marketing challenge is to market 'responsible consumption' so successfully, that managed degrowth leading towards more sustainable patterns of production and consumption becomes a pathway we can collectively identify with and wish to take. Until we reach that point, perhaps what the discipline needs to do is to borrow a popular phrase within societal marketing practice and say 'Please use marketing responsibly'.

Professor Ken Peattie

Introduction

I have been surrounded by the most interesting and inspirational writers for many years of my academic career, often I have wondered at their line of thought and depth of reasoning. This edited text presents a range of the most pioneering work around ethical approaches to marketing with contributions from the most respected and esteemed researchers in the field many of whom I am proud to call my friends.

The ethical marketing movement has enjoyed a long and steady evolution for many years, my 1992 fair trade papers are amongst my most cited and I am proud to say that at the time I was simply labelled as a hippy by academics and including my closest friends. So, here we are after many years with an international collection of ethical marketing contributions that are truly inspiring and incredible to read. Just pick a chapter, dip in and out, recognise the authors name and read that chapter first, or connect with the chapter title and go on to read something halfway into the book.

This text offers readers a wide and inspiring perspective on how powerful marketing can have a positive and ethically impact on society. It brings together a wealth of internationally acclaimed academics who share their thoughts on a broad range of ethical approaches to marketing.

With the continued and unwavering criticism of marketing across the globe, with accusations of persuasion, exploitation and manipulation and more this body of work aims to open the minds of the reader to the constructive and progressive approaches of ethical marketers. This text reframes the way we think about marketing and society with a range of emotional and motivational topics written by world leading academics from across the globe, bringing together the great minds of ethical academics in a profound and dynamic monography. The range of scholars includes new and upcoming academic given the opportunity to publish their work alongside eminent scholars.

Contributions support the notion that marketing is good for society and impacts on consumer wellbeing, lifestyle, communities and positive consumer behaviours. This text asks the reader to think differently, feel the change that is rapidly developing in marketing through the interconnections of personal ethical values which are becoming interdependent with professional marketing values.

Carolyn Strong

https://doi.org/10.1515/9783110659566-203

Contents

Mike Marinetto

1 Apathy in the UK? The New Lifestyle Political Activism of Ethical Consumerism

Introduction

Can shopping can change the world? Or to put it another way: can consumer choices exert pressures on companies and even governments to create social change? To help us think about these questions, I invite the reader to think back in time. Specifically, to the late eighteenth century and to the eastern seaboard of North America.

It was one of the most notorious acts of political vandalism and direct action in British history. In September and October 1773, seven ships carrying East India Company tea from China, were sent to the American colonies: four were bound for Boston, and one each for New York, Philadelphia, and Charleston. The various ships bound for British America held more than 2,000 chests containing nearly 600,000 pounds of tea. In December a group of political agitators known as the Sons of Liberty forcibly boarded the four merchant ships in the Boston Harbour. Around seventy men, some dressed as Native Americans, threw $18,000 worth of tea overboard into the Boston Harbour. Unbeknown to the Sons of Liberty at the time, they unleashed a social, political, and economic firestorm that would result, some two-and-a-half years later, in the Declaration of Independence (Unger 2012, p. 5–7).

It was not so much the quality of the tea that motivated this historic act of vandalism. The good burghers of Boston were somewhat incensed by the British parliament's imposition of a tax on all imported tea by colonial (that is, American) merchants. And there was a supplementary caveat which added to colonial fury: the British East India Company could import Chinese tea to America without paying any tax. This not only disadvantaged colonial merchants but was also regarded as an undemocratic imposition by politicians unelected by Americans, which inspired the tea party slogan: no taxation without representation. The British Parliament responded in 1774 with an iron fist, befitting the world's first modern super-power. Inter alia, the government passed laws from London which ended local self-government in Massachusetts and closed commerce in Boston. Further protests followed, culminating in the American Revolutionary War or the American War of Independence. The war started in 1775, unsurprisingly, near Boston.

For historians, the Boston Tea Party was the decisive catalyst in the revolution that freed the American colonies from British rule. But those events of 1774 in Boston were the climax of a wider and longer struggle against British rule. And tea, or more specifically taxes levied on tea, were often the focus, although not the only cause, of the anti-colonial struggle. In this pre-revolutionary struggle, we find the earliest, possibly first, examples of politically motivated consumerism.

https://doi.org/10.1515/9783110659566-001

In the 1760s, a subterranean protest movement surfaced against the new taxes imposed on the colonies from London. A particular strategy used by the colonist agitators was to organise boycotts against the consumption of British tea. One of the leaders of the movement, the lawyer and activist and eventual founding father, John Adams, demanded it a patriotic duty to abstain from drinking tea. And alternatives to a British brew emerged. Activists in New England even produced domestic, homegrown tea and during the revolution itself tea drinking declined, and coffee eventually became the drink of choice for colonists loyal to the new flag. It was in these early skirmishes of the American Revolutionary War which saw the birth of ethical consumerism. This historical episode suggests, anecdotally, how ethical consumerism can in fact spearhead and have a role in significant social and political change. But this historically arrived at 'hypothesis' needs to be fleshed out and updated.

Two hundred and fifty years after the Boston Tea Party, ethical consumerism is now a staple feature of today's world and is very much part of the commercial landscape. For proponents, there is a case to be made that it can empower people to act politically against irresponsible forces, namely, multinational companies or even governments. Here, consumerism exerts 'social control'. Ethical buyers are at the forefront of a new style of politics, less reliant on political parties and working instead through lifestyle choices. This new form of politics is concerned with single issue causes rather than broad programmes of reform. We have an alternative style of political activism.

The chapter will attempt to assess the potential influence and impact of ethical consumerism today. It will focus on how ethical consumerism works and the crucial role of pressure groups in organising consumers. But there are inevitably inbuilt limits to ethical consumerism as political activism. This will lead us to explore alternatives, arguing that a more powerful statement would be to change our lifestyles, to consume less. Here, I make the case for a radical consumerism.

Never Mind the Ballots . . . Here Comes the Ethical Consumer

There is a widely held view that political apathy is endemic in Western democracies like the UK, a fact characterized by the decline in voter turnout at general elections. For example, the elections of 2001 and 2005 in the UK produced the lowest levels of voter turnout since the First World War. The UK Elections that took place during the 1950s saw around 80 per cent of voters participating in the ballots. But in recent times the average turnout has levelled off at just over two-thirds of the electorate. At in the recent 2019 election, 67.3 per cent of the registered electorate bothered to vote, down 1.5 per cent from the 2017 election. The historical trajectory of voting patterns, as a measure of public engagement and involvement, suggests that Britain's population is becoming a passive citizenry or at worst an indolent and apathetic citizenry, disengaging from politics and therefore wider civil society.

That could be one conclusion which could be drawn from voter behaviour. However, there is a different interpretation about the decline in voting. We may be no less apathetic today but the population is channelling its activism via other channels. This is the conclusion reached by political geographer Charles Pattie and his colleagues from Sheffield University. They used empirical data to dismiss the popular and rather pessimistic claim that Britain is becoming more apathetic. They conducted a major survey in the early 2000s of civic attitudes and engagement of the British public. The authors called this survey a Citizen Audit.

The evidence from Pattie et al.'s Citizen Audit survey suggests Britain, at the start of the twenty-first century, is far from conforming to this gloomy prognosis about the state of the civic body politic. Active citizenship is still very much in evidence amongst the populous and there exists a strong normative commitment towards citizenship (Pattie et al. 2003). But the range of activism and public engagement has widened and is not just focused on voting. Admittedly, the British public is less involved in 'traditional' party politics, although the growth in the membership of the Labour party under the former leader Jeremy Corbyn has bucked this trend to an extent. Pattie et al. note:

> While there can be no doubt that some people do pay out for others to become engaged, on average people engage in three forms of political action over 12 months, of which giving money is only one. The average citizen engages in two additional forms of political action. Furthermore, while membership of organisations may be passive, in the sense that apart from paying out a membership subscription no further engagement in the organisation takes place, the evidence from the Citizen Audit suggests that a significant proportion of people give their time to associational life. (2003, p. 632)

The other key conclusion to take from the Citizenship Audit is that political engagement in the twenty-first century is more individualistic than in the past. Active citizens tend to prioritise single-issue causes like climate change and people are also still locally active. The Citizen Audit clearly reveals that Britain is definitely not in the grip of political apathy. And one such issue that supports Pattie's conclusions is the growth of ethical consumerism.

Ethical consumerism, essentially, is the conscious application of specific ethical principles and criteria to the everyday, often mundane activity of shopping. This covers the consumption not only of goods bit also services. This can take on the following forms: Firstly, there are ethical boycotts of products associated with companies or countries that have an ethically dubious reputation. Secondly, it involves positive purchasing or buycotting which favours ethical products (energy saving light bulbs), involving the conscious purchase of products that were made without harming or exploiting humans, animals or the natural environment. Buycotting also involves favouring businesses that operate under social rather than market principles.

And certainly, in recent years, there has been a distinct growth and expansion of consumers looking to buy ethically. Consumer spending on green goods from Fairtrade food to eco-friendly travel grown significantly. The ethical market in the UK was worth £46.8bn in 2011. Sales of ethical goods and services grew by 8.8 per cent in 2014 according to the Co-operative Group's annual *Ethical Consumerism Report*. While it remains a small proportion of the total annual consumer spend of around £700 billion, the report shows the growth in ethical consumerism continues to outstrip the market as a whole.

But is ethical consumerism a well-intentioned commercial activity or part of a lose political movement in the same way as the American Tea Party? According to Clarke et al. (2007), ethical consumerism is indeed a 'political phenomenon'. As a political act, it deploys ideas about corporate responsibility in the pursuit of, what Clarke *et al* call, classic political objectives: mobilizing collective agents, lobbying and claim making. They suggest that ethical consumerism is also something that can work hand in hand with other collective modes of activism. The political rationale is that buying ethically can result in social change, Noreena Hertz the self-proclaimed campaigning academic, and so-called Nigella Lawson of economics, is someone who early on in the new century latched on to the potential power of ethical consumerism when it was very much at a nascent stage of development. For Hertz, the commercial growth and expansion of ethical consumerism has more than economic implications, making the case for the way that consumerism can be used to change the behaviour of companies. Hertz' assumes that in the modern economy consumers have more potential influence over the business sector than governments.

Hertz makes the rather uncontroversial claim that despite the long battle for universal suffrage, the general voting public is becoming weary and disillusioned by mainstream democratic and party politics. People are, in Hertz' words 'disengaging from traditional politics'. This is not a specifically British disease but something blighting mature Western democracies. But echoing the findings from Sheffield University's Citizen Audit, Hertz argues that the decline of democratic participation does not amount to an inexorable spiral of political apathy and disengagement from politics. Political activism and interest in social causes is finding other, alternative outlets: 'It is because of the fact that instead of showing up at the voting booth to register their demands and wants, people are turning to corporations. The most effective way to be political today is not cast your vote at the ballot box but to do so at the supermarket or at a shareholder's meeting. Why? Because corporations respond.' (2001, p. 190) In fact, Hertz goes a step further.

Hertz argues that ethical consumerism and consumer choices at the supermarket are more effective in pressuring companies when compared to the leviathan bureaucracy that is the central state. To drive this point home, Hertz points to the genetically modified (GM) food controversy of the 1990s. Whilst governments dithered about the potential health benefits or otherwise of GM foods, the main supermarkets pulled GM products from their shelves in the wake of consumer unrest.

And then there is the example of the sweatshop controversy embroiling Nike and Reebok. Governments did hardly anything to prevent or reform the corporate practice of contracting out production to overseas facilities in developing countries where wages are low, and regulations close to non-existent. But it was corporations responding to consumer boycott campaigns that came up with innovative plans for dealing with child labour.

Clearly there is a public distrust and concern over corporate power and the moral negligence of the commercial practices of the world's largest companies. And, partly in response to these wider public concerns, corporations are taking a more prominent role in society, attempting to alleviate poverty and to promote social justice and environmental sustainability. Corporate social responsibility policies and practices have now gone mainstream. Few of the Fortune 500 companies will not have significant CSR programmes. But Hertz is aware the corporate social turn is far from being wholehearted and remains a practice that is strategically rather than ethically driven: 'Their contribution to society's over- all needs will always remain marginal, and their contribution to welfare will never be comprehensive. Unlike politicians who are charged with looking after their citizens' interests, these corporations have no such mandate. Their motives are commercial rather than moral, and so will be subject to market vagaries'. (2001, p. 192)

It seems that with ethical consumerism, people are taking the matter of reforming capitalism and the harbingers of global capital (corporations) into their own hands. For Hertz, people are demanding that corporations demonstrate more ethical practices – governments are either unwilling or unable force such companies to make such changes. And says Hertz, these are not the demands of what she calls 'the brown rice-eating sandal-wearing brigade', but of wide- spread demands amongst consumers for corporate social responsibility, transparency and integrity. Hertz quotes one survey which revealed that 60 per cent of British consumers are prepared to boycott companies or products because of ethical standards. In America, the number of would-be product boycotters is higher according to Hertz: around 75 per cent of American would boycott companies for selling products made in sweatshops.

Government in Hertz' reckoning is secretly happy for consumer boycotts to manifest themselves: 'And while corporations, bidden by consumers, are increasingly taking on the role of global politicians, what are politicians doing? They are tacitly endorsing consumer activism. Consumer politics is the new politics, and politicians are stepping aside to make space so that consumers can become to an ever-greater extent agents of political change.' (2001, p. 191) So how does ethical consumer boycotting work and is it as effective as Hertz makes out?

Ethical Consumerism as Boycotting

One of the formative studies of ethical consumerism in the field of business ethics is Craig Smith's 1990 book *Morality and the Market: Consumer Pressure for Corporate Accountability*. The book is concerned with how market mechanisms and pressures can regulate businesses to behave responsibly. This broad social and philosophical question is explored through a specific analysis of ethical consumerism. Here Smith is concerned to address a number of key social concerns and issues about the impact of ethical consumerism: 'whether consumer sovereignty does affect social responsibility in business, the method by which this is achieved, and the success or potential of this method – whether consumer sovereignty does affect social responsibility in business' (1990, p. 278).

Key to the success of ethical consumerism is information. Ethical consumers come to rely first and foremost on the information furnished by product labelling. There is evidence to suggest that the number of products – especially foods – that are providing ethical signals and sustainable information labels for consumers is growing. Ethical labelling has even become a victim of its own success. There is evidence to suggest the proliferation of ethical labelling on products is confusing rather than informing consumers. A Which? Survey in 2010 found ethical labels were recognized by around 20 per cent of consumers. The effectiveness of labelling is questionable. But modern digital social media offer a way through the labelling morass.

For Smith (1990), labelling and product information are not enough to harness the power of consumers. The process of encouraging and informing consumers about their ethical choices also depends on the activities of pressure groups. They provide the strategic and informational know-how for raising the awareness of consumers about issues and for mobilizing their shopping habits. Probably one of the best and most notorious examples of how consumers can be mobilized at the hands of pressure groups and activists is the Nestlé baby milk scandal and subsequent boycott.

The Nestlé boycott's origins go back to the economic post-war boom. One of the major health developments in these years saw a major shift in the West from breast-feeding to bottle-feeding. By the 1950s, breastfeeding was regarded as something for and of the subaltern classes. The practice was considered old-fashioned and for mothers who could not afford infant formula. Breast feeding in the post-war years was also discouraged by medical practitioners and the media. In this vacuum, companies marketed and sold formulae baby milk as a convenient alternative to breast-feeding. Hence a whole industry emerged. And even today infant formula remains a $11.5-billion market. In fact, the founder of Nestlé, the pharmacist Henri Nestlé, invented baby formula in 1867. Using twentieth century advertising, and medical support, formula milk become a mass market product. In contrast to breastfeeding, the use of infant formulae, bottled milk was sold as being more convenient and less messy. The use of bottle-feed at the time was supported by science given the impression it was more nutritious and a better alternative to breast milk – of course, today, we know this is false. This is how companies that developed infant formula milk marketed their new product – a mixture of modern convenience and science.

The baby formulae business ran into a major demographic problem. With growing prosperity in the West during the 1960s, birth rates fell and invariably so did sales of formulae milk. And this was a highly lucrative market that companies were loathe to relinquish. Hence, Nestlé as leaders of the bottled milk market began the search for new markets (Krasny, 2012). Nestlé looked to developing countries, and thus began an aggressive marketing campaign aimed at new mothers, using samples to win them over to the bottled feeding. The marketing and selling, by Nestlé, of infant formula in Africa, South America, and south Asian countries had direct health consequences. According to one New York Times report from 1984, the sale of formulae milk in the developing world was a flagrant abuse of infant health: 'Critics of Nestle have contended that in poor countries it has been selling infant formula, a substitute for breast feeding, without regard to its proper use. The critics say illiteracy and poor sanitary conditions, including a lack of refrigeration and clean water, can lead to misuse of the formula, causing dietary deficiencies and serious illness.'

Pressure groups and NGOs were crucial in raising awareness about the formulae industry's – led by companies such as Nestlé – exploitative marketing and selling practices (Smith 1990). For instance, the New Internationalist exposed Nestlé's marketing in a 1973 pamphlet *Babies Mean Business*. It described how the company got mothers from the developing world dependent on baby formula. It was the UK based War On Want pressure group's leaflet *The Baby Killer* published in 1974, that helped raise international consciousness about the baby formula industry and galvanised the boycott campaign against Nestlé products. The campaign against Nestlé became the longest running consumer boycott in history. As well as mobilising consumers, the boycott campaign also drew in trade unions, faith groups, student unions, universities.

The organization of consumers does not just rely on collective actors (namely, pressure groups). In a media saturated world, individual agents have helped raise awareness and organizing consumers. These individual agents can be termed, to use Howard Becker's term, 'moral entrepreneurs'. These are leading or high-profile figures who act as crusaders for certain causes. And it would be easy to regard the moral entrepreneur as 'a meddling busybody, interested in forcing his own morals on others. But this is a one-sided view. Many moral crusades have strong humanitarian overtones . . . He believes that if they do what is right it will be good for them' (Becker 1995, p. 169). These moral entrepreneurs are celebrities. And there has been no shortage of celebrity backing of the Nestlé boycott, including A-List actors Emma Thompson, Felicity Kendal, and Julie Waters.

Organising boycotts is one thing but what about their impact? The most pertinent concern that Smith attempts to address about ethical consumerism is whether consumer sovereignty does affect social responsibility in business. We can see in the Nestlé boycott that the targeted company had accepted certain international marketing standards. In 2017, Nestlé's published a document of its Procedures for the Implementation of the WHO International Code of Marketing of Breast Milk Substitutes. However, Mike Mulller (2013) the author the original War on Want milk scandal report of 1974, *Baby Killer*, is sceptical about the whether the campaign has been truly successful: 'However, for Nestlé and the rest of the global food industry, the baby milk scandal has grown up rather than gone away. The industry today stands accused of harming the health of whole nations, not just their babies. New York mayor Michael Bloomberg has committed his own money to a campaign against unhealthy food, comparing this to his fight against the tobacco industry'. And so, the campaign and boycott against Nestlé is still operational to this day – with it being more of an online based campaign organised by International Nestlé Boycott Committee.

The Political Limits of Boycotting

The ongoing and unending story of the Nestlé boycott underlines limitations to how far ethical consumerism, especially ethical boycotts, can exert social control on business. The Nestlé boycott is still relevant for the simple reason that it has, even after forty years, not achieved all of its aims. There have been some triumphs, but it is uncertain as to whether it was the boycott itself that caused Nestlé to agree to certain demands from pressure groups. Boycotts may contribute only to a limited extent to any success. As Smith notes, boycotts need to be part of a broader range of tactics and strategies – they are not sufficient on their own. As Smith acknowledges ethical consumer action should not be seen in isolation from other tactics and these other tactics are crucial for consumer boycotts to have any traction on companies.

As Craig Smith argues in *Morality and the Market* there are several reasons why the power of consumer boycott campaigns is always circumscribed. There are a number of factors that weaken the power of markets in the social control of business. There are for a start various whitewashing tactics employed by companies to counteract boycotts. They can also use corporate social responsibility to deflect any criticisms or take part in third party activities organised by the likes of NGOs to show they are attempting to address consumer concerns. Nothing substantive may change despite the boycotters efforts to demand compliance with ethical standards. This seems to be the case with the Nestlé boycott campaign.

One of the main weaknesses of boycott campaigns is that not all companies are vulnerable to consumer boycotts, argues Smith. The most vulnerable companies are those businesses that are consumer-oriented and focused. These are companies whose commercial model depends on selling products to consumers. Some of the companies with the worst track records, in terms of environmental and social impact, are neither consumer-facing or dependent on a retail market. The oil extraction services company Halliburton is one such company, which is often included in top lists of the most unethical companies. This business has no high street presence as it provides services for the oil extraction industry – making it highly culpable in environmental degradation. Halliburton is also regarded as profiteering from war – specifically the Iraq War. Since the war started in 2003, Halliburton has benefited from $39.5 billion worth of federal contracts. How can consumer boycotts target such a divisive and compromised company? Boycotts against Halliburton would be useless. And this is a company whose impact on the global sphere and its potential contribution to human misery far outweighs that of Nestlé's.

So how effective are consumer boycotts when targeting companies that are vulnerable to such politically motivated consumer behaviour? Smith makes the rather paradoxical claim: consumer boycotts may be successful in the social control of business without being effective. For Smith, consumer boycotts may fail to apply commercial pressures on companies that are targeted for their irresponsibility or negligence. Evidence seems to suggest that consumer boycotts have a negligent impact on the bottom-line – whether the company being targeted is Nestlé for its complicity in the baby milk scandal or Barclays Bank for investing in apartheid South Africa. The consumer boycott exerts limited influence in making companies more responsible – unable to hit home where it matters: in profits. But the consumer boycott may still be a success in forcing an ethical agenda on companies. How so?

For Smith, the influence of ethical boycotts rests with its symbolic influence. Here, moral pressure exerted via the force of the symbolic protest of the boycott may be enough to achieve change. Smith argues that symbolic boycotts succeed because of how they impact on the corporate image, undermining the idea that targeted companies are fine moral actors. These boycotts also distract executives and managers, displacing the routines of commercial activities. According to Smith, it is moral obligation working with markets that leads to ethical control over business. The market operating through consumer choice – or the avoidance of certain purchases – still has an important role to play in the control of companies. Hence, ethical purchase behaviour in the form of boycotts can provide a deterrent, encouraging corporate social responsibility, or curbing corporate excesses (1990, p. 284).

We need to be realistic about the ethical boycotter and not get caught in the type of hyperbolic claims made by the cheerleaders of ethical consumerism – Noreena Hertz being an example. Not all consumers are enfranchised or have the economic earning power to boycott particular companies or goods. The role of legislation should not be overlooked as a means to reforming the corporate sector and in acting as a bulwark against corporate power – consumers do not necessarily trump government despite Noreena Hertz' claims. As Smith notes: 'It is important not to overstate the potential of the market for the social control of business. The role of politics . . . should not be forgotten. Many issues are particular to government and legislative action. Many issues could not be resolved by ethical purchase behaviour because the firms involved are not susceptible to it' (1990, p. 284). In such cases, the role of government, rather than the aggregated decisions of ethical consumers, is more decisive and crucial. Boycotting is not the whole story. There is another form of ethical consumerism, which relies on a positive form of action.

From Political Boycotting to Ethical Buycotting . . . (and Dualcotting)

Not all forms of ethical consumerism are about the avoidance of companies and goods. There is 'buycotting' – which I have already referred to as positive purchasing which favours ethical products and businesses. Boycotting and buycotting are both forms of ethically motived consumerism. But there are fundamental differences between these two forms of ethical consumerism? According to Lisa Nielson these two ethical consumer practices, or what she terms political consumerism, differ in substantive ways: 'Boycotts are often favoured by activist groups who lean toward protest strategies, and buycotters are more oriented toward rewarding strategies . . . In addition, boycotts commonly target single businesses, whereas buycotts are usually multitarget (for example, union-made products). These differences raise the question of how much uniformity we should expect among political consumers' (Nielson 2010, p. 215).

There are also differences when it comes to the attitudes and psychological makeup of those with a tendency to buycotting as opposed to boycotting. According to Copeland (2014), consumers who boycott are likely to be reward or goal-oriented individuals. Lisa Neilson's research, in this respect, offers further insights into the characteristics and psychological make-up of buycotters. Her study reveals how buycotters trust official institutions and sources of information, especially that emanating from media bodies. And this makes sense. As Smith showed, ethical consumerism, especially the positive variety, is dependent on information about the ethical sourcing and origins of products. The buycotter will be someone who trusts official sources of information whether from the media or government. As Neilson observes: 'An individual with greater levels of generalized trust should be more likely to believe and act on information that is shared. As well, without the media attention afforded to boycotts, generalized trust might replace evidence of collective action as motivation for buycotting' (Neilson 2010, p. 216). Neilson logically extends this point by noting that the average buycotter will tend to trust political institutions. The simple reason being that boycotting is associated with trust in governing institutions and politicians: those who engage in such action believe governments will be responsive and attentive to their activism. Hence, they are motivated to act as boycotters convinced that politicians will be listening and willing to act on what they hear.

The purpose of buycotting is to harness consumer choice as a way of contributing to the broader commonweal. The motives behind such consumer behaviour tends to be altruistic rather than punitive. Again, this is perfectly logical and makes sense on a psychological and social level. Buycotting certainly requires a greater conscious effort and is demanding for the consumer. To shop ethically as a buycotter often comes at 'the cost of lost convenience, higher prices, and lessened choice, to consume in a way that supports desirable business practices.' (Nielson 2010, p. 217) Neilson's conclusion relies on simplistic psychological tropes: the person with an altruistic personality will be attracted to the supportive purpose of buycotting. The boycotter on the other hand is a competitive type.

What happens when the same consumer engages in both boycotting and buycotting which is not beyond the realms of possibility in the real world outside of the abstract confines of the academic paper? This has a name: 'dualcotting'. Studies conducted by both Neilson and Copeland demonstrate political consumerism can often involve boycotting and boycotting. More than one-third of the respondents in Neilson's sample survey were political consumers in 2002–2003. According to Copeland there are a number of distinct social-economic characteristics which predict dualcotting behaviour. There is the obvious characteristic of education and political interest, which are key resources for dualcotting and this is also the case for boycotting and buycotting. But Copeland goes on to say: 'On the other hand, many predictors associated with dualcotting are not associated with the acts alone, including: income, gender, external efficacy, strength of party identification and strength of ideology. Unlike boycotting and buycotting, dualcotting is characterized by higher levels of income and higher levels of external efficacy.' (2014, p. 184–185) Copeland also claims dualcotters are more likely to be female.

Indeed, research consistently shows politicised consumer behaviour is gendered. Politically and ethically motivated consumerism is something that young professional women tend to engage in more than their male counterparts. For Neilson, the reason is simple: political consumerism can be integrated easily into familiar, day-to-day activities which means not conforming to male-dominated political roles or demands: 'This explanation is more applicable to buycotting because boycotting is more likely to take place as part of a structured organization.' (2010, p. 217) But with boycotting there are no gender differences.

Neilson concludes from her findings that politicised buyer behaviour is ubiquitous: 'Given the ubiquity of socially responsible products in today's marketplace, political consumerism appears to be becoming more mainstream. This may motivate further examination of the role of political consumerism as a means of social change.' (2010, p. 225) To explore this further we return to boycotting. The question is whether consumer boycotting can result in meaningful social change is one worth exploring, demanding further reflection.

No Holidays in the Sun ... Boycotting Consumption and the Rise of 'Flygsam'

American journalist Orge Castellano in a 2018 article confidently claimed that buy-cotting is the new political activism of the twenty-first century:

> Nowadays, a new mode of political activism has emerged, the reverse modality of boycott: The Buycott, which is, actively buying products that respect certain values or ethics in order to generate a movement towards fairer production processes, both from an environmental and human point of view. Today, consumer activism not only focuses on stop buying a certain product or brand but on making conscious, ethical purchases. These two behaviours, both active and passive, integrate what is known as *conscious consumption* or *political consumption*.   [sic.]

The ethical market keeps growing, exponentially so. Between 2011 and 2017, it doubled. The ethical market is worth over £83.33bn, with the average household spending £1,238 on ethical goods in 2017. And who or what is your average ethical consumer? The annual *Ethical Consumer Markets Report* shows young people in particular are turning towards more sustainable shopping. Millennials are at the vanguard of ethical consumerism – whether it is veganism, or sustainable tourism. The young professionally educated class is shopping with its heart and not only its pocket. A key concern for the ethical shopper is the environment, especially climate change. Research by the Ethical Consumer in 2017 found that around 49 per cent of those under twenty-four having avoided a product or service due to its environmental impact.

Thus, we must be on the brink of major change at the hands of socially aware consumers? The growth of ethical consumption – the boycotting phenomenon outlined above – should be a welcome. And in the future buycotting is likely to grow and feature in the mainstream economy. If all things remain equal, the onward and upward trajectory of ethical consumption is likely to result in lasting and fundamental change for the better. Changes to society, the economy at large and to the agents of capitalism – corporate businesses – are likely to ensue. Ethical consumerism, as it becomes a fixture of the economy, will ensure that capitalism will become more responsible. That is the theory.

But does ethical consumption really help address some the world's most pressing problems? Take boycotting. There are limits to the impact of ethical consumerism. One failing of buycotting is that it may actually exacerbate the greatest threat facing humanity in the twenty-first century: the threat of thermo-environmental Armageddon. The Canadian journalist Naomi Klein in her 2015 book *This Changes Everything: Capitalism vs the Climate* states the scale of the problem. She argues that climate change is not about carbon or greenhouse gases. Rather climate change boils down to a battle between capitalism and the planet: 'that the idea and commitment to perpetual growth is incompatible with ecological limits and that . . . the triumph of market logic, with its ethos of domination and fierce competition, is paralysing almost all serious efforts to respond' (Gillespie 2016). But since Klein published her book the hegemony of unfettered free markets has come under the most severe existential reappraisal since the raising of the Iron Curtain.

The popular rise of the Extinction Rebellion environmental pressure group is a testament to the growing sense of crisis around climate change. This is an issue that cuts across party political affiliations and ideologies. It seems unusual to find Margaret Thatcher, the now dead paramour of 80s neo-liberalism, giving a speech at the UN General Assembly in 1989 decrying the problems of environmental degradation and climate change. Nearly thirty years later another woman, this time a Swedish teenager addressed the same UN General Assembly with this warning: 'We are in the beginning of a mass extinction. And all you can talk about is money and fairy tales of eternal economic growth'. Greta Thunberg, the neophyte teenage spiritual spokesperson of modern environmentalism, has inspired a climate change movement. The school climate strikes, which she began in August 2018, saw 1,659 strikes planned for March 15 in 105 countries planned in 2019. The agenda is clear: buying fair trade coffee and green lightbulbs and electric cars is not necessarily the answer to the problem. To use Thunberg's words: 'If solutions within this system are so difficult to find then maybe we should change the system itself'. Or to use the popular epigram so beloved of Extinction Rebellion activists: 'system change not climate change'.

For Thunberg and Extinction Rebellion activists, it seems quite clear what is the problem: global unregulated markets. And driving this global system is unfettered spending and buying by shoppers. So quite clearly, ethical consumption does not deal with the obvious concern of the climate activists: producing too many goods to feed ever greater consumer demand and the search for ever more growth. The need for system change means that consumers, even ethical boycotting, is part of the problem. Buycotting does nothing to address the issue of overconsumption, for it is part of the vicious circle of overconsumption, even if its products are ethically soured. The idea is that anti- rather than ethical consumption is the ultimate answer solution.

And there have been, even before the rise of Extinction Rebellion, examples of anti-consumerist activism and lifestyle advocates. Freeganism or dumpster diving is one such example – a lifestyle of anti-consumerism that is very much a fringe lifestyle choice. But anti-consumerism is moving from the margins. Take air travel. There is evidence travellers are turning against flying because of environmental concerns. According to a recent survey by Swiss bank UBS, the Swedish concept of 'flygskam' or 'flight shame' is gaining popular appeal. Of those surveyed by UBS, one in five had reduced the number of flights they took over the last year because of climate concerns. UBS commented on the basis of their survey that the expected growth in passenger numbers could be halved as climate concerns grow. The flygskam phenomenon just goes to underline how the climate crisis and activists such as Extinction Rebellion have raised objections to an economic system addicted to growth and consumption.

The climate crisis has raised society-wide doubts about an economy dependent on economic growth. The environment and its finite sources are unable to withstand the infinite desire for economic growth and consumer appetites for more. Increasing levels of pollution and now seeming irreversible climate change are twin catastrophes that await humanity. The American business ethicist Roger Bucholz argues, writing before even Greta Thunberg was born, that industrial societies need to roll back economic growth in order to secure the planet for future generations. For our economy, which has become dependent on consumer industries, cutting back on consumption to save the planet will mean one thing: the sacrifice of jobs, careers and livelihoods. Hardly a vote winning strategy for any politician seeking to be elected. For Bucholz there is some light at the end of the ecological tunnel: 'But if consumption does need to be constrained and circumscribed, and the science of climate change suggests this is an immediate necessity, then the impact on jobs and the economy can be moderated. This can be done by investing in investing in technologies and services that enhance the environment.' (Bucholz 1998, p. 881)

Conclusion: Consume to Oblivion?

It remains to be seen whether the adult world is ready or prepared for these ecological-saving measures to roll back growth. Politicians, ever lagging behind, are unprepared and unwilling and too unimaginative to embrace the necessary measures. But as I write this conclusion to my chapter the pandemic has forced governments to constrain economic activity to deal with the COVID-19 health crisis. The break in economic activity has seen concrete benefits for the environment. But the ever-present threat of climate change and specifies depletion still remain – despite the pandemic breaks on economic activity. Global capitalism at this moment in history is all too hegemonic – our material interests as individuals are wrapped up and closely intertwined with the global status quo at the expense of nature. After all the Western consumer is the dominant interest group in the global world order. And not just our interests but also our sense of wellbeing relies on ever growing prosperity and wealth. We have no sense of meaning outside shopping and our fetish for commodities, in part, because of the omnipresent advertising industry. Advertisers tell us we are masters of our destiny. And in this universe ethical consumerism, whether buycotting and dualcotting, is just another choice we make.

The science of climate change suggests our survival means that we may have no other choice but to boycott endless consumption and disavow ourselves from the lifestyles we have been accustomed to in the West; and switching to ethically sourced commodities will make little or no difference. This could even add to ecological problems. But for the system change needed to avoid climate change a more fundamental transformation is required, according to ecologist Tom Oliver in his 2020 book *The Self Delusion*. We in the West need to redefine how we relate to nature vis a vis our identities. We need to identify ourselves, not as independent self-maximisers, but as fragile human beings intimately determined by, and joined to the ecology. The more assertive and independent we try to become as consumers the more we are likely to obliterate ourselves.

References

Becker, H. S. (1995), 'Moral entrepreneurs: The creation and enforcement of deviant categories' in N.J. Herman (ed.), D*eviance: a Symbolic Interactionist Approach* (Lanham MD: Rowman & Littlefield).

Buchholz, R. A. (1998), 'The ethics of consumption activities: a future paradigm?', *Journal of Business Ethics*, vol. 17, no. 8, pp. 871–82.

Castellano, O. (2018), 'Why 'Buycotting' is The New Form of Political Activism', *Medium*, 27 June 2018 (Link: https://medium.com/@orge/why-buycott-is-the-new-form-of-political-activism-a85a746756e3).

Clarke, N., Barnett, C., Cloke, P. and Malpass, A. (2007), 'Globalising the consumer: doing politics in an ethical register', *Political Geography*, vol. 26, no. 3, pp. 231–49.

Copeland, L. (2014), 'Conceptualizing Political Consumerism: How Citizenship Norms Differentiate Boycotting from Buycotting', *Political Studies* vol. 62 (S1), pp. 172–86.

Gillespie, P. (2016), 'Naomi Klein argues climate change is a battle between capitalism and the planet', *Irish Times*, 14th May 2016 (Accessed 17.1.20: https://www.irishtimes.com/opinion/naomi-klein-argues-climate-change-is-a-battle-between-capitalism-and-the-planet-1.2647166)

Hertz, N. (2001), 'Better to shop than to vote?', *Business Ethics: A European Review*, vol. 10, no. 3, pp. 190–93.

Krasny, J. (2012). 'Every Parent Should Know The Scandalous History Of Infant Formula', *Business Insider*, 25th June 2012. (Accessed 16.1.20: https://www.businessinsider.com/nestles-infant-formula-scandal-2012-6?r=US&IR=T#the-bad-publicity-sparked-a-global-boycott-of-nestl-11).

Klein, N. (2015), *This Changes Everything: Capitalism vs. the Climate* (London: Penguin).

Mueller, M. (2013), 'Nestlé baby milk scandal has grown up but not gone away', *Guardian* 13th Feb 2013 (Accessed 18.1.20: https://www.theguardian.com/sustainable-business/nestle-baby-milk-scandal-food-industry-standards).

Neilson, L. A. (2010), 'Boycott or buycott? Understanding political consumerism', *Journal of Consumer Behaviour* vol. 9, no. 3, pp. 214–27.

Oliver, T. (2020), *The Self Delusion: The Surprising Science of How We Are Connected and Why That Matters* (London: W&N).

Pattie, C., Seyd, P. and Whiteley, P. (2003), 'Civic Attitudes and Engagement in Modern Britain', *Parliamentary Affairs*, vol. 56, no. 4, pp. 616–33.

Smith, N. C. (1990), *Morality and the Market: Consumer Pressure for Corporate Accountability*, (London; New York: Routledge).

Unger, H. G. (2012), *American Tempest: How the Boston Tea Party Sparked a Revolution* (Cambridge, Mass.: Da Capo Press).

Miriam McGowan and Louise M. Hassan

2 The Usefulness of the Social Identity Approach to Social Marketing

Introduction

The vast majority of social marketing literature has ignored the potential usefulness of an identity perspective for behaviour change. A scan through the index of social marketing texts or a search of the contents of the journal *Social Marketing Quarterly* reveal the lack of attention paid to social identity within the social marketing literature base. This chapter aims to show the relevancy of social identity for behaviour change using literature across the marketing discipline that has applied a social identity approach within contexts of interest to those working in social marketing. Given the dearth of literature within social marketing that is based, in particular, on a social identity approach, this chapter begins by outlining what an identity is and the basic tenants of the social identity approach. The chapter then discusses extensions to the social identity approach, alongside the motives for social identification and its outcomes. Given the vast literature base within psychology and allied fields, a number of general principles related to identification have been identified and these are discussed in detail. The latter sections of the chapter then move on to the contexts of social marketing and document research findings that show the utility of the social identity approach for social marketing.

What is Identity?

Individuals have both a personal identity and a social identity. The personal identity comprises of characteristics that make the individual unique and distinguish her from others, such as being extrovert or enjoying the outdoors (Hornsey 2008; Turner et al. 1994). These idiosyncratic characteristics relate to attitudes, behaviours, memories and emotions (Hornsey 2008). A person's social identity is made up of characteristics that the individual shares with other members of a specific social group (Hornsey 2008; Turner et al. 1994). Such social groups can range from males, mothers, members of a particular football club, to brands such as Apple or Harley Davidson. In this chapter, social identity is defined as 'that part of an individual's self-concept which derives from his knowledge of his membership of a social group (or groups) together with the value and emotional significance attached to that membership' (Tajfel 1981, p. 255). Recent work stresses the multi-dimensionality of social identity (e.g., Ashmore et al. 2004; Johnson et al. 2012; Wolter and Cronin Jr. 2015). Specifically, the cognitive dimension of social identity captures the 'cognitive

https://doi.org/10.1515/9783110659566-002

connection between the definition of [a social group] and the definition a person applies to himself or herself' (Wolter and Cronin Jr. 2015, p. 401), while affective social identity captures group members' feelings about their oneness with the group (Johnson et al. 2012). Cognitive and affective social identity are correlated (Johnson et al. 2012; Smith et al. 2007) and initial findings by Johnson et al. (2012) suggest that cognitive social identity can positively impact affective social identity.

Research on the social identity approach dates back to the early 1970s (e.g., Tajfel 1972, 1978; Tajfel et al. 1971). Since then the social identity approach has been successfully applied within the consumer behaviour literature (e.g., Kang et al. 2015; Lam et al. 2013; Stokburger-Sauer et al. 2012), made possible because brands have a personality (Aaker 1997) and are associated with descriptive attributes, values and traits (Keller 1993). Consumers' perception of a brand's personality is partially shaped by people associated with the brand, characteristics associated with prototypical brand users, the company's employees, or the brand's endorsers (Aaker 1997). If consumers regard the brand personality as similar to themselves, they can define themselves through the brand and identify with it (Lam et al. 2013). The social identity approach has also been applied within the organisational behaviour literature (e.g., Bergami and Bagozzi 2000; Johnson et al. 2012; Wolter and Cronin Jr. 2015), as not only do employees define themselves through their membership in an organisation (Mael and Ashforth 1992), but consumers can also regard themselves as symbolic members of the company (Bhattacharya and Sen 2003).

The following two sections offer a brief overview of social identity theory and self-categorisation theory and key propositions of each, relevant to this chapter. This overview includes: the finding that being allocated into a group is enough to create a sense of belongingness to that group; group members' desire for positive value distinctiveness; the distinction between social and personal identity; as well as the depersonalisation of group members' (self)perception, attitudes and behaviours. Given the large body of research the social identity approach has generated, it is not possible to provide a comprehensive discussion of it all. However, a number of review articles exist which offer a more detailed description of the theories and the research they sparked (e.g., Hornsey 2008).

Social Identity Theory

Social identity theory was initially developed to explain intergroup relations and social change (e.g., Tajfel 1974, 1978, 1982a, b). Tajfel later focuses on how socio-structural variables impact social change, by exploring how group members respond to challenges to their social identity, posed by their group's relative status (high or low status or power), the perceived nature of the intergroup status difference (secure or not; legitimate or not; stable or unstable), and their belief about the nature of the social structure (e.g., Tajfel and Turner 1979; see Ellemers et al. 1999, for a review). However, this section only focuses on two core propositions of social identity theory relevant to this chapter. Firstly, merely allocating people into a group is enough to create a sense of group membership, which in turn influences individuals' behaviour. Secondly, people have a need for a positive self-concept, and use the group membership to obtain it. The need for a positive self-concept further causes group members to seek to establish positive value distinctiveness of their ingroup over an outgroup. This section examines these two propositions in greater detail.

Social identity theory originates from a series of 'minimal group studies', in which participants are allocated into groups based on minimal or arbitrary criteria (e.g., Billig and Tajfel 1973; Tajfel 1970; Tajfel et al. 1971). In an early study Tajfel et al. (1971) set out to evidence that the mere act of being allocated into distinct groups, into 'us' and 'them' respectively, can induce intergroup behaviours such as ingroup favouritism and discrimination against the outgroup. To test this prediction, Tajfel et al. (1971) randomly allocated participants into groups, allegedly based on their performance in an estimation task (study 1) and aesthetic preference for painters (study 2). Participants are informed of their group membership and the alleged reason for their allocation. Participants are then tasked to distribute money, which they can either give to members of their own group ('ingroup') or members of a group they do not belong to ('outgroup'). There is no face-to-face interaction between participants, meaning participants do not know who is in their group, the group has neither history nor projected future, and group allocation is based on trivial criteria (Hornsey 2008; Tajfel 1970). Taken together, participants' choice to allocate money is based entirely on group membership. It is possible for participants to allocate money using different strategies: the maximum joint profit strategy (allocating money in a way which maximizes the total, combined amount awarded to the ingroup and outgroup), the maximum ingroup profit strategy (allocating money in a way which awards the highest amount of money to the ingroup) or the maximum difference profit strategy (allocating money in a way which maximizes the difference in money awarded to ingroup and outgroup, the difference being in favour of the ingroup). In short, participants can pursuit a rational and self-serving strategy, which results in maximum benefit for all, or choose an intergroup differentiation strategy, which favours their ingroup over the outgroup. Consistently, Tajfel et al. (1971) find that participants allocate money in line with the maximum difference profit strategy in favour of the ingroup. This means participants allocate money in such a way as to maximize the difference between the two groups, in favour of the ingroup, even if this results in less money for both groups (Tajfel et al. 1971). It follows that merely mentioning a group is enough to create a sense of group membership, which influences individuals' behaviour, even if the group allocation is openly random. The first proposition, which states that allocating people into a group creates a sense of group membership that influences individuals' behaviour, is thus supported. See Brewer (1979) for a discussion of replication studies.

The second proposition from social identity theory is that group members have a need for positive social identity. Before going into greater detail on this proposition it is helpful to briefly outline the social comparison theory (Festinger 1954), the theory from which this proposition arises. Tajfel (1981) criticises Festinger's (1954) theory, recognising the restrictive focus on inter-individual comparisons, because this narrow focus causes the social comparison theory to fail to account for individuals' membership in groups. Yet clear parallels between the theories can be drawn. Festinger's (1954) social comparison theory revolves around three key statements. Firstly, Festinger argues that people have a need to evaluate their opinions (e.g., whether one's opinion towards organic food is correct) and abilities (e.g., whether one's running speed is relatively fast or slow). People will therefore engage in behaviours that offer an accurate appraisal of their abilities and test the correctness of their opinions (Festinger 1954). Secondly, people evaluate their opinions and abilities by comparing themselves against others, but only if objective, non-social means of comparison are not available (Festinger 1954). Lastly, Festinger (1954) proposes a unidirectional drive upward in regard to ability, meaning that people wish to perform better than others. Importantly, this drive is not present for opinions, as there is no such thing as a 'better' opinion (Festinger 1954). Similar to Festinger, Tajfel (1972) believes that people evaluate themselves through comparison, in particular by comparing their ingroup with an outgroup. In fact, Tajfel (1981) claims that the significance of one's membership in a group is only achieved through the comparison against another group. However, Tajfel (1972) disagrees with Festinger's notion that people always prefer objective, non-social comparisons. Tajfel (1972) proposes that objective measures are often not available, and that a high social consensus can replace an 'objective' measure of correctness, especially when evaluating group characteristics. In addition, Tajfel disagrees with Festinger's proposition that people compare themselves to relatively similar others. Instead Tajfel (1972) believes that in an intergroup situation the ingroup is compared against a maximally different outgroup. The basis of comparison is therefore not whether or not the groups are similar, but the perceived legitimacy of the relationship between the groups (Tajfel 1972). Further, because individuals' group membership impacts their self-evaluation, and individuals have a general need for a positive self-concept (e.g., Brown et al. 1988; Epstein 1973), Tajfel (1972, 1981) concludes that group members want their group to be valued more favourably than the outgroup. If the ingroup is evaluated more favourably than the outgroup, the ingroup is understood to have positive value distinctiveness, which in turn boosts members' self-esteem and sense of self-worth (Turner et al., 1979). This corresponds to Festinger's (1954) third proposition, according to which people want to do better than others. In social identity theory the need for positive value distinctiveness is expected to bias group members' perceptions, evaluations and behaviours in favour of the ingroup (Turner et al. 1979). Individuals are also more likely to become or remain part of a group that offers a positive social identity, due to the potential positive consequences for their self-evaluation (Turner 1975).

A core tenant of social identity theory is that merely being allocated to a group fosters a sense of group membership. Tajfel (1982a) defines a group based on external and internal criteria. External criteria are outside designations of the group members, such as people using Apple products, or employees in a particular company. Internal criteria refer to members' group identification, which arises from a sense of awareness of membership, the sense that this awareness is related to some value connotations, and an emotional investment in the awareness and evaluations (Tajfel 1982a). At times a third criteria may be necessary, namely that an outside source acknowledges the group (Tajfel 1982a). Tajfel and Turner (1979, p. 40) focus more on the internal criteria when they define a group as 'a collection of individuals who perceive themselves to be members of the same social category, share some emotional involvement in this common definition of themselves, and achieve some degree of social consensus about the evaluation of their group and of their membership of it'. Turner and Reynolds (2003, p. 137) conclude that a social group is 'a body of real people that acts in the world; it is a social system. The members interact, behave and have relationships with each other. They share an identity, have goals, are interdependent, and they have social structures'.

Beyond a broad ingroup vs. outgroup distinction, the literature also highlights one type of outgroup, namely dissociative group (i.e. groups individuals do not wish to be misidentified with, see Berger and Heath 2008; White and Dahl 2007). In particular, individuals are strongly motivated to avoid exhibiting views, attitudes, behaviours, or being associated with products and services, that might lead others to misidentify them as members of such dissociative groups.

Types of Social Groups

There is not yet an agreed upon typology of social groups. However, Lickel et al. (2000) distinguish between intimacy groups (e.g., family, small group of friends), task groups (e.g., work groups, committees), social categories (e.g., women) and loose associations (e.g., standing in line together in a queue). These groups differ in their duration, permeability, and the level of interaction between groups. For example, intimacy groups are small and characterised by long duration and high levels of interaction, but are low in permeability. In contrast, social categories are large, of very long duration, but very low in permeability. Lickel et al. (2000) further distinguish between dynamic groups and social categories. In dynamic groups members are bound together by patterns of interdependence instead of similarity (e.g., family members). In contrast, members of social categories (e.g., gender, nationality) share certain characteristics and are grouped into the social category because of them (Lickel et al. 2000). Using a cluster analysis Deaux et al. (1995) further distinguish between five types of social identities, namely personal relationships (e.g., daughter, grandfather), vocations/avocations (e.g., student, musician), political affiliations (e.g., Labour, political independent), ethnic/religious groups (e.g., German, Christian) and stigmatized groups (e.g., homeless person, retired person). Relationship identities are predicted by three properties, namely ascribed – achieved, active – passive, relational – nonrelational, and early in life – late in life see Deaux et al. 1995, p.288. Stigma groups can be described according to whether they are harmless or threatening, common or uncommon, preventable or unpreventable and active or passive. For example, retired people are deemed to not be dangerous, but a person with AIDS is regarded as dangerous. The authors believe that they failed to include the correct properties for ethnicity/religion and political affiliation, as the results for these social identities are inconclusive.

Reed et al. (2012) distinguishes between objective membership groups (e.g., gender or family), culturally determined membership groups (e.g., ethnicity and religion), groups based on abstracted role ideals (e.g., mother, friend, philanthropist), groups based on the association with a known individual (e.g., a graduate advisor), or on an individual not known personally (e.g., Angela Merkel). Consumers may also identify with brands or companies (e.g., Lam et al. 2013; Stokburger-Sauer et al. 2012). In keeping with Licker's (2000) typology, brands and companies are considered intimacy groups, as consumers can form a relationship with them (Schultz Kleine et al. 1995). In the typology proposed by Reed et al. (2012) brands or companies represent a group based on the association with a person not known personally.

Following the death of Tajfel in 1982, Turner developed the self-categorization theory (e.g., Turner 1985; Turner et al. 1987). The social identity approach is based on the idea that the individual cannot be regarded as an isolated entity, but must be seen as part of society, acting in an 'intersubjective world of shared social meaning' (Turner and Oakes 1986, p. 240). Self-categorization theory reflects this interconnectedness when proposing that people's self-concept is a 'system of cognitive representations of self, based upon comparisons with other people and relevant to social interaction' (Turner and Oakes 1986, p. 241). People categorise themselves and others into social categories based on similarity to one and dissimilarity from another social category (Tajfel 1981; Turner et al. 1994). Social categorisation thus allows individuals to segment, classify and order their social environment (Tajfel and Turner 1979; Turner and Oakes 1986). Further, by offering a system of (self)reference social categories enable individuals to define their place in the world (Tajfel and Turner 1979; Turner and Oakes 1986). Social categories are defined as 'psychological representations in the mind; they are cognitive structures which people use *to define themselves*' and others (Turner and Reynolds 2003, p. 137). Given the similarity between Tajfel's (1982) definition of social groups and the above definition of social categories, the terms social group and social category are used interchangeably in this chapter.

Motives Underlying Social Identification

Social groups are characterised by social norms which shape group members' attitudes and behaviours (Abrams et al. 1990; Turner 1991). When individuals self-categorise into a social group, the norms, values and beliefs of this group become internalised by group members, allowing the norms, values and beliefs to guide individuals' attitudes and behaviours (Hogg and Turner 1987). This is possible because, following their self-categorisation, individuals experience a shift in self-perception, causing them to think of themselves in terms of their group membership rather than in terms of their idiosyncratic characteristics (Turner, 1985). This 'depersonalisation' (Turner 1984b), has consequences for individuals' attitudes, and behaviours (Hogg and Turner 1987; Smith and Henry 1996). In particular, group members adopt attitudes, beliefs and behaviours that are in line with those of their ingroup, to increase their similarity to other ingroup members (Rabinovich et al. 2012). Group members do this as social reality is created through social consensus and information which has been agreed upon is regarded as true (Turner 1991). To avoid undermining this social consensus and to avoid social exclusion group members adopt attitudes and behaviours that conform to their social group (Abrams et al. 1990; Haslam et al. 1999; Rabinovich et al. 2012; Turner et al. 1994). In addition, new information is interpreted by relating it to existing group-specific knowledge and theories (Tajfel 1982b). Oyserman (2009) refers to the motivation to interpret one's environment in line with one's group membership as procedural readiness. For example, if consumers read an ambiguously written review, they will interpret it in favour of 'their' brand.

Abrams and Hogg (2003) highlight the importance of three motives underlying social identification, namely the need for positive self-esteem, the need to reduce uncertainty and to obtain or maintain self-meaning. Further, Brewer's (1991) model of optimal distinctiveness proposes two additional motives, the need for uniqueness and for belongingness. This section outlines each of the five motives.

Need for Positive Self-esteem

A core assumption of the social identity approach, which can be traced back to the social comparison theory (Festinger 1954), is that individuals strive to achieve and/or maintain a positive self-concept (Tajfel and Turner 1979). Social identity refers to that part of individuals' self-concept, which derives from their group membership, and the group obtains its (positive or negative) value partially through intergroup comparison. Based on this premise, social identity theory predicts that group members strive to obtain positive value distinctiveness (Tajfel and Turner 1979). In other words, an important motive underlying social identification is group members' need to obtain and maintain a positive self-concept or self-esteem. The importance of self-esteem is best illustrated by the consequneces of its absence, given that a lack of self-esteem can result in a number of negative outcomes ranging from psychological distress, mental disorders, and substance abuse, to lower post-operative survival rates (see Mann et al. 2004 for an overview). The need for positive self-esteem may lead individuals to self-enhance. Self-enhancement refers to the motivation to 'maintain or increase the positivity, or decrease the negativity, of the self' (Reid and Hogg 2005, p. 804).

Need for Uncertainty Reduction

Hogg (2000) claims that '[p]eople need to feel certain about their world and their place within it; certainty renders existence meaningful and gives one confidence in how to behave, and what to expect from one's physical and social environment' (p. 227). In contrast, subjective uncertainty arises if individuals are unsure about their thoughts, perceptions, emotions and actions, or do not feel confident in their sense of self (Hogg 2000). Uncertainty is linked to loss of control and results in aversive feelings ranging from unease to fear, making the need to reduce uncertainty a powerful motive (Hogg 2000; Mullin and Hogg 1999). The subjective uncertainty hypothesis states that self-categorisation is well suited to reduce subjective uncertainty (Hogg 2000). Not only does self-categorisation offer a meaningful self-definition, but it also provides guidelines for prototypical attitudes, beliefs and behaviours, thus reducing people's uncertainty regarding what to think and how to act (Hogg 2000). Because other ingroup members are also expected to adhere to these prototypes, subjective uncertainty regarding one's interaction with others is also reduced (Hogg 2000). In support of this argument, Hogg et al. (2007) find that participants identify most strongly with a social group when they are high in uncertainty and the group is high in entitativity. Group entitativity, which is captured as 'how much of a group do you feel they are' refers to a group's clear boundaries, internal homogeneity, social interaction, clear internal structure, common goals, and common fate (Hogg et al. 2007). Mullin and Hogg (1999) and Hogg et al. (2010) report similar findings, namely that uncertainty leads to an increase in identification.

Need for Self-meaning

Individuals wish to render their world subjectively meaningful, as this allows them to act in an adaptive manner and interact with others (Abrams and Hogg 2003). Self-categorisation theory is based on the assumption that individuals categorise themselves and others into social categories, 'a system of orientation which helps to create and define the individual's place in society' (Tajfel 1981, p. 255). In addition, for individuals to engage in social comparison they must first know who they are themselves (Abrams and Hogg 2003). Only once individuals have a reference point of who they are, can they evaluate themselves against others or an outgroup (Abrams and Hogg 2003).

Not only must individuals be clear on who they are, but their sense of self must also be coherent (Swann et al. 2003). People make sense of their surrounding and social interactions by relating them back to themselves (Swann et al. 2003). A coherent sense of self is therefore crucial to meaningfully interpret one's environment because '[p]eople's self-views represent the lens through which they perceive reality, lending meaning to all experience' (Swann et al. 2003, p. 368). Without a coherent self-view, individuals are unsure about how to respond to the (social) world, and will find organizing experiences, predicting future events or engaging in social interactions difficult (Swann et al. 2003). Indeed, a self-view that lacks coherence undermines psychological functioning, and may result in negative emotions (Chandler et al. 2003; Sani 2005). To satisfy their need for a coherent sense of self, individuals are motivated to seek out people who confirm their pre-existing self-views (Swann et al., 2003). They may do this by displaying identity cues (e.g., through branded clothes), selectively interacting with people in social contexts (e.g., specialised brand communities), seeing more confirmatory evidence than there actually is, and selectively paying attention to or encoding identity-consistent information (Swann et al. 2003). By signalling who they are consumers also ensure that others know how to interact with them, thus allowing interpersonal interactions to proceed smoothly (Swann et al. 2003).

Need for Belongingness and Distinctiveness/Uniqueness Needs

Humans have a fundamental need for belongingness, which causes them to form lasting, positive and significant interpersonal relationships (Baumeister and Leary 1995). Baumeister and Leary (1995) argue that the need for belongingness is beneficial for individuals' survival and reproduction, and helps protect their resources from external threats. Being deprived of belongingness has been shown to negatively affect people's health (e.g., DeLongis et al. 1988; Goodwin et al. 1987). Further the need for belongingness results in goal-directed behaviours, as individuals seek out and develop interpersonal relationships (Baumeister and Leary 1995).

In addition to their need for belongingness, people have the conflicting need for uniqueness and individuation (Brewer 1991). On the one hand, social inclusion alleviates the isolation associated with being extremely individuated, as individuals feel uncomfortable when they perceive themselves to be too dissimilar to others (e.g., feeling embarrassed when over or under dressed). On the other hand, feeling too similar to others is equally uncomfortable (e.g., when wearing identical dresses at a function), as individuals have a need for clear self-definition (Brewer 1991). There is thus an ongoing tension between these conflicting needs. Individuals who are highly distinct from others feel the need to belong and strive to become more similar to other members of their group. In contrast, individuals who are immersed in a large and overly-inclusive group feel the need to differentiate themselves from it. This phenomenon is apparent in Apple discussion forums, where many users perceive the brand as too mainstream nowadays. Instead of identifying with Apple as a whole, these users choose to identify with the sub-brand 'iMac', which is perceived to be used mainly by creative professionals.

Outcomes of Social Identification

The influence of social identity on consumers' attitudes and behaviours is well established. In particular, social identification has been shown to lead to greater preference for identity-linked products and services (e.g., Reed 2004), purchase intention (e.g., Madrigal 2000), brand loyalty (e.g., Stokburger-Sauer et al. 2012), increased product utilization (Ahearne et al. 2005), repurchase of identity-linked products (e.g., Kuenzel and Halliday 2008), willingness to pay (Homburg et al. 2009), and participation in online chats (Dholakia et al. 2004). Social identification further leads to positive word of mouth (e.g., Tuškej et al. 2013), brand advocacy (Stokburger-Sauer et al. 2012), extra-role behaviour (e.g., Ahearne et al. 2005), and charitable giving (e.g., Winterich et al. 2009).

A number of reasons have been given for the above observed effects. Firstly, the higher consumers' level of cognitive social identity the more they have depersonalised (Hogg and Turner 1987; Turner 1985). It follows that there is a positive relationship between consumers' level of cognitive social identity and the degree to which they have internalised the group's norms, values, and beliefs. Terry and Hogg (1996) find support for this, by showing that group norms predict participants' intention to engage in identity-related behaviours. However, this effect is only present for highly identified group members, who feel greater normative pressure from other group members. Oyserman (2009) proposes a model of identity based motivation, which focuses on the motivational pull that exists towards identity-congruent actions and cognitive procedures. According to Oyserman (2009), identities carry within them a procedural and action readiness. Procedural readiness refers to group members' readiness to make sense of the world by taking into account the salient social identity's norms, values and goals (Oyserman 2009). Action readiness refers to the readiness to engage in behaviours through which desired identities can be achieved and undesired identities can be avoided (Oyserman 2009). Finally, once a choice becomes linked to a social identity the choice becomes automatized and does not require further reflection (Oyserman 2009). Therefore, the identity-based motivation model predicts that when brands or products become linked to an identity these brands or products are preferred, independently of any evaluative judgment (Oyserman 2009).

Faced with a large and fragmented body of literature on downstream consequences of social identification, Reed et al. (2012) summarise them into five principles, which help understand identity-based (consumer) behaviour. Firstly, the salience principle states that the more salient a social identity is, the more likely the identity is to influence subsequent attitudes and behaviours (Reed et al. 2012). Secondly, the identity association principle predicts that when a stimulus (such as a brand or product) becomes associated with a social identity there is a – at times undeliberate – transfer of meaning and affect from the identity to the associated stimulus (Reed et al. 2012). This principle is based on earlier findings on associative self-anchoring (Gawronski et al. 2007), implicit egotism (Jones et al. 2004), mere ownership effect (Nuttin 1987), and name letter branding (Brendl et al. 2005). Across slightly different contexts these studies show that once an object becomes associated with the self, a positive affective transfer takes place from the self to the object, resulting in a more positive response to the object. Brendl et al. (2005) replicate this affective transfer for brands with the same first letters as respondents' first name, resulting in a preference for these brands. Their findings further suggest that this transfer is affect based, as the effect disappears when the respondents are told to think about the reasons for their preference. In contrast, the affective transfer is present when respondents are told to trust their feelings (Brendl et al. 2005). Further, the strength of this effect increases with the positivity of individuals' self-esteem (Gawronski et al. 2007; Perkins and Forehand 2012). Finally, Mercurio and Forehand (2011) show that when a specific social identity is activated at the time when new information is learnt, the new information becomes associated with this identity, thereby influencing participants' response to the information.

The third principle, referred to as the relevance principle, argues that an activated social identity impacts individuals' response to a stimulus only if the stimulus is of relevance to the identity (Reed et al. 2012). There are different ways in which this relevance may express itself. A stimulus has object relevance if it helps define or symbolise the identity (Reed 2004). For example, a dress or makeup may help a female consumer define her identity as a woman. Stimuli that signal or reinforce one's social identity in the eye of others have symbolic relevance (Belk 1988; Shavitt and Nelson 2000). For example, a jumper branded by one's football club has symbolic relevance for a football fan. A stimulus has goal relevance when it relates to an issue or belief important to a social identity (Reed et al. 2012). For example, organic food or Quorn products have goal relevance for environmentalists. Action relevant stimuli allow people to engage in behaviours or actions related to the particular social identity. For example, a knife by Tojiro Senkou may have action relevance for a chef, as it allows her to enact this social identity. Lastly, a stimuli's evaluation relevance captures whether the meaning of a social identity is precise and clear enough to guide consumer behaviour, as without evaluation relevance there is no basis to make a choice. For example, if a young and urban consumer is searching for an outfit she may choose between multiple brands offering the imagery of being young and urban (e.g., Calvin Klein and Reiss). The lack of identity-related norms does not offer an adequate basis to choose between Calvin Klein and Reiss.

The verification principle is based on the finding that people wish to engage in behaviours that are consistent with their social identity (Reed et al. 2012). According to this principle people monitor if they are identity-consistent and strive to correct any behaviours that are not (Reed et al. 2012). The need to verify one's identity is particularly strong if the social identity is threatened (Avery 2012; Swann et al. 2007) and individuals believe they are capable of obtaining their desired identity-consistent behaviour (Reed et al. 2012). Lastly, given that people tend to have multiple social identities these identities may conflict (Reed et al. 2012). The identity conflict principle states that individuals are motivated to reduce identity conflict by making the conflicting social identity less salient (Reed et al. 2012).

Making the Case Why Social Identification is Important Within Social Marketing and Behaviour Change Contexts

A very limited literature base within social marketing explores the utility of the social identity approach despite a recognition in social marketing for the power of peer pressure and other social forces. Bhattacharya and Elsbach (2002) claim that identification had previously not been studied in the social marketing literature (until their study) and therefore despite the history of the social identity approach, its use in social marketing is fairly short.

A general premise on the need to take account of social groups within the highlighted contexts is that there is often a well defined ingroup. For instance, smokers, vegans, boycotters of a brand and thus there are corresponding outgroups for instance non-smokers, meat-eaters, or buycotters of a brand. Some of these corresponding groups might in fact be dissociate groups rather than neutral outgroups. Indeed, research by Earle and Hodson (2017) indicates that some beef lovers regard vegetarians as a dissociative group. The nature and strength of identification we have with the groups that we belong to will (referring back to the principles discussed earlier) affect our attitudes and behaviours and, importantly for social marketers, the potential that we might want to change our behaviour. Moving from an ingroup (that you view positively with clear understanding of the prototypes associated with being a member) to seeing as important to your self-concept of a group that you don't know might be painful (e.g., transitioning from a smoker to an ex-smoker). Therefore, understanding social identification is important in order to determine not only how important current group membership is to individuals, but also to help individuals to redefine the self, as this is part and parcel of (permanently) changing their behaviour and the group(s) to which they belong. Furthermore, Mols et al. (2015) in critiquing nudge theory advocates that behaviour change approaches can be even more successful if a social identity approach is also incorporated because 'promoting lasting behaviour change need to engage with people not as individual cognitive misers, but as members of groups whose norms they internalise and enact' (Mols et al. 2015, p. 81).

Of further importance is the need for collective action to address the challenges of climate change. Research within social marketing is moving towards understanding the motives for collective action (e.g., Summers and Summers 2017) and a social identity perspective is relevant here. For instance, the green-feminine stereotype that exists within society results in men having lower intentions to adopt green behaviours due to gender-identity maintenance (Brough et al. 2016). Thus, knowing how to use the social identity approach to overcome such bias, in this instance through changing the traditional branding of green products to include a more masculine image presentation, will have benefits to wider society.

We now turn our focus to research within social marketing that has applied the social identity approach in some form. Relevant findings from consumer research studies, where these have clear linkages to social marketing contexts, are also considered. It is not intended that this section is a narrative or exhaustive review of the literature, but rather that it gives some insight into the general applicability of the social identity approach to the topics at hand. Indeed, there is much work to be undertaken in these contexts with authors still calling for the need for increased understanding of the role of social identity in shaping responses to, for instance, anti-smoking campaigns (Baig et al. 2017).

Consumers respond asymmetrically to messages directed at their ingroup (i.e. groups they belong to) versus outgroups (i.e. groups they do not belong to; Aaker et al. 2000) or dissociative groups (i.e. groups they do not wish to be misidentified with; Berger and Heath 2008). In other words, consumers respond favourably to marketing strategies explicitly targeting them, but respond negatively to messages targeting customer segments they regard as dissociative groups (termed the dissociative group effect), especially if they identify strongly with their ingroup (White and Dahl 2007). This dissociative group effect arises because people want to have a positive and distinctive self-view and hence seek to distance themselves from products, brands or behaviours that would mis-represent them.

In social marketing, individuals were found to engage in more positive public behaviour (recycling) after learning that a dissociative group is known to recycle (White et al. 2014). However, this behavioural assimilation is not due to the above negative dissociative group effect having been reversed but is driven by consumers' concern for their ingroup's image in the eyes of others. Individuals therefore recycle – in public – to present their ingroup in a positive light (White et al. 2014). Berger and Rand (2008) also show the power of dissociative groups in health communication contexts. Through a series of field studies, they found that if a risky health behaviour was associated with a dissociative group, it leads consumers to make healthier choices, including reduced alcohol and lower fat food consumption.

In the context of recycling, Trudel et al. (2016) find consumers to are more likely to recycle a product if that product is linked to their identity. These authors show that consumers are motivated to avoid 'trashing' an identity-linked product because 'placing an identity-linked product in the trash is symbolically similar to trashing a part of the self', which would signal to yourself that you must be worthless (p. 246). In particular, when people make (or failed to make) prosocial choices, they not only show significant others as to the type of person they are, but such choices also serves a self-signalling function (Bodner and Prelec 2003).

Examining views of smokers and non-smoker from the perspective of the corporate social responsibility of tobacco companies in Indonesia, Arli et al. (2015) find smokers to have higher levels of consumer-company identification than non-smokers but didn't find that consumer-company identification influenced company evaluation. A broader study by Deng and Xu (2017) examined the fit of corporate social responsibility initiatives as well as product valence on consumer-company identification which acted as a mediator onto a range of outcomes including purchase intention. The results of the study were that consumer-company identification did play an important mediating role. Thus, the importance of consumer-company identification in corporate social responsibility contexts may be context dependent. Examining purchase behaviour separately of products that make environmental or ethical claims, Bartels and Onwezen (2014) find that social identification explained intentions for both types of purchase behaviour alongside demographics and other factors. Overall, these results concur with the earlier discussion that identification encourages identity consistent behaviours.

We now move on to discuss the linkage between social groups and promotion activities. In a field experiment Champniss et al. (2016) find that a social identity perspective had value in closing the intention-behaviour gap that has been found within ethical and sustainability contexts (see Hassan et al., 2016 for a discussion and review of the intention-behaviour gap). In particular, Champniss et al. (2016) find that when a brand asked consumers to act in a sustainability-related manor, consumers did so regardless of their individual attitudes if involved in a social group that had sustainability objectives. That is, for these consumers there was a high behaviour-identity congruency, which meant that they were more inclined to respond favourably to the brands request. In a health communication context, Baig et al. (2017) utilised a social identity perspective to explore support for anti-tobacco advertising amongst different subgroups within society (teens, gays, lesbians and bisexuals, African Americans, or Latinos). Their hypothesis was that campaigns which were targeted at in-group members would receive more support compared to out-group members. Results of two national experiments in the United States show that support for anti-smoking advertising targeting teens was generally high across participants in general. But with the exception of the teen group, there was increased support for in-group anti-smoking advertainments within the gays, lesbians and bisexuals, African Americans, and Latinos groups in comparison to outgroup members. Therefore, in-group membership may affect responses to health campaigns and the health behaviour norms of in-group members are important to understand in the context of developing campaign messages. Similar conclusions are found from the work of Moran and Sussman (2014) who draw on Comello's (2013) prisim model that explores the relationship between one's identity and media use. Moran and Sussman (2014) examined the efficacy of social identity targeting, which they refer to as constructing communications that target a specific group that the individual identifies with, on anti-smoking beliefs amongst adolescents. They propose that adverts which target based on a social identity approach are more effective at instilling anti-smoking beliefs. They identified eleven different peer groups and assessed anti-smoking beliefs one week after showing an advert that was/was not linked to a membership peer group. They find that the adolescents had stronger anti-smoking beliefs if the advert they saw targeted an ingroup. These collection of studies emphasize the importance of targeting social marketing messages at ingroup members and therefore including a consideration of social groups as part of the social marketing development and planning phase of any social marketing programme.

Examining differences in collective self-esteem for individuals who had more/less favourable attitudes towards drinking, Kropp et al. (2004) find different effects to those hypothesized – that public and private collective self-esteem were higher for those who had less favourable attitudes towards drinking. Reed et al. (2007) drew on the social identity approach as well as injunctive norms to understand alcohol consumption. They show the relevancy of strength of identification as a moderator of the relationship between acceptability of heavy drinking amongst social group members and alcohol consumption for three social groups (friends, peers, and fraternity/sorority members), while controlling for demographic factors.

Together the results of the studies discussed in this section show that group membership, or willingness to avoid some groups, shapes behaviour even in the case of groups that are newly formed. In particular, identification can directly explain attitudes and intentions. Furthermore, the strength with which one identifies with a group can act to enhance or dampen effects. Lastly, there are consistent findings that social identification is important in understanding consumer views, attitudes and behaviours across health contexts.

Conclusion and Reflections

This chapter has focused on outlining the basic tenants of the social identity approach as well discuss the limited literature to date that purports to apply this approach within social marketing. Yet of note is that research on social identity has so far paid scant attention to the need to distinguish between cognitive and affective social identification. Affective social identification (capturing how positive individuals feel about their social group) has beneficial effects on positive emotions leading to stronger motivation to engage in prosocial behaviours. On the other hand, cognitive social identification (capturing the degree of cognitive connection between the definition of a social group and the definition applied to the self) shapes views, attitudes and behaviours consistent with the social group. Emerging research evidences the separate and independent roles of these two forms of identification, with cognitive identification influencing 'what-to-do' and affective identification generating 'what-to-feel' information. As such both cognitive and affective social identifications need to be considered for effective application in social marketing.

One important note to bear in mind regarding the application of social identity in social marketing is the need to understand the underlying motivations that might shape current an individual's behaviours and the willingness for adopting lasting behaviour change. In this respect, an alignment is needed between the social marketing motivations that might drive behavioural change and the motives underlying social identification (need for positive self-esteem; need for uncertainty reduction; need for self-meaning; need for belongingness and distinctiveness/uniqueness needs).

In conclusion, we hope that the potential of the social identity approach for enhancing understanding of behavioural change at the individual and group-level inspires future research in this area. It is clear from the cited studies, that have already begun to link the social identity approach within social marketing studies, that there is much potential for new insights to be gained into attitude formation, behaviour and the development of effective social marketing campaigns.

References

Aaker, J. L., 1997. Dimensions of brand personality. *Journal of Marketing Research*, *34*(3), pp.347–356.

Aaker, J.L., Brumbaugh, A. M. and Grier, S. A., 2000. Nontarget markets and viewer distinctiveness: The impact of target marketing on advertising attitudes. *Journal of Consumer Psychology*, *9*(3), pp.127–140.

Abrams, D. and Hogg, M. A., 2003. Collective identity: Group membership and self-conception. In: Hogg, M. A. and Tindale, C. (eds.) *Blackwell Handbook of Social Psychology: Group Processes*. Malden, M. A.: Blackwell Publishing. pp.425–460.

Abrams, D., Wetherell, M., Cochrane, S., Hogg, M. A. and Turner, J. C., 1990. Knowing what to think by knowing who you are: Self-categorization and the nature of norm formation, conformity and group polarization. *British Journal of Social Psychology*, *29*(2), pp.97–119.

Ahearne, M., Bhattacharya, C. B. and Gruen, T., 2005. Antecedents and Consequences of Customer–Company Identification: Expanding the Role of Relationship Marketing. *Journal of Applied Psychology*, *90*(3), pp.574–585.

Arli, D., Rundle-Thiele, S., and Lasmono, H., 2015. Consumers' evaluation toward tobacco companies: implications for social marketing. *Marketing Intelligence and Planning*, *33*(3), pp.276–291.

Ashmore, R. D., Deaux, K. and McLaughlin-Volpe, T., 2004. An organizing framework for collective identity: Articulation and significance of multidimensionality. *Psychological Bulletin*, *130*(1), pp.80–114.

Avery, J., 2012. Defending the markers of masculinity: Consumer resistance to brand gender-bending. *International Journal of Research in Marketing*, *29*(4), 322–336.

Baig, S. A., Pepper, J. K., Morgan, J. C., and Brewer N. T., 2017. Social identity and support for counteracting tobacco company marketing that targets vulnerable populations. *Social Science and Medicine*, *182*, pp.136–141.

Bartels, J., and Onwezen, M. C., 2014. Consumers' willingness to buy products with environmental and ethical claims: the roles of social representations and social identity. *International Journal of Consumer Studies*, *38*(1), pp.82–89.

Baumeister, R. F. and Leary, M. R., 1995. The need to belong: Desire for interpersonal attachments as a fundamental human motivation. *Psychological Bulletin*, *117*(3), pp.497–529.

Belk, R. W., 1988. Possessions and the extended self. *Journal of Consumer Research*, *15*(2), pp.139–168.

Bergami, M. and Bagozzi, R. P., 2000. Self-categorization, affective commitment and group self-esteem as distinct aspects of social identity in the organization. *British Journal of Social Psychology*, *39*(4), pp.555–577.

Berger, J. and Rand, L., 2008. Shifting signals to help health: Using identity signaling to reduce risky health behaviors. *Journal of Consumer Research*, *35*(3), pp.509–518.

Berger, J., and Heath, C., 2008. Who drives divergence? Identity signaling, outgroup dissimilarity, and the abandonment of cultural tastes. *Journal of personality and social psychology*, *95*(3), 593–607.

Bhattacharya, C. B. and Sen, S., 2003. Consumer-company identification: A framework for understanding consumers' relationships with companies. *Journal of Marketing*, *67*(2), pp.76–88.

Bhattacharya, C. B., and Elsbach, K. D., 2002. Us versus them: The roles of organizational identification and disidentification in social marketing initiatives. *Journal of Public Policy and Marketing*, *21*(1), pp.26–36.

Billig, M. G. and Tajfel, H., 1973. Social categorization and similarity in intergroup behavior. *European Journal of Social Psychology*, *3*(1), pp.27–52.

Bodner, R. and Prelec, D., 2003. Self-signaling and diagnostic utility in everyday decision making. *The Psychology of Economic Decisions*, *1*, pp.105–126.

Brendl, C. M., Chattopadhyay, A., Pelham, B. W. and Carvallo, M., 2005. Name letter branding: Valence transfers when product specific needs are active. *Journal of Consumer Research*, *32*(3), pp.405–415.

Brewer, M.B., 1979. In-group bias in the minimal intergroup situation: *A cognitive-motivational analysis. Psychological Bulletin*, *86*, pp.307–324.

Brewer, M. B., 1991. The social self: On being the same and different at the same time. *Personality and Social Psychology Bulletin*, *17*(5), pp.475–482.

Brough, A. R., Wilkie, J. E., Ma, J., Isaac, M. S., and Gal, D., 2016. Is eco-friendly unmanly? The green-feminine stereotype and its effect on sustainable consumption. *Journal of Consumer Research*, *43*(4), pp.567–582.

Brown, J. D., Collins, R. L. and Schmidt, G. W., 1988. Self-esteem and direct versus indirect forms of self-enhancement. *Journal of Personality and Social Psychology*, *55*(3), pp.445–453.

Champniss, G., Wilson, H. N., Macdonald, E. K., and Dimitriu, R., 2016. No I won't, but yes we will: Driving sustainability-related donations through social identity effects. *Technological Forecasting and Social Change*, *111*, pp.317–326.

Chandler, M. J., Lalonde, C. E., Sokol, B. and Hallett, D., 2003. Personal persistence, identity development and suicide: A study of native and non-native North American adolescents. *Monographs of the Society for Research in Child Development*, *68*(2), i–138.

Comello, M. A., 2013. Conceptualizing the intervening roles of identity in communication effects: The prism model. In D. Lasorsa and A. Rodriguez (Eds.) *Identity and communication: New agendas in communication* (pp.168–188). New York, NY: Routledge.

Deaux, K., Reid, A., Mizrahi, K. and Ethier, K. A., 1995. Parameters of social identity. *Journal of Personality and Social Psychology, 68*(2), pp.280–291.

DeLongis, A., Folkman, S. and Lazarus, R. S., 1988. The impact of daily stress on health and mood: Psychological and social resources as mediators. *Journal of Personality and Social Psychology, 54*(3), pp.486–495.

Deng, X., and Xu, Y., 2017. Consumers' responses to corporate social responsibility initiatives: The mediating role of consumer–company identification. *Journal of Business Ethics, 142*(3), pp.515–526.

Dholakia, U. M., Bagozzia, R. P. and Pearo, L. K., 2004. A social influence model of consumer participation in network- and small-group-based virtual communities. *International Journal of Research in Marketing, 21*(3), pp.241–263.

Earle, M. and Hodson, G., (2017). What's your beef with vegetarians? Predicting anti-vegetarian prejudice from pro-beef attitudes across cultures. *Personality and Individual Differences*, Vol. *119*, pp.52–55.

Ellemers, N., Spears, R. and Doosje, B., 1999. *Social Identity: Context, Commitment, Content.* Oxford: Blackwell.

Epstein, S., 1973. The self-concept revisited: Or a theory of a theory. *American Psychologist, 28*(5), pp.404–416.

Festinger, L., 1954. A theory of social comparison processes. *Human Relations, 7*(2), pp.117–140.

Gawronski, B., Bodenhausen, G. V. and Becker, A. P., 2007. I like it, because I like myself: Associative self-anchoring and post-decisional change of implicit evaluations. *Journal of Experimental Social Psychology, 43*(2), pp.221–232.

Goodwin, J. S., Hunt, W. C., Key, C. R. and Samet, J. M., 1987. The effect of marital status on stage, treatment, and survival of cancer patients. *Journal of the American Medical Association, 258*(21), pp.3125–3130.

Haslam, S. A., Oakes, P. J., Reynolds, K. J. and Turner, J. C., 1999. Social identity salience and the emergence of stereotype consensus. *Personality and Social Psychology Bulletin, 25*(7), pp.809–818.

Hassan, L. M., Shiu, E. and Shaw, D., 2016. Who says there is an intention–behaviour gap? Assessing the empirical evidence of an intention–behaviour gap in ethical consumption. *Journal of Business Ethics, 136*(2), pp.219–236.

Hogg, M. A. and Turner, J. C., 1987. Intergroup behaviour, self-stereotyping and the salience of social categories. *British Journal of Social Psychology, 26*(4), pp.325–340.

Hogg, M. A., 2000. Subjective uncertainty reduction through self-categorization: A motivational theory of social identity processes. *European Review of Social Psychology, 11*(1), pp.223–255.

Hogg, M. A., Meehan, C. and Farquharson, J., 2010. The solace of radicalism: Self-uncertainty and group identification in the face. *Journal of Experimental Social Psychology, 46*(6), pp.1061–1066.

Hogg, M. A., Sherman, D. K., Dierselhuis, J., Maitner, A. T. and Moffitt, G., 2007. Uncertainty, entitativity, and group identification. *Journal of Experimental Social Psychology, 43*(1), pp.135–142.

Homburg, C., Wieseke, J. and Hoyer, W. D., 2009. Social identity and the service–profit chain. *Journal of Marketing, 73*(2), pp.38–54.

Hornsey, M. J., 2008. Social identity theory and self-categorization theory: A historical review. *Social and Personality Psychology Compass, 2*(1), pp.204–222.

Johnson, M. D., Morgeson, F. P. and Hekman, D. R., 2012. Cognitive and affective identification: Exploring the links between different forms of social identification and personality with work attitudes and behavior. *Journal of Organizational Behavior, 33*(8), pp.1142–1167.

Jones, J. T., Pelham, B. W., Carvallo, M. and Mirenberg, M., 2004. How do I love thee? Let me count the Js: Implicit egotism and interpersonal attraction. *Journal of Personality and Social Psychology, 87*(5), pp.665–683.

Kang, J., Alejandro, T. B. and Groza, M. D., 2015. Customer–company identification and the effectiveness of loyalty programs. *Journal of Business Research, 68*(2), pp.464–471.

Keller, K. L., 1993. Conceptualizing, measuring, and managing customer-based brand equity. *Journal of Marketing, 57*(1), pp.1–22.

Kropp, F., Lavack, A. M., Silvera, D. H., and Gabler, J. R., 2004. Alcohol consumption among university students: a multi-country study of attitudes, values, identity, and consumer influence. *Journal of Nonprofit and Public Sector Marketing, 12*(2), pp.1–28.

Kuenzel, S. and Halliday, S. V., 2008. Investigating antecedents and consequenes of brand identification. *Journal of Product and Brand Management, 17*(5), pp.293–304.

Lam, S. K., Ahearne, M., Mullins, R., Hayati, B. and Schillewaert, N., 2013. Exploring the dynamics of antecedents to consumer–brand identification with a new brand. *Journal of the Academy of Marketing Science, 41*(2), pp.234–252.

Lickel, B., Hamilton, D. L., Wieczorkowska, G., Lewis, A., Sherman, S. J. and Uhles, A. N., 2000. Varieties of groups and the perception of group entitativity. *Journal of Personality and Social Psychology, 78*(2), pp.223–246.

Madrigal, R., 2000. The influence of social alliances with sports teams on intentions to purchase corporate sponsors' products. *Journal of Advertising, 29*(4), pp.13–24.

Mael, F. and Ashforth, B. E., 1992. Alumni and their alma mater: A partial test of the reformulated model of organizational identification. *Journal of Organizational Behavior, 13*(2), pp.103–123.

Mann, M., Hosman, C. M., Schaalma, H. P. and de Vries, N. K., 2004. Self-esteem in a broad-spectrum approach for mental health promotion. *Health Education Research, 19*(4), pp.357–372.

Mercurio, K. R. and Forehand, M. R., 2011. An interpretive frame model of identity-dependent learning: The moderating role of content-state association. *Journal of Consumer Research, 38*(3), pp.555–577.

Mols, F., Haslam, S. A., Jetten, J., and Steffens, N. K., 2015. Why a nudge is not enough: A social identity critique of governance by stealth. *European Journal of Political Research, 54*(1), pp.81–98.

Moran, M. B., and Sussman, S., 2014. Translating the link between social identity and health behavior into effective health communication strategies: An experimental application using antismoking advertisements. *Health communication, 29*(10), pp.1057–1066.

Mullin, B.-A. and Hogg, M. A., 1999. Motivations for group membership: The role of subjective importance and uncertainty reduction. *Basic and Applied Social Psychology, 21*(2), pp.91–102.

Nuttin, J. M., 1987. Affective consequences of mere ownership: The name letter effect in twelve European languages. *European Journal of Social Psychology, 17*(4), pp.381–402.

Oyserman, D., 2009. Identity-based motivation: Implications for action-readiness, procedural-readiness, and consumer behavior. *Journal of Consumer Psychology, 19*(3), pp.250–260.

Perkins, A. W. and Forehand, M. R., 2012. Implicit self-referencing: The effect of nonvolitional self-association on brand and product attitude. *Journal of Consumer Research, 39*(1), pp.142–156.

Rabinovich, A., Morton, T. A., Postmes, T. and Verplanken, B., 2012. Collective self and individual choice: The effect of inter-group comparative context on environmental values and behaviour *British Journal of Social Psychology, 51*(4), pp.551–569.

Reed, A. 2004., Activating the self-importance of consumer selves: Exploring identity salience effects on judgments. *Journal of Consumer Research, 31*(2), pp.286–295.

Reed, A., Forehand, M. R., Puntoni, S. and Warlop, L., 2012. Identity-based consumer behavior. *International Journal of Research in Marketing, 29*(4), pp.310–321.

Reed, M. B., Lange, J. E., Ketchie, J. M., and Clapp, J. D., 2007. The relationship between social identity, normative information, and college student drinking. *Social Influence, 2*(4), pp.269–294.

Reid, S. A. and Hogg, M. A., 2005. Uncertainty reduction, self-enhancement, and ingroup identification. *Personality and Social Psychology Bulletin, 31*(6), pp.804–817.

Sani, F., 2005. When subgroups secede: Extending and refining the social psychological model of schism in groups. *Personality and Social Psychology Bulletin, 31*(8), pp.1074–1086.

Schultz Kleine, S., Kleine, R. E. and Allen, C. T., 1995. How is a Possession "Me" or "Not Me"? Characterizing Types and an Antecedent of Material Possession. *Journal of Consumer Research, 22*(3), pp.327–343.

Shavitt, S., and Nelson, M. R., 2000. The social identity function in person perception: Communicated meanings of product preferences. In: Maio, G. R. and Olson, J. M. (eds.) *Why we evaluate: Function of attitudes*. Mahwah, NJ: Erlbaum. pp.27–57.

Smith, E. R. and Henry, S., 1996. An ingroup becomes part of the self: Response time evidence. *Personality and Social Psychology Bulletin, 22*(6), pp.635–642.

Smith, E. R., Seger, C. R. and Mackie, D. M., 2007. Can emotions be truly group level? Evidence regarding four conceptual criteria. *Journal of Personality and Social Psychology, 93*(3), pp.431–446.

Stokburger-Sauer, N., Ratneshwar, S. and Sen, S., 2012. Drivers of consumer-brand identification. *International Journal of Research in Marketing, 29*(4), pp.406–418.

Summers, J., and Summers, J., 2017. Motivating intention to take action on behalf of an out-group: implications for the use of advocacy messages in social marketing strategies. *Journal of Marketing Management, 33*(11–12), pp.973–1002.

Swann Jr, W. B., Rentfrow, P. J., and Guinn, J. S., 2003. Self-verification: The search for coherence. *Handbook of self and identity*, 367–383.

Swann, W. B., Chang-Schneider, C. and McClarty, K., 2007. Do our self-views matter? Self-concept and self-esteem in everyday life. *American Psychologist, 62*(2), pp.84–94.

Tajfel, H. and Turner, J. C., 1979. An integrative theory of intergroup conflict. In: Austin, W. G. and Worchel, S. (eds.) *The Social Psychology of Intergroup Relations*. Monterey, CA: Brooks/Cole. pp.33–47.

Tajfel, H., 1970. Experiments in intergroup discrimination. *Scientific American, 223*(5), pp.96–103.

Tajfel, H., 1972. La categorisation sociale [Social categorization]. In: Moscovici, S. (eds.) *Introduction a la psychologie sociale*. Paris: Larousse. pp.272–302

Tajfel, H., 1974. Social identity and intergroup behaviour. *Social Science Information*, 13, pp.65–93.

Tajfel, H., 1978. *Differentiation Between Social Groups: Studies in the Social Psychology of Intergroup Relations*. London: Academic Press.

Tajfel, H., 1981. *Human groups and social categories: Studies in social psychology*. Cambridge: Cambridge University Press.

Tajfel, H., 1982a. Social psychology of intergroup relations. *Annual Reviews of Psychology, 33*(1), pp.1–39.

Tajfel, H., 1982b. *Social identity and intergroup relations*. Reprint. Cambridge: Cambridge University Press, 2010.

Tajfel, H., Billig, M. G., Bundy, R. P. and Flament, C., 1971. Social categorization and intergroup behaviour. *European Journal of Social Psychology, 1*(2), pp.149–178.

Terry, D. J. and Hogg, M. A., 1996. Group norms and the attitude-behavior relationship: A role for group identification. *Personality and Social Psychology Bulletin*, *22*(8), pp.776–793.

Trudel, R., Argo, J. J. and Meng, M. D., 2016. The recycled self: consumers' disposal decisions of identity-linked products. *Journal of Consumer Research*, *43*(2), pp.246–264.

Turner, J. C. and Oakes, P. J., 1986. The significance of the social identity concept for social psychology with reference to individualism, interactionism and social influence. *British Journal of Social Psychology*, *25*(3), pp.237–252.

Turner, J. C. and Reynolds, K. J., 2003. The social identity perspective in intergroup relations: Theories, themes, and controversies. In: Brown, R. and Gaertner, S. (eds.) *Blackwell Handbook of Social Psychology: Intergroup Processes*. Malden, MA: Blackwell. pp.133–152.

Turner, J. C., 1975. Social comparison and social identity: Some prospects for intergroup behaviour. *European Journal of Social Psychology*, *5*(1), pp.1–34.

Turner, J. C., 1985. Social categorization and the self-concept: A social cognitive theory of group behavior. In: Lawler, E.L. (eds.) *Advances in group processes: Theory and research* (Vol. 2). Greenwich, CT: JAI Press. pp.77–122

Turner, J. C., 1991. *Social influence: Mapping social psychology series*. Belmont, CA: Thomson Brooks/Cole Publishing Co.

Turner, J. C., Hogg, M. A., Oakes, P. J., Reicher, S. D. and Wetherell, M. S., 1987. *Rediscovering the social group: A self-categorization theory*. Oxford: Blackwell.

Turner, J. C., Oakes, P. J., Haslam, S. A. and McGarty, C., 1994. Self and collective: Cognition and social context. *Personality and Social Psychology Bulletin*, *20*(5), pp.454–463.

Turner, J., Brown, R. J. and Tajfel, H., 1979. Social comparison and group interest in ingroup favouritism. *European Journal of Social Psychology*, *9*(2), pp.187–204.

Tuškej, U., Golob, U. and Podnar, K., 2013. The role of consumer–brand identification in building brand relationships. *Journal of Business Research*, *66*(1), pp.53–59.

White, K., and Dahl, D. W., 2007. Are all out-groups created equal? Consumer identity and dissociative influence. *Journal of Consumer Research*, *34*(4), pp.525–536.

White, K., Simpson, B. and Argo, J. J., 2014. The motivating role of dissociative out-groups in encouraging positive consumer behaviors. *Journal of Marketing Research*, *51*(4), pp.433–447.

Winterich, K. P., Mittal, V. and Ross Jr, W. T., 2009. Donation behavior toward in-groups and out-groups: The role of gender and moral identity. *Journal of Consumer Research*, *36*(2), pp.199–214.

Wolter, J. S. and Cronin Jr., J. J., 2015. Re-conceptualizing cognitive and affective customer-company identification: the role of self-motives and different customer-based outcomes. *Journal of the Academy of Marketing Science*, *44*(3),pp.397–413.

P. K. Noushad, S. Sreejesh and Justin Paul

3 Social Responsibility Communication of Corporates: A Consumer Marketing Perspective

Introduction

In recent years, since it is closely associated with a company's long-term success and sometimes even its existence, Corporate Social Responsibility has been gaining a noteworthy fascination among the stakeholders, particularly among the consumers (Vaaland, Heide and Grønhaug 2008). Corporate Social Responsibility denotes the 'actions that appear to further some social good, beyond the interests of the firm and that which is required by law' (McWilliams and Siegel 2001, p. 117). In this era, consumers are more socially aware of the activities of their firms from where they purchase products or avail services and it, in turn, prompt the companies to do favourable Corporate Social Responsibility activities (Bonilla-Priego, Najera and Font 2011; de Grosbois 2012; Smerecnik and Andersen 2011), and it becomes a common phenomenon in most parts of the world. With the advent of non-traditional communication media, consumers are better aware of the Corporate Social Responsibility actions of the company; and hence, they usually update even a minute developments occurring in the atmospheric areas of Corporate Social Responsibility (Berens and Popma 2014; Schmeltz 2014). If the consumers consider better responsibility from the company's Corporate Social Responsibility actions, the company will gain more support from the community and the consumers. This action oriented towards social responsibility help these firms to gain consumer trust, awareness, and reputation. This knowledge about the benefits of Corporate Social Responsibility directed companies to do very serious actions in the Corporate Social Responsibility domain. For example, the global giant Johnson and Johnson's Corporate Social Responsibility efforts focusing on reducing the adverse impact on the planet and their call for healthy lifestyle attracted the attention of millions of people across the world. Similarly, Bosch's model of Corporate Social Responsibility is different, where the company invested half of its R&D budget in environmental conservation technology. Yet another Corporate Social Responsibility effort from New Belgium Brewing Company, where the company made attempts to follow a sustainable business by adopting solar panels to support their power needs, and also an aerobic digester system to convert waste water into energy, and motivated their employees in their company base to use bikes to get around. Though the company do very serious Corporate Social Responsibility actions, sometimes it will give expected results, because of the failure of effective strategy for communicating Corporate Social Responsibility activities. Hence, it is expected that if the company wishes

https://doi.org/10.1515/9783110659566-003

desired results, there is a need for properly planned and adequate Corporate Social Responsibility communication strategy, which can eventually bring out some company-favouring responses from the consumers (Sen and Bhattacharya 2001). The importance of Corporate Social Responsibility communication is also emphasised in the literature that 'businesses cannot hope to enjoy concrete benefits from Corporate Social Responsibility unless they intelligently communicate about their initiatives to relevant stakeholders' (Maignan and Ferrell 2004, p. 17), specifically very focused Corporate Social Responsibility communication strategies and appropriate approaches needed to attract the consumers' attention with respect to company's Corporate Social Responsibility efforts. Hence, in this chapter, we follow a consumer marketing perspective of Corporate Social Responsibility communication and presenting a framework for effective Corporate Social Responsibility communication, that further enhances the theoretical and practical insights in the domain of Corporate Social Responsibility communication.

Corporate Social Responsibility Communication Framework

In Figure 3.1 we suggested a comprehensive Corporate Social Responsibility communication framework and divided into four stages: pre-communication, communication design, communication execution, and post-communication. Within the circles, we presented the numbers which show the important priorities of the firm during each stage of their Corporate Social Responsibility communication. In addition to this, each stage of their Corporate Social Responsibility communication, there is a need to examine or assess the effectiveness. Here the study presumes that the failure to assess the efficacy lead to the failure in Corporate Social Responsibility communication. In the following sections we elaborate Figure 3.1 in detail and substantiate the actions required in each stage of Corporate Social Responsibility communication.

Pre-Communication Stage

In the pre-communication stage of Corporate Social Responsibility communication, the company should have to decide in advance what information is to be communicated to the stakeholders, particularly to the consumers. Pre-communication stage includes various decisions relating to the content of the message, the communication strategies, the medium of communication, the expectations of the stakeholders about company's Corporate Social Responsibility initiatives, and the evaluation criteria of the message. The main purpose of this stage is to identify the possible drawbacks of the company's Corporate Social Responsibility communication system in

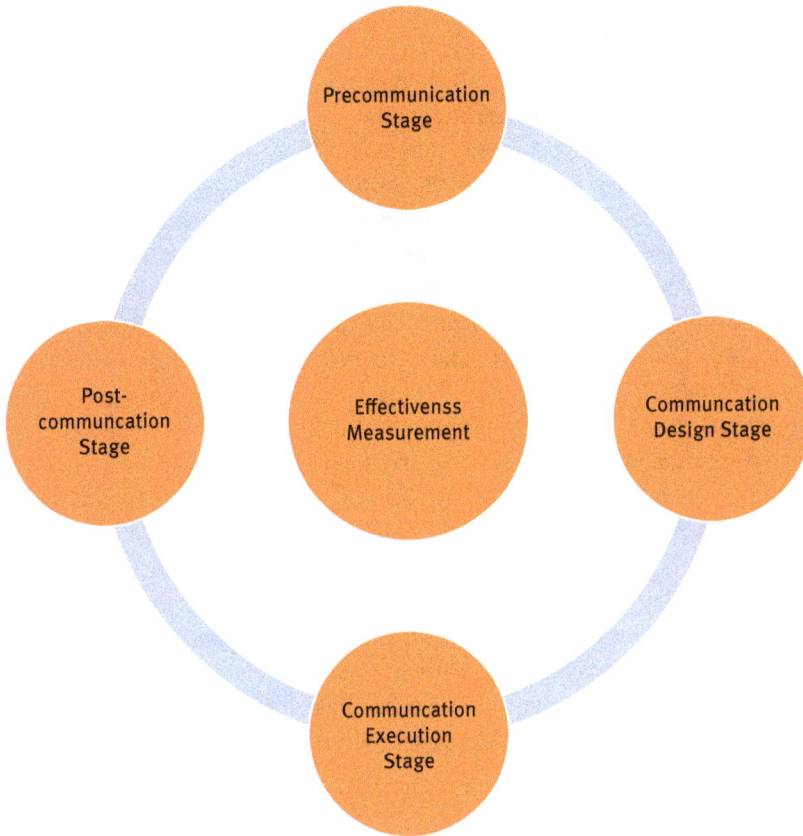

Figure 3.1: Corporate Social Responsibility communication framework on a consumer marketing perspective.
Source: Author Compilation

advance, and to eliminate them before the actual communication process begins. Pre-communication is thus undertaken: (1) to establish awareness among the stakeholders regarding the Corporate Social Responsibility initiatives of the company, and (2) to reduce the level of stakeholder skepticism.

Corporate Social Responsibility Communication Content

While deciding the content of the Corporate Social Responsibility communication messages, the company should be particularly cognizant about various aspects of the message to be communicated such as accessibility of information to the stakeholders, attractiveness of the message, richness of information, interactivity of the message, and credibility and transparency of the information. Accessibility of Corporate Social

Responsibility information to the stakeholders is a significant prerequisite for attaining the objectives of Corporate Social Responsibility communication (Hong and Kim 2004). Chaudhari and Wang (2007) rightly pointed out that the behaviour of the consumers towards various companies exceptionally relied upon their accessibility towards the Corporate Social Responsibility information. Thus, the companies should be vigilant in ensuring that their Corporate Social Responsibility information is highly accessible to the stakeholders. This can be easily attained by the company by publishing their Corporate Social Responsibility information on the 'home' page or 'about us' page of their corporate websites (Dincer and Dincer 2010). Corporate Social Responsibility information of a company should also be attractive to the stakeholders. Attractiveness of Corporate Social Responsibility information can create a good impression about the company in the minds of the stakeholders (Aiezza 2015). Companies can ensure the attractiveness of their Corporate Social Responsibility information in different ways, say for example, by using a multiple channel for communicating Corporate Social Responsibility such as both corporate website and social media pages of the company at the same time (Belinda, Westerman, and Bergman 2018; Cao, Peng and Ye 2019). In order to be attractive, the Corporate Social Responsibility message of the company should also be filled with richer information that is adequately required by the stakeholders (Saat and Selamet 2014). Instead of limiting Corporate Social Responsibility information into text messages alone, the company can use various other multimedia forms such as videos, audios, and animated contents for ensuring the richness of information. Corporate Social Responsibility communication is said to be complete and perfect, only if there are some possibilities for interaction in between, the company and the stakeholders (Moreno and Capriotti 2009). Interactivity is more related with the media selection decisions of the company. The most important factor determining the content of the Corporate Social Responsibility message more acceptable among the stakeholders is the credibility and transparency of the Corporate Social Responsibility messages. Credibility issues in Corporate Social Responsibility communication arise, when a company fails to publish the whole truth regarding its Corporate Social Responsibility initiatives by omitting important information (Devin 2016). Hence, in the pre-communication stage, it is the responsibility of the company to maintain the required minimum quality of the content of Corporate Social Responsibility information to be communicated to the stakeholders, by way of ensuring accessibility, attractiveness, information richness, interactivity and, credibility and transparency of the message.

Corporate Social Responsibility Communication Strategies

Corporate Social Responsibility communication strategies refer to various modes of communication the company indents to apply for the purpose of transmitting their Corporate Social Responsibility initiatives to the stakeholders. The basic question that a company required to consider while deciding its communication strategy is whether their mode of communication should be unidirectional or bidirectional in nature (Kent and Taylor 2016). On the basis of the direction or flow of message between the stakeholders and the company, the Corporate Social Responsibility communication strategies can be broadly classified into two as asymmetric Corporate Social Responsibility communication strategy and symmetric Corporate Social Responsibility communication strategy (Kollatt and Farache 2017). The Asymmetric Corporate Social Responsibility communication strategy is unidirectional in nature, where the objective of the company is just to inform the stakeholders about their Corporate Social Responsibility activities; whereas in the case of symmetric Corporate Social Responsibility communication strategy, which is bidirectional in nature, the company expects an interaction-oriented dialogue from the stakeholders and to involve and engage them as a part of the company's Corporate Social Responsibility initiatives.

While deciding the Corporate Social Responsibility communication strategies, the company should consider two basic factors such as the objective of Corporate Social Responsibility communication and the media used for communicating Corporate Social Responsibility initiatives. If the objective of the company is confined only on using Corporate Social Responsibility communication just as an informing tool, for instance, as in the case of some controversial companies (Grygiel and Brown 2019), the company is better to apply the asymmetric Corporate Social Responsibility communication strategy; whereas if the company aims to elaborate its Corporate Social Responsibility communication as device to collect the opinion of the stakeholders about its Corporate Social Responsibility performances, then it needs to apply the symmetric strategy. If the media utilized by the company covers some conventional forms of communication such as newspapers and periodicals, it will restrict the company from using the symmetric strategy, but allow to use only asymmetric strategy, because it lacks the possibility of interactivity among the communicating parties; rather, if the company uses non-traditional media of communication such as corporate websites and social media pages that permit them to apply the symmetric strategy of Corporate Social Responsibility communication.

Corporate Social Responsibility Communication Media

As in the case of any forms of communication, Corporate Social Responsibility can likewise be transmitted by making use of different types of communication media. The entire Corporate Social Responsibility communication media can be broadly classified into two as traditional media and non-traditional media (Korschun and Du 2013). The decision between either to use traditional media or to use non-traditional media for Corporate Social Responsibility communication is a crucial one, because it is capable of affecting the attitude of the targeted audience. Non-traditional media, such as social media and corporate websites, used as a Corporate Social

Responsibility communication device enable the companies in creating rapid relationship with stakeholders (Colleoni 2013). In addition to this, they have the advantages of easily reaching a mass audience with greater speed, but with lowest cost. They also offer greater flexibility in communication by easily editing the communicated content with least restrictions.

Traditional media such as mass media and print media, on the other hand, are perceived among the stakeholders as a symbol of public trust and confidence (Perks, Farache, Shukla and Berry 2013). Even though the importance of traditional media as a communication device is under question, particularly in today's digitally dominated communication world, previous studies show that it still maintains its credibility as an ideal device for Corporate Social Responsibility communication. Hence, in pre-communication stage, the companies should be very much cautious in making decisions regarding the media selection of Corporate Social Responsibility communication. It is advisable to use both traditional and non-traditional media for communicating the Corporate Social Responsibility initiatives of the company as far as possible (Mercadé-Melé, Molinillo and Fernández-Morales 2017).

Expectations of Stakeholders

Expectations of stakeholders about the Corporate Social Responsibility policies of a company is a relevant factor to be considered in the pre-communication stage of Corporate Social Responsibility communication. It is a basic idea to be kept in the minds of the Corporate Social Responsibility policy makers that there should be a similarity or congruence in between the causes selected by the companies to implement their Corporate Social Responsibility programs and the courses of the business activities (Berens and Popma 2014). It is because, the stakeholders always expect the company's contribution from Corporate Social Responsibility activities in the same areas where the company actually operates. For example, a company undertaking business such as forestry and plantation will be highly acknowledged among the stakeholders, if it is implementing environmental protection-related activities as part of Corporate Social Responsibility initiatives. If the expectations of stakeholders gone wrong, they will be tended to doubtfully watch the activities of the companies. This situation will lead to stakeholder skepticism (Du, Bhattacharya and Sen 2010). Hence, in the pre-communication stage itself the company should consider the expectations of the stakeholders in order to gain acceptability to their Corporate Social Responsibility communication.

Corporate Social Responsibility Communication Evaluation Criteria

Company's overall Corporate Social Responsibility performances have an ultimate impact on various business outcomes such as business returns, competitive advantage, financial performance, and corporate reputation (Du et al. 2010; Ettinger, Grabner-Kräuter and Terlutter 2018; Porter and Kramer 2006; Brown and Dacin 1997). All these outcomes are the results of various responses of the customers. Thus, during the pre-communication stage, the company should decide in advance how do they intend to measure the effectiveness of their Corporate Social Responsibility programs.

In short, in the pre-communication stage of Corporate Social Responsibility communication, the company prepares a blue print of its entire Corporate Social Responsibility communication framework. It is a crucial stage in the sense that any weakness happening on account of pre-communication will seriously affect the entire Corporate Social Responsibility -related strategies of the company.

Corporate Social Responsibility Communication Design Stage

Designing Corporate Social Responsibility communication is the key issue in the Corporate Social Responsibility communication framework (Aakhus 2011). It demonstrates how the Corporate Social Responsibility communication message of a company looks like and, in this manner, it must cover all the basic components of a Corporate Social Responsibility message in the wake of thinking about the special features of the targeted audience, as it is necessary to ensure stakeholder engagement (Aakhus and Bzdak 2015). Corporate Social Responsibility communication design is the process of developing the themes of the Corporate Social Responsibility messages to be passed on to the stakeholders by forming a mental picture of the actual Corporate Social Responsibility initiatives of a company that gives importance to the physical arrangement of the elements in the Corporate Social Responsibility communication message so that this mental idea may be effectively presented. It gives specific importance to the question how Corporate Social Responsibility communication message is to be framed (Craig and Tracy 2014). Hence, Corporate Social Responsibility communication design should include the three steps, as follows:
1. Identification of the distinct characteristics of the stakeholders
2. Classification of the stakeholders based on their distinct characteristics
3. Framing Corporate Social Responsibility messages on the basis of types of stakeholders

Identification of the Distinct Characteristics of the Stakeholders

From consumer marketing point of view, stakeholder's distinctive characteristics, in the light of a persuasive message background, can substantially be explained with the help of two psychological theories, construal level theory (Liberman and Trope 1998), and regulatory focus theory (Higgins 1997).

Construal Level Theory

Construal level theory presumes that the interpretation of a message is highly affected by the psychological distance of an object or an event (Liberman and Trope 1998). According to the construal level theory, if the psychological distance between the individual and the object is high, then it will be construed in a more abstract nature; however, if the psychological distance and the object are very short, then it will be construed in a more concrete level (Liberman and Trope 1998; Trope and Liberman 2003). An object is said to be construed in abstract nature, if it is interpreted in terms of its general and superordinate features; whereas concrete construal refers to representing an object in terms of its specific and subordinate features (Liberman and Trope 1998; Trope 1989). That means, abstract construal is represented by peripheral information, however, concrete construal is represented by a detail-oriented information (Line, Hanks and Zhang 2016). Psychological distance is a multi-dimensional concept, which includes temporal distance (short term vs. Long term), spatial distance (nearby vs, far-away), social distance (ingroup vs. outgroup), and hypothetical distance (probable vs. unlikely) (Trope, Liberman and Wakslak 2007).

Regulatory Focus Theory

According to the regulatory focus theory, two types of motivational systems may co-occur in every individual, in particular, a promotion-focus system and a preventions-focus system (Higgins 1997). Promotion-focus system is connected with an individual's desire for advancement, growth and accomplishment; while, prevention-focus system is concerned with that of an individual's security, safety, and responsibility aspiration (Crowe and Higgins 1997). Subsequently, promotion-focused individuals are more inclined to pursue positive outcomes; on the other hand, prevention-focused individuals are more prepared to avoid negative outcomes (Higgins 1997).

An individual may express regulatory focus systems either as a chronic behavior or as a situational behavior (Crowe and Higgins 1997). As a chronic behavior, the regulatory focus is a personality tendency that is framed gradually in the process of the growth of an individual; while, regulatory focus as a situational behavior is a personality tendency initiated incidentally because of the pressure of some momentary situations (Cui and Ye 2017). In short, the chronic regulatory focus system is long-term and constant in nature, whereas, situational momentary regulatory focus system is short-term in nature.

While designing Corporate Social Responsibility communication messages, it is fundamental to consider the distinct characteristics of the stakeholders in the light of both construal level theory and regulatory focus theory. Stakeholders may exhibit different behaviors, according to their chronic and situational behaviors. These behavioral variations have a prominent role while considering whether company designs their Corporate Social Responsibility messages for a short run or for a long run.

Classification of the Stakeholders Based on their Distinct Characteristics

On the basis of construal level theory and regulatory focus theory, individuals are classified into different categories. Each type of individual possesses some special characteristics and features that have importance in their information processing. Hence, the type of stakeholders showing a particular regulatory orientation or a specific level of abstraction is to be differently dealt when designing the Corporate Social Responsibility communication messages of the company.

Abstract and Concrete-Level Stakeholders

According to the construal level theory, stakeholders may fall either in the abstract level category or in concrete level category, on the basis of their information processing attitude. Abstract level stakeholders evaluate Corporate Social Responsibility messages at a high level of construal that requires the company to provide information in such a manner that gives an overall impression about the entire Corporate Social Responsibility initiatives of the firm; whereas, the stakeholders belonging to concrete level of construal interprets Corporate Social Responsibility information at a low level, where the company should have to present their messages by pinpointing a detailed picture of their Corporate Social Responsibility performances with the help of all supporting contexts (Irmak, Wakslak, and Trope 2013).

Promotion-Focused and Prevention-Focused Stakeholders

Regulatory focus theory classifies stakeholders into two groups, promotion-focused stakeholders, and prevention-focused stakeholders, based on their regulatory orientations towards evaluating a Corporate Social Responsibility message. Promotion-focused stakeholders are characterized by a focus on hopes, aspirations, and the attainment of positive outcomes, and prevention-focused stakeholders character-ized by a focus on responsibilities, duties, and the avoidance of negative outcomes (Higgins 1997). In other words, the promotion-focused stakeholders are focused to-wards the orientations, either a positive benefit from a message being attained or a positive benefit from a message not being attained; while the prevention-focused stakeholders are focused towards the orientations, either a negative benefit from a message not being attained or a negative benefit from a message being attained (Lee and Aaker 2004).

Framing Corporate Social Responsibility Messages on the Basis of Types of Stakeholders

Message framing is a process of persuading the perception of a particular message audience about a particular issue such as Corporate Social Responsibility initiatives of a company (Waller and Conaway 2011). While framing Corporate Social Responsi-bility communication messages, companies should consider the type of stakeholders on the basis of their level of construal and regulatory orientation towards evaluating a message.

Abstract and Concrete Messages

Companies can frame Corporate Social Responsibility communication messages into different ways, generally as abstract level messages and concrete level messages, con-sidering the level of abstraction of the stakeholders while they are evaluating a mes-sage (Line et al. 2016). As construal is multi-dimensional concept (Trope et al. 2007), different dimensions of psychological distance can also be made use of framing Cor-porate Social Responsibility messages. For example, Line et al. (2016) called attention to that the Corporate Social Responsibility message can be framed as universally ben-eficial message and locally beneficial message (social distance) as well as short-term benefitted message and long-term benefitted message (temporal distance).

Gain-Framed and Loss-Framed Messages

Corporate Social Responsibility communication messages can be framed in at least two ways, in a gain-framed manner and in a loss-framed manner, by considering the regu-latory orientations of the stakeholders (Rothman and Salovey 1997). A gain-framed message focuses on the positive outcomes of a particular cause, that is, that highlights the positive consequences of engaging in Corporate Social Responsibility initiatives; and a loss-framed message focuses on the negative outcomes of a particular cause, that is, that highlights the negative consequences if the Corporate Social Responsibility initiative is not undertaken (White, MacDonnell and Dahl 2011).

As the two important variables in Corporate Social Responsibility communication design, both the construal level at which the messages are appraised and the regulatory focus of an individual has inherent relationships (Lee, Keller and Sternthal 2010; Aaker and Lee 2001). When involving a lower-level, concrete construal the stakeholder is actually trying to evaluate the feasibility of a particular Corporate Social Responsibility message, in the same manner, a loss-framed Corporate Social Responsibility message is describing the feasibility of undertaking a particular Corporate Social Responsibility initiative and specify how such activity is to be done. This is true in the case of abstract construal and promotion focus orientation also, in the sense that a higher-level, abstractly construed Corporate Social Responsibility message manipulate the desirability of a particular message to that of a gain-framed Corporate Social Responsibility message describing the desirability of a Corporate's socially responsible initiatives by specifying why such activity is to be done. Hence, while designing Corporate Social Responsibility communication messages, the designers should try to understand the congruence between the construal level and the regulatory orientations so as to reap maximum business benefits.

Communication Execution Stage

At this stage, the company is making every effort to implement the message of Corporate Social Responsibility communication designed for the target audience during the previous stage. Corporate Social Responsibility communication execution is the process of selecting suitable media to convey a detailed and comprehensive information about the Corporate Social Responsibility initiatives of a company, to its stakeholders. The main purpose of this stage is to ensure the information available to the stakeholders, particularly to the consumers, so as to maximize benefit to the company on account of Corporate Social Responsibility (Du et al. 2010). This is not an easy attempt, where the company has to face some specific challenges while communicating its Corporate Social Responsibility activities to the stakeholders (Dawkins 2004). These challenges include lack of awareness among the stakeholders regarding the Corporate Social Responsibility activities of a company, consumer skepticism and negative reactions from the media (Du et al. 2010; Dawkins 2004).

The problem of lack of awareness about the Corporate Social Responsibility initiatives among consumers and the negative reactions from the media are the results of the wrong media selection decision of the company. In this regard, in order to increase consumers' knowledge about a specific company's Corporate Social Responsibility and positive reactions from them, the company should have to ensure that the communication media is approachable and credible to the stakeholders

(Berens and Popma 2014; Pomering and Johnson 2009). Consumer skepticism arises when there is any difference in the expectations of the consumers about the genuineness of firm's Corporate Social Responsibility performance and the company's claims in the form of Corporate Social Responsibility reports. (Lewis 2003). It may happen because different stakeholders expect different initiatives from the company about their Corporate Social Responsibility policies (Dawkins 2004). The concept of skepticism may be defined as a tendency of the consumers to distrust the company's claim and to raise questions about the communicative intentions of the corporates on account of their Corporate Social Responsibility performances (Obermiller and Spangenberg 1998; Pirsch, Gupta and Grau 2006). Skepticism and credibility are inversely related, in the sense that when credibility increases, skepticism will reduce (Schmeltz 2014). Hence, the company should try to increase the credibility of their Corporate Social Responsibility claims by transparently communicating their Corporate Social Responsibility information (Podnar and Golob 2007). In short, in order to overcome various challenges of Corporate Social Responsibility communication, the company should be very much careful about their media selection decision.

Corporate Social Responsibility Communication Media

A company uses different media of communication through which its Corporate Social Responsibility information is disseminated (Du et al. 2010). Specifically, these media can be broadly classified into two categories as, internal and external Corporate Social Responsibility communication media. Internal Corporate Social Responsibility communication media represent the workforce of the company, who are considered as a strong spokesperson of the company's Corporate Social Responsibility initiatives (Dawkins 2004), and such communication are treated as one of the strategic approaches of the companies towards their Corporate Social Responsibility communication systems that is helpful in reducing stakeholder skepticism (Schmeltz 2014). Moreover, it has the benefit of flexibility and cost effectiveness.

On the other hand, the external Corporate Social Responsibility communication media of a company are considered as a tool guaranteeing corporate legitimacy that emerges as a result of the innate relationship between a company and its stakeholders (Colleoni 2013). They can be broadly classified, on the basis of the type of communication devices used, as traditional media and non-traditional or digital media (Korschun and Du 2013). Traditional media comprises of the annual reports of the company and various mass media such as different forms of print media of communication. These media reports may be prepared and published by the company itself, or by a third party. Consumer perception and attitude towards the traditional media reports of a company varies, according to its style of preparation and publication (Folkes and Kamins 1999). Berens and Popma (2014) illustrate this situation as, when such reports are prepared by the company, but published by a third party, it will be more effective than a report prepared as well as published by the company itself; even though, the traditional media reports are most effective when prepared as well as published by a third party, there is a possibility of perceiving it as a public relation document sponsored by the company. Still, they are considered to be a symbol of consumer trust in the case of Corporate Social Responsibility communication.

Digital media platforms of Corporate Social Responsibility communication popularly cover the corporate websites and the social media pages of the company. The corporate websites and social media pages serve almost a same purpose, but there are some differences in between these two, in the manner they are treating the content of Corporate Social Responsibility information. In other words, corporate websites provide information relating to the Corporate Social Responsibility initiatives of a company in a general perspective along with all other company-related relevant information (Sones, Grantham and Vieira 2009). On the contrary, social media pages of a company can be specifically designed for the sole purpose of transmitting its Corporate Social Responsibility information alone (Crişan and Zbuchea 2015). In other words, a company can create a specific Facebook or Twitter page of its own for attracting the stakeholders.

In the context of Corporate Social Responsibility communication, social media, which is otherwise called as Web 2.0 platforms, play a critical role because that enable to establish a strong relationship between the company and the stakeholders, by interacting in between from across the globe (Colleoni 2013; Chan and Guillet 2011). In addition to this, social media carries better viral features, hence would reach to the mass audience very rapidly compared to other competitive platforms. Moreover, it facilitates the companies use relatively inexpensive, flexible and advanced communication tools and hence, generate better customer outcomes. Different from other media, social media adds flexibility in Corporate Social Responsibility communication by providing necessary information to its customers and also generate their responses towards the same. In short, social media can have both one-way and two-way communication possibilities, which is considered to be an inevitable condition for stakeholder engagement.

Post-Communication Stage

Corporate Social Responsibility communication efforts of a company are said to be effective only if it can accomplish its desired objectives (Kim, Kang, and Mattila 2012). Post-communication stage of Corporate Social Responsibility communication incorporates the evaluation of the effectiveness of Corporate Social Responsibility communication strategies designed and executed by the company. It indicates the reachability of the implemented Corporate Social Responsibility communication effort of a company among the stakeholders and its effect on their purchase or investment behaviours. It is an important stage in the Corporate Social Responsibility communication framework because, it is necessary to estimate the benefits gained by the company against the investments made in its Corporate Social Responsibility initiatives.

It is an accepted conviction among the corporates that the companies actively involving in the Corporate Social Responsibility initiatives can enjoy critical business benefits, if they are able to share it with the stakeholders effectively (Du et al. 2010). These benefits are apparent from its impact on the major areas of business discipline such as marketing, finance and investment, and human resources. In the marketing area, various studies reported different types of business benefits of Corporate Social Responsibility communication such as corporate reputation (Morsing, Schultz and Nielsen 2008), competitive advantage (Marcus and Anderson, 2006), profit maximisation (Husted and Salazar 2006), consumer loyalty (Sanclemente-Téllez 2017) and many more. The business benefits concerning finance and investment area that a company expects on account of its Corporate Social Responsibility performance as shown by previous studies included return on equity and return on assets (Peloza 2009), profit maximisation (Lin, Yang and Liou 2009), and other financial-related benefits in general (say for example, Uadiale and Fagbemi 2012; McWilliams and Siegel 2000). Human resource department of a company considers Corporate Social Responsibility communication as a tool to attract young and talented employees (Belinda et al. 2018; Duthler and Dhanesh 2018).

It is better to consider the message-related outcomes to measure the effectiveness of the Corporate Social Responsibility communication practices of a company, even though all the above mentioned business benefits are very much helpful for the same purpose. Two such important outcomes are attitude towards message and recommendation intention. According to cognitive dissonance theory (Festinger 1957), attitudinal change in an individual occurs when he is trying to make some deliberate changes in his current situations. In line with this, when the consumers get satisfied their expectations about a company through its socially responsible performances, it will lead to a change in the attitude of the consumers towards that particular company (Anghelache 2014). That means, if consumers show positive attitudes towards a company, it can be considered as an indication of the effectiveness of a company's Corporate Social Responsibility communication efforts.

Consumers usually express their loyalty towards a company in two ways, either in the form of repurchase intention or in the form of recommendation intention. Both repurchase intention and recommendation intention are different in their effect on the company. Repurchase intention is concerned with the actual purchasing behaviour of a customer by actually spending his/her amount, whereas recommendation intention is related to the behaviour of a customer for complimenting the company or the product by referring it to other people (Jin and Su 2009). Altunel and Erkurt (2015) defines recommendation intention as 'an indirectly measured loyalty in the conative stage which could be measured by observing the buying behaviour of the consumers'. Consumers will show a higher level of recommendation intention behaviour when they are highly satisfied with the Corporate Social Responsibility message communicated by the company (Al-Ansi, Olya and Han 2018; Altunel and Erkurt 2015). In short, as the message-related outcomes directly related with the qualitative features of Corporate Social Responsibility communication, both the message attitude and recommendation intention can serve as an important tool to be used in the post-communication stage.

Conclusion

Corporate Social Responsibility communication framework covers different stages beginning from planning of communication to the evaluation of its effectiveness. The company should be careful about the 'between-the-line' readings of the consumers regarding their communicated contents. Thus, in order to ensure the effectiveness of the Corporate Social Responsibility communication, the company should frame each stage with utmost care.

References

Aaker, J. L., and Lee, A. Y. (2001). "I" seek pleasures and "we" avoid pains: The role of self-regulatory goals in information processing and persuasion. *Journal of Consumer Research*, *28*(1), 33–49.

Aakhus, M. (2011). Crafting interactivity for stakeholder engagement: Transforming assumptions about communication in science and policy. *Health physics*, *101*(5), 531–535.

Aakhus, M., and Bzdak, M. (2015). Stakeholder engagement as communication design practice. *Journal of Public Affairs*, *15*(2), 188–200.

Aiezza, M. C. (2015). "We may face the risks" . . . "risks that could adversely affect our face." A corpus-assisted discourse analysis of modality markers in CORPORATE SOCIAL RESPONSIBILIIY reports. *Studies in Communication Sciences*, *15*(1), 68–76.

Al-Ansi, A., Olya, H. G., and Han, H. (2019). Effect of general risk on trust, satisfaction, and recommendation intention for halal food. *International Journal of Hospitality Management*, *83*, 210–219.

Altunel, M. C., and Erkurt, B. (2015). Cultural tourism in Istanbul: The mediation effect of tourist experience and satisfaction on the relationship between involvement and recommendation intention. *Journal of Destination Marketing and Management*, *4*(4), 213–221.

Anghelache, V. (2014). Factors which determine the level of job satisfaction for kindergarten teachers. Preliminary study. *Procedia-Social and Behavioral Sciences*, *127*, 47–52.

Belinda, C. D., Westerman, J. W., and Bergman, S. M. (2018). Recruiting with ethics in an online era: Integrating corporate social responsibility with social media to predict organizational attractiveness. *Journal of Vocational Behavior*, *109*, 101–117.

Berens, G., and Popma, W. T. (2014). Creating consumer confidence in CORPORATE SOCIAL RESPONSIBILITY communications. In *Communicating corporate social*

    responsibility: Perspectives and practice (pp. 383–403). Emerald Group Publishing
    Limited.

Bonilla Priego, M. J., Najera, J. J., and Font, X. (2011). Environmental management decision-making
    in certified hotels. *Journal of Sustainable Tourism, 19*(3), 361–381.

Brown, T. J., and Dacin, P. A. (1997). The company and the product: Corporate associations and
    consumer product responses. *Journal of marketing, 61*(1), 68–84.

Cao, F., Peng, S. S., and Ye, K. (2019). Multiple large shareholders and corporate social
    responsibility reporting. *Emerging Markets Review, 38*, 287–309.

Chan, N. L., and Guillet, B. D. (2011). Investigation of social media marketing: how does the hotel
    industry in Hong Kong perform in marketing on social media websites? *Journal of Travel and
    Tourism Marketing, 28*(4), 345–368.

Chaudhri, V., and Wang, J. (2007). Communicating corporate social responsibility on the internet:
    A case study of the top 100 information technology companies in India. *Management
    Communication Quarterly, 21*(2), 232–247.

Colleoni, E. (2013). CORPORATE SOCIAL RESPONSIBILITY communication strategies for
    organizational legitimacy in social media. *Corporate Communications: An International
    journal, 18*(2), 228–248.

Craig, R. T., and Tracy, K. (2014). Building grounded practical theory in applied communication
    research: Introduction to the special issue. *Journal of Applied Communication Research, 42*(3),
    229–243.

Crişan, C., and Zbuchea, A. (2015). CORPORATE SOCIAL RESPONSIBILITY and Social Media: Could
    Online Repositories Become Regulatory Tools for CORPORATE SOCIAL RESPONSIBILITY Related
    Activities' Reporting? In *Corporate social responsibility in the digital age* (pp. 197–219).
    Emerald Group Publishing Limited.

Crowe, E., and Higgins, E. T. (1997). Regulatory focus and strategic inclinations: Promotion and
    prevention in decision-making. *Organizational behavior and human decision processes, 69*(2),
    117–132.

Cui, W., and Ye, M. (2017). An Introduction of Regulatory Focus Theory and Its Recently Related
    Researches. *Psychology, 8*(06), 837.

Dawkins, J. (2004). Corporate responsibility: The communication challenge. *Journal of
    communication management, 9*(2), 108–119.

De Grosbois, D. (2012). Corporate social responsibility reporting by the global hotel industry:
    Commitment, initiatives and performance. *International Journal of Hospitality Management,
    31*(3), 896–905.

Devin, B. (2016). Half-truths and dirty secrets: Omissions in CORPORATE SOCIAL RESPONSIBILITY
    communication. *Public Relations Review, 42*(1), 226–228.

Dincer, C., and Dincer, B. (2010). An investigation of Turkish small and medium-sized enterprises
    online CORPORATE SOCIAL RESPONSIBILITY communication. *Social Responsibility Journal,
    6*(2), 197–207.

Du, S., Bhattacharya, C. B., and Sen, S. (2010). Maximizing business returns to corporate social
    responsibility (CORPORATE SOCIAL RESPONSIBILITY): The role of CORPORATE SOCIAL
    RESPONSIBILITY communication. *International journal of management reviews, 12*(1), 8–19.

Duthler, G., and Dhanesh, G. S. (2018). The role of corporate social responsibility (CORPORATE
    SOCIAL RESPONSIBILITY) and internal CORPORATE SOCIAL RESPONSIBILITY communication in
    predicting employee engagement: Perspectives from the United Arab Emirates (UAE). *Public
    Relations Review, 44*(4), 453–462.

Ettinger, A., Grabner-Kräuter, S., and Terlutter, R. (2018). Online CORPORATE SOCIAL
    RESPONSIBILITY communication in the hotel industry: Evidence from small hotels.
    International Journal of Hospitality Management, 68, 94–104.

Festinger, L.: 1957, A Theory of Cognitive Dissonance (Stanford University Press: Stanford, California).

Folkes, V. S., and Kamins, M. A. (1999). Effects of information about firms' ethical and unethical actions on consumers' attitudes. *Journal of Consumer Psychology, 8*(3), 243–259.

Grygiel, J., and Brown, N. (2019). Are social media companies motivated to be good corporate citizens? Examination of the connection between corporate social responsibility and social media safety. *Telecommunications Policy, 43*(5), 445–460.

Higgins, E. T. (1997). Beyond pleasure and pain. *American psychologist, 52*(12), 1280–1300.

Hong, S., and Kim, J. (2004). Architectural criteria for website evaluation – conceptual framework and empirical validation. *Behaviour and Information Technology, 23*(5), 337–357.

Husted, B. W., and de Jesus Salazar, J. (2006). Taking Friedman seriously: Maximizing profits and social performance. *Journal of Management studies, 43*(1), 75–91.

Irmak, C., Wakslak, C. J., and Trope, Y. (2013). Selling the forest, buying the trees: The effect of construal level on seller-buyer price discrepancy. *Journal of Consumer Research, 40*(2), 284–297.

Jin, Y., and Su, M. (2009). Recommendation and repurchase intention thresholds: A joint heterogeneity response estimation. *International Journal of Research in Marketing, 26*(3), 245–255.

Kent, M. L., and Taylor, M. (2016). From Homo Economicus to Homo dialogicus: Rethinking social media use in CORPORATE SOCIAL RESPONSIBILITY communication. *Public Relations Review, 42*(1), 60–67.

Kim, E. E. K., Kang, J., and Mattila, A. S. (2012). The impact of prevention versus promotion hope on CORPORATE SOCIAL RESPONSIBILITY activities. *International Journal of Hospitality Management, 31*(1), 43–51.

Kollat, J., and Farache, F. (2017). Achieving consumer trust on Twitter via CORPORATE SOCIAL RESPONSIBILITY communication. *Journal of Consumer Marketing, 34*(6), 505–514.

Korschun, D., and Du, S. (2013). How virtual corporate social responsibility dialogs generate value: A framework and propositions. *Journal of Business Research, 66*(9), 1494–1504.

Lee, A. Y., and Aaker, J. L. (2004). Bringing the frame into focus: the influence of regulatory fit on processing fluency and persuasion. *Journal of personality and social psychology, 86*(2), 205–218.

Lee, A. Y., Keller, P. A., and Sternthal, B. (2009). Value from regulatory construal fit: The persuasive impact of fit between consumer goals and message concreteness. *Journal of Consumer Research, 36*(5), 735–747.

Lewis, S. (2003). Reputation and corporate responsibility. *Journal of Communication Management, 7*(4), 356–366.

Liberman, N., and Trope, Y. (1998). The role of feasibility and desirability considerations in near and distant future decisions: A test of temporal construal theory. *Journal of personality and social psychology, 75*(1), 5–18.

Lin, C. H., Yang, H. L., and Liou, D. Y. (2009). The impact of corporate social responsibility on financial performance: Evidence from business in Taiwan. *Technology in Society, 31*(1), 56–63.

Line, N. D., Hanks, L., and Zhang, L. (2016). Sustainability communication: The effect of message construals on consumers' attitudes towards green restaurants. *International Journal of Hospitality Management, 57*, 143–151.

Maignan, I., and Ferrell, O. C. (2004). Corporate social responsibility and marketing: An integrative framework. *Journal of the Academy of Marketing science, 32*(1), 3–19.

Marcus, A. A., and Anderson, M. H. (2006). A general dynamic capability: does it propagate business and social competencies in the retail food industry? *Journal of Management Studies, 43*(1), 19–46.

McWilliams, A., and Siegel, D. (2000). Corporate social responsibility and financial performance: correlation or misspecification? *Strategic management journal*, *21*(5), 603–609.

McWilliams, A., and Siegel, D. (2001). Profit maximizing corporate social responsibility. *Academy of Management Review*, *26*(4), 504–505.

Mercadé-Melé, P., Molinillo, S., and Fernández-Morales, A. (2017). The influence of the types of media on the formation of perceived CORPORATE SOCIAL RESPONSIBILITY. *Spanish Journal of Marketing-ESIC*, *21*, 54–64.

Moreno, A., and Capriotti, P. (2009). Communicating CORPORATE SOCIAL RESPONSIBILITY, citizenship and sustainability on the web. *Journal of Communication Management*, *13*(2), 157–175.

Morsing, M., Schultz, M., and Nielsen, K. U. (2008). The 'Catch 22'of communicating CORPORATE SOCIAL RESPONSIBILITY: Findings from a Danish study. *Journal of Marketing Communications*, *14*(2), 97–111.

Obermiller, C., and Spangenberg, E. R. (1998). Development of a scale to measure consumer skepticism toward advertising. *Journal of consumer psychology*, *7*(2), 159–186.

Peloza, J. (2009). The Challenge of Measuring Financial Impacts from Investments in Corporate Social performance. Journal of Management, 35(6),1518–1541.

Perks, K. J., Farache, F., Shukla, P., and Berry, A. (2013). Communicating responsibility-practicing irresponsibility in CORPORATE SOCIAL RESPONSIBILITY advertisements. *Journal of Business Research*, *66*(10), 1881–1888.

Pirsch, J., Gupta, S., and Grau, S. L. (2006). A framework for understanding corporate social responsibility programs as a continuum: An exploratory study. *Journal of business ethics*, *70*(2), 125–140.

Podnar, K., and Golob, U. (2007). CORPORATE SOCIAL RESPONSIBILITY expectations: the focus of corporate marketing. *Corporate communications: An international journal*, *12*(4), 326–340.

Pomering, A., and Johnson, L. W. (2009). Advertising corporate social responsibility initiatives to communicate corporate image: Inhibiting scepticism to enhance persuasion. *Corporate Communications: An International Journal*, *14*(4), 420–439.

Porter, M. E., and Kramer, M. R. (2006). The link between competitive advantage and corporate social responsibility. *Harvard business review*, *84*(12), 78–92.

Rothman, A. J., and Salovey, P. (1997). Shaping perceptions to motivate healthy behavior: the role of message framing. *Psychological bulletin*, *121*(1), 3.

Saat, R. M., and Selamat, M. H. (2014). An examination of consumer's attitude towards corporate social responsibility (CORPORATE SOCIAL RESPONSIBILITY) web communication using media richness theory. *Procedia-Social and Behavioral Sciences*, *155*, 392–397.

Sanclemente-Téllez, J. C. (2017). Marketing and Corporate Social Responsibility (CORPORATE SOCIAL RESPONSIBILITY). Moving between broadening the concept of marketing and social factors as a marketing strategy. *Spanish Journal of Marketing-ESIC*, *21*, 4–25.

Schmeltz, L. (2014). Introducing value-based framing as a strategy for communicating CORPORATE SOCIAL RESPONSIBILITY. *Social Responsibility Journal*, *10*(1), 184–206.

Sen, S., and Bhattacharya, C. B. (2001). Does doing good always lead to doing better? Consumer reactions to corporate social responsibility. *Journal of marketing Research*, *38*(2), 225–243.

Smerecnik, K. R., and Andersen, P. A. (2011). The diffusion of environmental sustainability innovations in North American hotels and ski resorts. *Journal of Sustainable Tourism*, *19*(2), 171–196.

Sones, M., Grantham, S., and Vieira, E. T. (2009). Communicating CORPORATE SOCIAL RESPONSIBILITY via pharmaceutical company web sites: Evaluating message frameworks for external and internal stakeholders. *Corporate Communications: An International Journal*, *14*(2), 144–157.

Trope, Y. (1989). Levels of inference in dispositional judgment. *Social Cognition*, *7*(3), 296–314.

Trope, Y., and Liberman, N. (2003). Temporal construal. *Psychological review*, *110*(3), 403–421.

Trope, Y., Liberman, N., and Wakslak, C. (2007). Construal levels and psychological distance: Effects on representation, prediction, evaluation, and behavior. *Journal of consumer psychology*, *17*(2), 83–95.

Uadiale, O. M., and Fagbemi, T. O. (2012). Corporate social responsibility and financial performance in developing economies: The Nigerian experience. *Journal of Economics and Sustainable Development*, *3*(4), 44–54.

Vaaland, T. I., Heide, M., and Grønhaug, K. (2008). Corporate social responsibility: investigating theory and research in the marketing context. *European Journal of Marketing*, *42*(9/10), 927–953.

Waller, R. L., and Conaway, R. N. (2011). Framing and counterframing the issue of corporate social responsibility: The communication strategies of Nikebiz. com. *The Journal of Business Communication (1973)*, *48*(1), 83–106.

White, K., MacDonnell, R., and Dahl, D. W. (2011). It's the mind-set that matters: The role of construal level and message framing in influencing consumer efficacy and conservation behaviors. *Journal of Marketing Research*, *48*(3), 472–485.

Lukas Parker, Linda Brennan, Sy Nurleyana Wafa, Nguyen Luu,
Nhat Tram Phan-Le and Shinyi Chin

4 Ethical and Social Marketing in Asia: A Multi-Country Perspective

Introduction

One of the main challenges and influences of social marketing strategies, interventions and campaigns is that of context. Macroenvironmental factors such as political, legal, economic, social, cultural, technological and other contextual all have an impact on how a campaign is developed, implemented and received, and ultimately impacts on the degree of success and failure. There are also more microenvironmental and local-ised contextual factors, like community, local institutions and even family dynamics that impact individuals' worldviews, attitudes, knowledge and the way they behave. With these in mind, this chapter evaluates social marketing in three countries in South-east Asia – Malaysia, Singapore, and Vietnam – in macro, micro and local contexts. The aim is to explore how social marketing is conducted in each country, and how case examples from each country provide an overview of social marketing practices in the region. Theories of social marketing applicable to the region are reviewed and extant research presented. This chapter builds on an earlier chapter by the authors (Parker, Brennan, and Nguyen 2015), and presents new material outlining social marketing practice in these three countries.

The unique and diverse characteristics of the three countries are explored. This chapter details how those aspects contribute to each country's social marketing strat-egies. The different levels of social marketing strategies are explained through the lens of the Behavioural Ecological Model adapted by Hovell, Wahlgren, and Gehrman (2002) from Bronfenbrenner's (1977) original ecological systems theory. The Behaviou-ral Ecological Model is conceptualised as a systems model, which means that social marketers look not only to individuals to develop their practice but also to broader societal and community level actors to facilitate change. Consequently, this chapter aims to provide a framework for thinking about social marketing that goes beyond behaviour change (Brennan and Parker 2014). This model is described at the theoreti-cal level and then explained using practical examples. The case examples include a wide range of social marketing campaigns tackling difficult issues, from food waste

Acknowledgement of funding: Professor Brennan is a Chief Investigator (CI) in the FightFoodWaste Cooperative Research Centre which is funded by the Australian Government through the Business Cooperative Research Centres Program. She is also a CI on Communicating Health Project which is funded by the National Health and Medical Research Council (grant number GNT1115496).

https://doi.org/10.1515/9783110659566-004

to human trafficking. Each of the exemplar countries implements social marketing in a unique way, taking into account varying cultural, social and political contexts.

Social Marketing Theories

Social Marketing at a Glance

Social marketing is a multi-layered enterprise that aims to rectify the perceived wrongs of the global society by creating positive social change (Brennan et al. 2014). Social marketing is founded in a Western business tradition and as such, often applies Western ideals of individual autonomy and decision-making to develop strategies for change (for example, Lee's (2019) rubric for social marketing planning) (Brennan et al. 2014). Social marketing in non-Western environments must adjust to different cultural, social and political contexts. There are some fundamentals of social marketing planning that can be adjusted to the context regardless of where social marketing practice is developed. These fundamentals of the social marketing process are depicted in Figure 4.1.

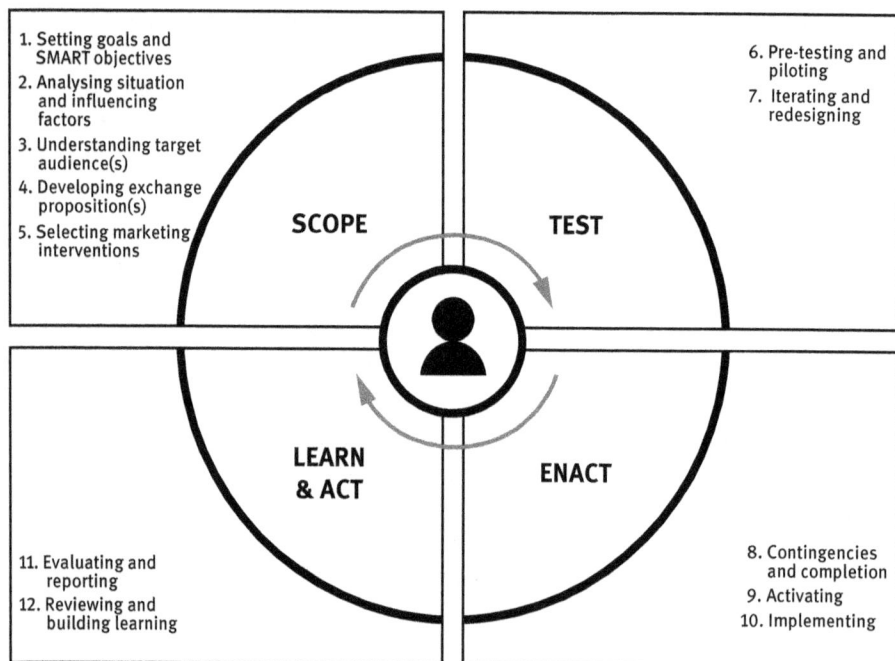

Figure 4.1: The social marketing planning process.
Adapted from: French (2010)

Generally, a social marketing organisation undertakes four key sets of activities. The first key area, and that which has the greatest priority, is the research and evaluation of the market (audience or customer) needs and *scoping* the market dynamics. The market and the social marketing issue must be at the centre of the social marketing organisation's activities. All successful campaigns start with baseline research and evaluation before designing activities that influence change. Secondly, the organisation will also research and evaluate its own capability in matching the needs of the market by pre-testing and piloting interventions as well as iterating and redesigning in response to feedback (*testing*). Thirdly, organisational influences and structures, the operating environment, and the social marketing context are all taken into account when *enacting* the social marketing program. Finally, the organisation learns from its activities and acts on those learnings, ensuring that program evaluation leads to improved outcomes for all (*learn and act*).

In an ideal world, a social marketing organisation develops their offering (program product, service, idea or concept) only *after* considering these four areas and the key learnings are fed back into a virtuous cycle of co-created outcomes between actors in the system (Brennan, Previte, and Fry 2016). In reality, this does not always occur, and many organisations have limited flexibility in adapting the core offering in response to changes throughout the system.

Systems in Social Marketing Practice and Influence

Systems thinking in social marketing is a relatively new way of looking at market dynamics (Brychkov and Domegan 2017). Systems thinking is an approach to social change and marketplace solutions that focuses on collaboration amongst market actors and *with* – rather than *for* – consumers (Brennan et al. 2016). Systems thinking argues that individual behaviours take place within an ecological system that consists of the totality of life (Brychkov and Domegan 2017). Life consists of historical, cultural, social, physical and environmental factors, all interdependently influencing the individual in terms of interactions, choices and behaviours. Behavioural ecologies are developed on the same principles as biological or environmental systems; everything is interrelated, and nothing operates without affecting something else within the system. How people participate in their ecologies depends on the interplay between the actors, their actions, interactions and reactions, and therefore there is a co-evolution (co-creation) of outcomes. Systems have multiple layers: conceptualised by Bronfenbrenner (1977) as chronosystem, macro system, exo system, meso system, and micro system (see Figure 4.2). (Figure 4.2 does not include chronosystem elements because while changes over time are pertinent to social marketing, the elements within the chronosystem are patterns developed over lifetimes. Consequently, these are not within the scope of being addressed by current social marketing campaigns.)

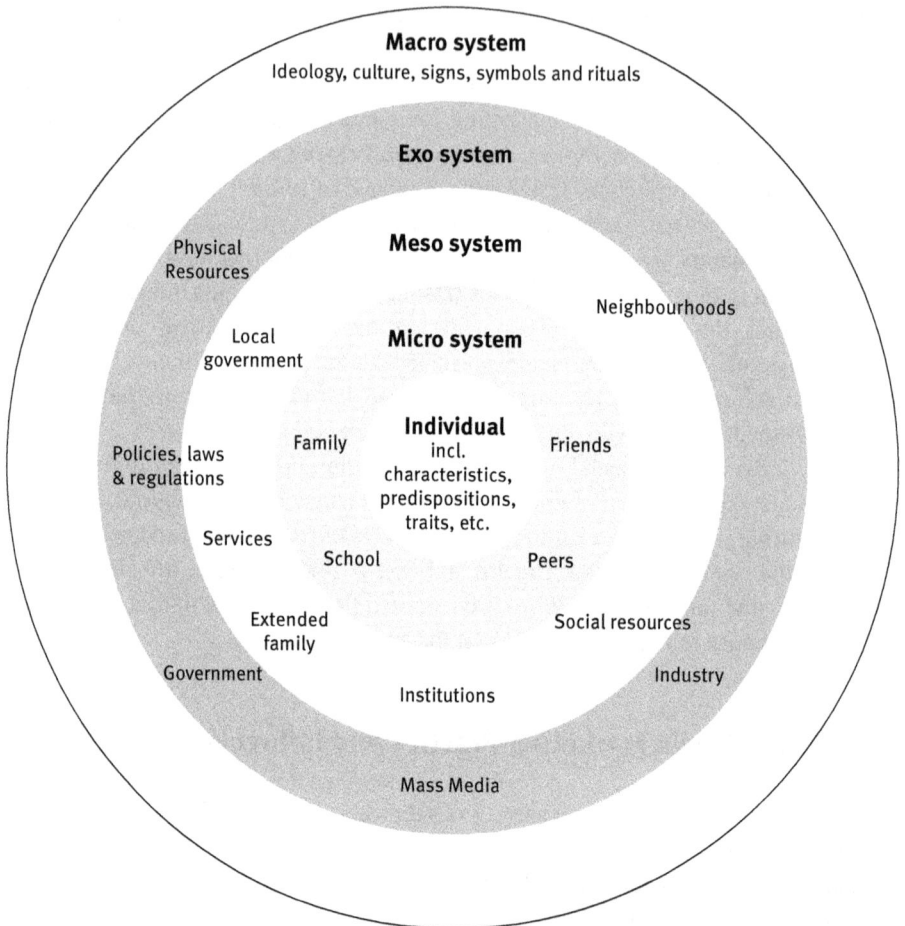

Figure 4.2: Ecological systems in social marketing.
Source: Brennan et al. 2014 (originally adapted from Bronfenbrenner)

Bronfenbrenner's (1977) ecological systems theory was proposed within the developmental psychology discipline. It applied a systems thinking lens to child development and family welfare. There have been several other models used in social marketing that seek to incorporate social and systemic factors in social marketing programs (for example, Domegan et al. 2016; Manika and Gregory-Smith 2017; Michie, Van Stralen, and West 2011). These models have some fundamental similarities. Firstly, they include a multi-lateral constituency for change. That is, actors in the system may come from various levels of the system. For example, public policy, consumers, service providers, families and communities might all be involved in co-creating change. Secondly, these models imply at least bi-directional influences throughout the system elements. For example, individuals are influenced by their families and families are influenced by individuals. Additionally, communities influence societal actors and public policymakers, often creating changes to public policy, and so on. Thirdly, the interplay between actors is complex and infinitely mutable with one act setting off changes within the system in sometimes unpredictable ways (see for example, Bolton, Cohen, and Bloom 2006; Cho and Salmon 2006; see also Ringold's (2002) social marketing research on the theme of 'unintended consequences'). This type of socio-ecological approach avoids blaming consumers for poor market choices, as individuals are often motivated by systemic influences of which they are not fully cognisant (Hoek and Jones 2011).

Although there are five layers in Bronfenbrenner's (1977) ecological system, this chapter primarily focuses on *macro, meso* and *micro*, because exo factors are largely beyond the control of social marketing practice (Brennan et al. 2014). This is not to imply that exo factors are unimportant. They can be extremely important. However, the focus of this chapter is to articulate where social marketing practice can be applied across the multiple layers in the system. It is necessary to note that there are complex and bi-directional relationships between factors from different layers of social marketing practices (Brennan et al. 2016). Thus, a successful social marketing campaign might have to be designed with considerations to activities and entities from multiple layers. *Upstream* influence of social marketing happens when the flow of activity is designed to affect the outer portion of the model, while the *downstream* influence is an inward flow of activities aimed at affecting individuals, their families and friends (Wood 2019). Additionally, *midstream* activities are designed to influence cooperation between mid-level entities (for example facilitating meso level actors to work with exo and/or macro-level actors). While many social marketing campaigns are spearheaded by both government and non-government entities, external agencies such as the United Nations often play a larger role in addressing socio-cultural (macro-level) issues, advocating the wellbeing of the entire population, such as poverty alleviation and children's rights. The social marketing examples presented later in this chapter will further demonstrate the multi-layered practices.

The *macro* (socio-cultural) factors are located in the outer layer and influence all other factors inside the system. They include tangible public policies, legal and regulatory frameworks, and the less tangible social systems (Wood 2019). In most cases, the outcome sought is to improve the population's social, economic or environmental wellbeing. This outcome involves advocating socio-cultural change to bring about some positive social outcome. While public policies can encourage or restrain social activities, they need to be facilitated and enforced by the legal and regulatory frameworks and infrastructure (Brennan et al. 2014). Social systems are complex structures of social mores, rituals, ideologies, norms and moral frameworks that are not defined in law but powerfully shape human actions, choices, and behaviours (Previte, Brennan, and Scott 2014). The actors involved at this level are those who shape structural conditions within the society, which includes regulators, politicians and policymakers. Examples of macro-level social marketing activities are policy advocacy or technical and financial assistance. These campaigns usually aim to create long term and larger economic, political, and cultural changes. They are often both upstream (for example seeking changes to macro level organisations activities) and downstream (for example seeking micro level organisational input or permission to act in the context).

The *meso* systems are the local and community layers that connect individuals in their micro systems and the outer macro systems (Brennan et al. 2014). The meso systems are the places and groups where individuals participate and perform. They could be formal settings such as communities, schools, workplaces, or informal, but more intimate, settings, such as families, friends, and neighbourhoods. Hence, the target audience of meso level social marketing is usually groups, organisations, or communities. Examples of marketing activities at this level are community and public information, public participation activities, exhibitions, conferences, or training programs. Social marketing campaigns in this category are likely to be midstream (for example strategy implementation to promote community wellbeing).

At the centre of the system, the micro layer contains individuals and their intimate settings. Social marketing at the micro level usually focuses directly on changing individual behaviours for social good. Various individual factors must be considered within a micro level social marketing campaign. They include individuals' biological factors, predispositions, attitudes (Lloyd et al. 2013; Thomson, Vandenberg, and Fitzgerald 2012), their personal factors and beliefs (Fry 2011), their adaptive roles within the micro and meso systems (Rimal and Real 2005), and their responses to marketing forces (Pettigrew et al. 2013). Many of the traditional marketing tools (for example, advertising, sale promotions, mobile marketing, social media marketing, direct marketing) can be adapted to micro level social marketing campaigns. Campaigns in this category are both upstream, where individual actions affect how communities and organisations operate (for example, influencing policymakers at meso and macro level), and downstream, where families support individual behavioural change.

Because of the interplay between these layers and the bi-directional influences, we have reframed the categories into socio-cultural, community, local and individual layers (see Table 4.1).

Southeast Asia at a Glance: Views from Malaysia, Singapore, and Vietnam

An Overview of Southeast Asia

Southeast Asia is dynamic, with 11 countries representing a diverse collection of cultures, economic and political systems and languages. In the interest of enabling easy comparison, we have elected to focus on three of these countries; Malaysia,

Table 4.1: Levels of social marketing and typical marketing activities.

Level	Type of SM objectives	Type of change sought	Typical audience	Type of decision making	Typical focus of social marketing activities
Socio-cultural Macro system	– Social change – Long term generational change	– Economic, political, cultural or traditional practice	Government policymakers and NGOs operating at a national or regional level	Group Political Policymaking	– Advocacy – Public policy negotiations – Public relations – Technical assistance – Financial assistance
Community Macro-Meso system	– Permission to act in the country or on the issue – Establishing a legal framework	– Organisational level decision making – Either active participation or non-interference in activities at next levels	Business and Provincial or local government NGOs operating within a specific SM context	Group Corporate Pragmatic	– Public communications – Publicity – Strategic partnerships and alliances – Seminars, consultations and meetings – Conferences and exhibitions
Local Meso-Micro system	– Access to and support for affected community members	– Referrals – Local support systems – Structural intervention development – Program development	Groups, communities, mass organisations such as unions and cooperatives	Group Participation Inclusive	– Sponsorships – Community participatory action – Training and education – Resource development – 'Sales' promotions – Online social marketing (information) – Freemiums and giveaways

(continued)

Table 4.1 (continued)

Level	Type of SM objectives	Type of change sought	Typical audience	Type of decision making	Typical focus of social marketing activities
Individual Micro system	– Prevention of, encouragement for, or cessation of behaviours	– Individual behaviours	Individuals (usually at risk)	Individuals within their social system (for example, collectivism, family decision making dynamics)	– Advertising – Social media – Mobile applications – Interpersonal interactions – Direct media such as notice boards, flyers, brochures, wearable marketing

Source: Adapted from Parker et al. (2015)

Singapore and Vietnam, as exemplars of this rich diversity. Malaysia is a country heading for high-income status, Singapore is a developed country with very high income, and Vietnam is a country at a lower middle-income position. The three countries represent various issues experienced by countries with different income levels within the region. As near neighbours, these countries share common challenges as well as having their own specific issues. Table 4.2 provides a summary of the main differences between the countries that affect the social marketing landscape.

All three countries are characterised by growing middle classes as a result of rapid economic development. With this economic growth, the investment in material wellbeing has increased the strain on environmental resources. The three countries are at different levels of development, but sustainability is often not the greatest priority for rapidly developing countries, like Malaysia and Vietnam. Population health and poverty alleviation are usually more salient goals (Brennan et al. 2013; Parker et al. 2015). Therefore, the 'correct' way to address socio-economic issues across three countries cannot be the same, given the fundamental differences between all three at the various levels.

There are various issues that require attention within the region, incorporating an array of political, economic, social, technological, legal and environmental. The sample cases presented in this chapter can be categorised as the following:

1. Addressing the side effects of economic development and modernisation, such as air pollution and waste disposal.
2. Alleviating poverty and providing access to basic necessities to those who are affected by rapid urbanisation.
3. Protecting the rights of those in need, such as children and specific sectors of the labour force.
4. Facing new challenges in the digital era including cybercrimes and internet safety.

While each category covers a wide range of issues, they all indicate the need for societal change. Addressing these challenges requires the involvement of all levels of society. Considering that each country operates differently, albeit being in the same region, the cultural and social make-up of the country affects how the issues are being tackled (see Table 4.3).

Contextual Case Studies

In order to illustrate the differences in systems being considered, following are country-specific case studies. These illuminate the uniqueness of challenges and approaches of each of the three countries.

Table 4.2: Social marketing landscape by country.

Country	Population (July 2018 est.)	Major religions	Languages	Median age	Birth rate (births/1000 population, 2018 est.)	Infant mortality rate (deaths/1000 live births, 2018 est.)	Population in urban areas of total population (2018)	Gross Domestic Product per capita (PPP) (2017 est.)	Political system
Malaysia	31,809,660	Islam, Buddhism, Christianity, Hinduism, Confucianism, Taoism	Bahasa Malaysia (official), English, Chinese (Cantonese, Mandarin, Hokkien, Hakka, Hainan, Foochow), Tamil, Telugu, Malayalam, Panjabi, Thai Note: Malaysia has 134 living languages – 112 indigenous and 22 non-indigenous; in East Malaysia, there are several indigenous languages; the most widely spoken are Iban and Kadazan	28.7	18.8	12.1	76%	$29,100	Federal parliamentary constitutional monarchy

Singapore	5,995,991	Buddhism, Christianity, Islam, Hinduism, Taoism, other	English (official), Mandarin (official), Malay (official), Tamil (official), other Chinese dialects (Cantonese, Hokkien, Hakka, Teochew), other	34.9	8.7	2.3	100%	$94,100	Parliamentary republic
Vietnam	97,040,334	Buddhism, Catholicism, Hoa Hao, Cao Dai, Protestantism, Islam	Vietnamese (official), English (increasingly favoured as a second language), some French, Chinese, and Khmer, mountain area languages (Mon-Khmer and Malayo-Polynesian)	30.9	15.2	16.7	35.9%	$6,900	Single-party communist state

Source: Selected statistics from the Central Intelligence Agency (2019)

Table 4.3: Summary of issues, opportunities and social marketing solutions.

Issue	Opportunity	Social Marketing Solution
Addressing the side effects of economic development and modernisation	To improve the potential for sustainable and safe development of lesser developed countries.	Depending on the particular issue, each side effect may require a different strategy. For example, reducing the impact of pollution will require upstream marketing strategies for legislation, mid-stream strategies for communication to enterprises and enforcement of laws. Improved housing for people without land may require financial and technical assistance (mid-stream strategies), in addition to community support and social infrastructure development. Lowering the road toll on urban roads might require upstream and midstream strategies for physical infrastructure and downstream strategies for individuals to behave safely.
Alleviating poverty	Increase affected populations and communities' access to sustainable development resources	Midstream and downstream strategies such as social enterprise development, equitable and sustainable micro-finance programs, training and education, technical assistance
Protecting the rights of those in need	Empowering disadvantaged groups and giving 'voice' to communities and marginalised groups	Mid-stream and downstream strategies including communication for development style campaigns
Facing new challenges in the digital era	Empowering people to be in control, while employing legislative, technical and enforcement protections	Downstream strategies would be needed to educate, remind and empower individuals. Upstream strategies to advocate for appropriate and coordinated legislative and technical controls that continue to foster open access to all users but provide protection where required.

Malaysia

Malaysia is a newly industrialised country with rapid economic growth in comparison to other developing countries. Due to this characteristic, Malaysia's populations are deeply impacted by globalisation and urbanisation processes, primarily those in the middle- and lower-income class (Tazreiter and Tham 2013). With the increasing cost of living and household financial commitments, these groups, especially the low-income group, continue to be susceptible to economic shocks (The World Bank 2019b). While the Malaysian government has successfully narrowed income disparities over the years, social struggles remain apparent, especially for those living in urban areas. Various social issues in Malaysia are currently being addressed by authorities and non-government organisations to promote better living, from health to personal financial freedom.

Among the prevalent social issues occurring at the macro level in Malaysia is the ill-treatment of domestic workers. It is a national issue that involves other neighbouring countries. Due to demanding urban lifestyles, many middle-class Malaysian women must work, resulting in the increased need for domestic workers for childcare or housekeeping (Carvalho 2019). On various occasions, domestic workers receive low wages, live in poor conditions, and in some rare cases, are physically abused by employers. Domestic workers grapple with a lack of legal protection and enforcement infrastructure to defend them from such violations. The Employment Act of 1955 unfortunately does not protect the rights of domestic workers. The Domestic Worker Draft Bill was later proposed in 2016 by the Domestic Workers Coalition. The Coalition comprises of various non-government bodies which aim to protect domestic workers from exploitation and abuse (Tan 2017). A case involving the death of a domestic worker from Indonesia due to abuse in 2018 has caused an uproar for the government to improve the law and the protection of domestic workers (Indramalar 2018). Due to the incident, the Indonesian government was reportedly proposing a moratorium on sending its citizens to work in Malaysia. Such cases call for urgent and better negotiations between both countries in reaching an agreement to protect the rights of the workers, which, to date, has proven to be difficult. Tenaganita (2020), a Non-Government Organisation (NGO) that promotes the rights of women, migrants and refugees in Malaysia, is actively advocating the protection of domestic workers. They create public awareness on domestic workers' rights through community events, while highlighting the need for change in how the group is being treated by policymakers.

The changing social dynamics around domestic work have also led to another challenge faced by Malaysian children, namely cybercrime and child poverty. Despite the national poverty rate being less than one per cent, a report by United Nations International Children's Fund (UNICEF) Malaysia (2018) indicated that the official figures do not reflect the actual situation. Reportedly, there are significant numbers of urban poor children who are malnourished and are not able to obtain early childhood education. However, this was refuted by the government, stating that food aid has been provided to poor children in schools around the country for more than a decade. Approximately 458,000 school children were recipients of the federal supplementary food scheme in 2018 alone (TODAY Online 2018). Nevertheless, it is established that every case of urban child poverty demands attention to ensure that children have access to broader opportunities. Through various social marketing activities, UNICEF Malaysia continues to collaborate with the government and private bodies to devise social wellbeing programs for those children affected, and at the same time involving the community at large in finding solutions to the problem. For example, UNICEF Malaysia has conducted programs that include university students working together to provide solutions to urban child poverty. Additionally, research awards are given to postgraduate researchers addressing the issue.

While there is a struggle to eliminate poverty in urban areas, a different dilemma is faced by those exposed to better opportunities. A widespread issue afflicting the nation at the micro level is cybercrimes involving children and the youth. With widespread internet penetration and increased access to social media, cybercrime is becoming more rampant (Hui et al., 2017). According to the Royal Malaysia Police, young people are especially vulnerable to online fraud and cybercrime (Waheed 2018). Young people are prone to online scams, fraud, and cyberbullying. For example, based on the National Study on School Cyber Safety, more than 70 per cent of school students were involved in some form of cyberbullying. Of that amount, only a small number of official reports were made to the Malaysian Communications and Multimedia Commission (MCMC) (Yazid 2017). It is believed that most of the victims decided not to report the incidents. Without proper education and awareness of cyber safety, this group is susceptible to potential threats that could negatively affect their future.

Individual practice of cyber safety largely depends on socio-environmental factors (Pitchan et al. 2018), and therefore requires support from all parties across many levels – family, school, community, and non-government and government agencies. To facilitate this, MCMC's 'Click Wisely' campaign was launched in 2012 to promote safety, security, and responsibility of using the internet. The campaign addresses all levels in the social system, from strengthening government policies to conducting awareness programmes at community centres and schools, as well as on social media and in mainstream advertising. Other government parties, such as CyberSecurity Malaysia (2020) and the National Cyber Security Agency (2020) launched similar programs to curb online fraud and promote cybersecurity. These campaigns provide avenues for the public to obtain information and support, to help safeguard them from online threats.

Singapore

Despite being the most regulated and advanced economy in Southeast Asia, Singapore has been grappling with its own societal level issues, notably human rights and food waste. As a regional hub with strong international links, it has developed into a destination for human trafficking, particularly labour and sex trafficking, and domestic servitude (Singapore Ministry of Manpower 2016). As of December 2017, there were 965,200 low-wage, documented migrant workers in Singapore; of these, a large number experienced labour trafficking (HOME 2019). The Singapore government has shown a significant effort to decrease human trafficking through the National Plan of Action Against Trafficking in Persons. Yet, the plan still does not meet minimum international standards in the area of trafficking (US Department of State 2017). At the societal level, Singapore's current labour law has no guaranteed minimum wage, employment contracts are not mandatory, and there are insufficient guidelines on working conditions. Migrant workers are specifically excluded from protection by the Employment Act (HOME 2019). At a meso-micro level, the challenges are twofold. Firstly, victims of human trafficking, including ill-treated migrant workers, are not equipped with the necessary awareness of available protective services (US Department of State 2017). Secondly, law-enforcement authorities did not effectively identify victims compelled into service (TWC2 2017). This leaves some victims unidentified and subject to punishment or deportation.

These societal challenges require comprehensive social marketing campaigns at all three levels. These campaigns include the development of formal policies to provide all victims with the right to robust protective services, strengthen the legal framework to enhance protection for victims, conduct law enforcement operations to increase investigations and prosecutions, and convict and severely sentence traffickers. At the meso level, partnerships with NGOs is necessary to establish support systems, intervention groups, and protective services for victims. Finally, at the micro level, downstream marketing campaigns can play an important role in increasing awareness of available protective services for victims and in educating front-line officials in investigations and prosecutions. Project X is one of the most active non-profit organizations that aims to advance the rights and representation of sex workers in Singapore and focus on meso and micro levels. Through their outreach campaigns and community centres, Project X provides aid and education to sex workers and offers a platform for sex workers to build their personal capacities to integrate into the local community.

Corporal punishment is supported by the legal system in Singapore. To date, this form of punishment is allowed in schools, families, alternative care settings, penal institutions, and law-enforcement offices (Farell 2019). This leads to social acceptance of uncontrolled violent practices such as domestic violence and child abuse. The legality and social acceptance of violent punishment not only violates its citizens' dignity and physical integrity and their right to equal protection under the law, but it also violates their education and health rights (Global Initiative to End All Corporal Punishment of Children 2015). In this context, social marketing campaigns can first influence at the meso level, focusing on changing social acceptance towards corporal punishment. This can be done through campaigns at schools, day care centres, and alternative care settings to raise awareness and provide alternatives and a reward rather than a punishment system. Secondly, at the micro level, there is a common dilemma between seeing corporal punishment as a good intention leading to better behaviour and long-term psychological effects on the victims (Chan 2018). Therefore, intervention and consultation play an important role in providing helpful and practical alternatives and prevent the use of corporal punishment. Established in 1995, PAVE (2020) is an organisation that aims to provide holistic impacts against interpersonal violence at all three levels. At the meso and micro levels, PAVE promotes public awareness towards interpersonal violence and provides services to individuals and families experiencing violence. At the macro level, research outputs and written feedback to the Singapore government contributed to the amendments of the Protection from Harassment Act.

Another social marketing issue in Singapore is that of food waste. Although advanced urban planning enables Singapore to afford an organised, trash-free, and unpolluted image, the food waste of up to 800,000 tons annually is pushing the limit of Singapore's already limited landfill (NEA 2019). Only 17 per cent of food waste was recycled in 2018 (NEA 2019). At the current rate, Singapore will need a new mass-incinerator every seven years and a new landfill facility every 30 to 35 years (Wan 2018). Given the landmass of Singapore, this is simply not feasible. At the micro level, 68.1 per cent of Singaporeans are unwilling to purchase food with an imperfect appearance or expired dates (Maria 2018). This magnifies the amount of food waste at the meso level throughout the whole food value chain, including farming, post-harvest processing, manufacturing, warehousing, transportation, trading, and distribution. Efforts have been made at micro levels to either address consumer perception towards 'imperfect' food or provide infrastructure for consumers to reduce waste. The National Environment Agency of Singapore (NEA) launched the 'Love your Food' campaign in 2015 to encourage smarter food purchase, storage, and preparation habits. Innovations such as tracking devices, dumpster diving, or food swapping have also been introduced. However, the current campaigns only address waste reduction and do not help to transform waste by means of recycling, reusing, or composting. Furthermore, guidelines and initiatives also need to be introduced to other stakeholders in the food supply chain to help them to eliminate waste through more effective forecasting, planning, producing, storing, and transporting food. Such guidelines also help meso-level actors to produce products from surplus food.

Vietnam

As a developing country, Vietnam faces complex issues of development as well as the side effects of development. One such side-effect is poverty. Although extreme poverty has been heavily reduced in Vietnam, it remains a problem in remote areas and amongst vulnerable groups of ethnic minorities, that require solutions tailored to meet the specific features of these communities. A successful example of poverty alleviation is the Northern Mountains Poverty Reduction project operated by the World Bank and the Vietnamese government. At the socio-cultural level, the project builds partnerships with government agencies, banks, agricultural extension systems, and other input-service providers. At the community and local levels, this project takes a community-driven approach by organizing Common Interest Groups (CIG) by connecting small and marginal producers, especially women and ethnic minorities, around livelihood activities such as farming, husbandry, fishing, or handicrafts. With these partnerships, the project enables the CIGs to assess capital, expertise, services and market linkages to start production and to sell their products. Infrastructure such as roads, bridges, and water irrigation systems are also built or repaired to increase market accessibility for the CIGs. Over eight years of operation, 192,000 households have directly benefited from the project. 13,568 CIGs were established with 157,000 members, creating more than US$24 million worth of products. Seventy-five per cent of these CIGs had a sustained increase in their production assets. Participants on average earn 16 per cent more income than non-participants (The World Bank 2019a). This success encourages the Vietnamese government to adopt the project's good practices into government policies and alternative approaches to poverty reduction.

Another side effect of development, airborne pollution, is severely affecting Vietnamese wellbeing, especially in Hanoi and Ho Chi Minh City. An important representation of air pollution is higher concentrations of fine particular matter (PM10 and PM2.5 indexes). In 2018, the number of days in Hanoi with PM indexes higher than the World Health Organization (WHO) recommendations was 232, and 164 days in Ho Chi Minh City[1] (GreenID 2019). According to WHO (2018), air pollution was linked to more than 60,000 deaths in Vietnam in 2016. The main source of air pollution in the cities is high density transportation and construction. Air pollution is also generated by nearby industrial, agricultural and handicraft village production, improper waste management, and thermal power plants.

In recent years, there have been various multilevel efforts from the local government, organisations, and individuals to tackle the issue. At the socio-cultural level, the Vietnamese government published the National Action Plan on Air Quality Management in 2016. The plan measures and investigates air pollution and the source of air pollution; and maps out solutions in the form of mechanisms, policies, and legislation (Vietnam News 2016). Hence the government has built and continues to build more air quality monitoring stations. The emission standards on new vehicles have also been raised, while other emission standards are under review. At the community and local levels, the participation and collaboration of various NGOs,

---

1 The data is measured by monitoring stations at the US Embassies in Hanoi and Ho Chi Minh City. The level of air pollution varied across different parts of the cities.

research institutions, and commercial organisations are necessary to reduce or limit the side effects of air pollution in Vietnam. For example, research institutions and commercial organisations are developing cheaper and more effective air monitoring systems, face masks, and air filtering systems. The PAMAir mobile application and website are introduced to provide location-based, real-time air quality updates and notify people to limit their outdoor activities if necessary. At the individual level, numerous campaigns and projects are organised by GreenID – an NGO – to raise awareness on air pollution and suggest feasible individual solutions. Another NGO, GreenHub, designs low-cost, low-emission stoves for households and small businesses. The above multilevel efforts have resulted in a slight improvement in air quality, but it is still far from significant (GreenID 2019). The complexity of air pollution requires solutions at all levels, managing and addressing the emission sources as well as finding cleaner alternatives.

In any country's social marketing strategy, at least one or all of the activities outlined in Table 4.1 may be required. This ranges from working with governments by providing technical assistance, to working with families and individuals to ensure that they understand and can behave in the manner that the social marketing intervention aims to achieve. Table 4.4 summarises the social marketing issues and activities across Malaysia, Singapore, and Vietnam that have been presented in this section.

Table 4.4: Layers of social marketing activity examples by country.

Level	Malaysia	Singapore	Vietnam
Socio-cultural Macro	Tenaganita advocates for the rights and protection of foreign domestic workers proposing changes to legal systems through public awareness programs (Tan 2017).	The National Environment Agency (NEA) works with various industry stakeholders to reduce food waste across the supply chain. They also launched an outreach program to encourage smart food purchase, storage and preparation habits that help consumers reduce food waste (NEA 2019).	The Vietnamese government published the National Action Plan on Air Quality Management which includes assessing air pollution and the source of air pollution to map out technical and legislative solutions (GreenID 2019).

Table 4.4 (continued)

Level	Malaysia	Singapore	Vietnam
Community-Local Meso	UNICEF Malaysia, the Malaysian government and private entities work together to find solutions to alleviate urban child poverty through the 'Children Without' campaign (UNICEF Malaysia 2018).	Child Protection Specialist Centre Singapore run Big Love protection centre that provides child-centric, family-focused and community-based support. Casework management and support services are conducted in clients' natural environments such as homes, schools, workplaces and within their communities (Big Love 2019).	Various institutions, corporations, and organisations such as FIMO, DL Corps, GreenHub, and GreenID collaborate to tackle air pollution with better air monitoring systems, communication channels, and air pollution reducing solutions (GreenID 2019). Northern Mountains Poverty Reduction project by the World Bank uses partnerships with government agencies, banks, agricultural extension systems, and other input-service providers to enable CIGs to access capital, expertise, services and market linkages to start production and to sell their products (The World Bank 2019a).
Individual Micro	The 'Click Wisely' campaign by the Malaysian Communications and Multimedia Commission rolled out a nationwide campaign to educate youth and the community on cyber safety (Waheed 2018).	The Project X is a non-profit organisation that aims to advance the rights and representation of sex workers in Singapore. They provide aid to sex workers, educate them about sexual health issues, bridge the community gap between sex workers and the public, and offer a platform for sex workers to build their personal capacities (The Project X 2019).	GreenID runs multiple campaigns to raise public awareness of air pollution. GreenHub offers low-cost, low-emission stoves for households and small businesses (GreenID 2019). Northern Mountains Poverty Reduction project by World Bank organises Common Interest Groups (CIG) connecting small and marginal producers around livelihood activities for extra incomes (The World Bank 2019a).

Conclusion

This chapter has used the Ecological Systems Theory to classify and explain social marketing interventions applicable at each level of the social marketing system. We have used the three countries as examples of social marketing practice that might be applicable to other Southeast Asian countries. The three countries – Malaysia, Singapore, and Vietnam – all face slightly different challenges when it comes to tackling social problems. Each country has its own priorities and is approaching issues in their own culturally and socially appropriate manner. Social marketing in this context can assist governments and non-government organisations to initiate, establish, develop and maintain programs that will have multi-level impact. The issues faced in developing countries where rapid social change is taking place are unique and need to be examined in further depth. This chapter provides a very brief insight into an exciting region where social marketing can be instrumental in producing positive social change.

References

Big Love (2019), Child Protection Specialist Centre, https://www.biglove.org.sg/ (last accessed: July 10, 2020).

Bolton, L. E., Cohen, J. B., and Bloom, P. N. (2006), Does marketing products as remedies create 'get out of jail free cards'?, *Journal of Consumer Research, 33*(1), 71–81.

Brennan, L., Binney, W., Parker, L., Aleti, T., and Nguyen, D. (2014), *Social Marketing and Behaviour Change: Models, Theory and Applications*, Cheltenham, UK: Edward Elgar Publishing.

Brennan, L., and Parker, L. (2014), Beyond behaviour change: social marketing and social change, *Journal of Social Marketing, 4*(3).

Brennan, L., Parker, L., Aleti-Watne, T., Fien, J., Duong, T. H., and Doan, M. A. (Eds.) (2013), *Growing Sustainable Communities: A Development Guide for Southeast Asia*, Prahran, Australia: Tilde University Press.

Brennan, L., Previte, J., and Fry, M.L. (2016), Social marketing's consumer myopia, *Journal of Social Marketing, 6*(3), 219–239.

Bronfenbrenner, U. (1977), Toward an experimental ecology of human development, *American Psychologist, 32*(7), 513–531.

Brychkov, D., and Domegan, C. (2017), Social marketing and systems science: past, present and future, *Journal of Social Marketing, 7*(1), 74–93.

Carvalho, R. (2019, 24 March), Domestic workers are the slaves of modern Asia. Are Hongkongers, Singaporeans and Malaysians ever going to change?, *South China Morning Post*, https://www.scmp.com/print/week-asia/society/article/3002942/domestic-workers-are-slaves-modern-day-asia-are-hongkongers (last accessed: July 10, 2020).

Central Intelligence Agency (2019), The World Factbook, *Central Intelligence Agency*, https://www.cia.gov/library/publications/the-world-factbook/ (last accessed: July 10, 2020).

Chan, W. C. (2018), Corporal Punishment of Children by Parents, *Singapore Academy of Law Journal*, 30, 545.

Cho, H., and Salmon, C. T. (2006), Unintended effects of health communication campaigns, *Journal of Communication*, *57*(2), 293–317.

CyberSecurity Malaysia (2020), http://www.cybersecurity.my (last accessed: July 13, 2020)

Domegan, C., McHugh, P., Devaney, M., Duane, S., Hogan, M., Broome, B. J., Layton, R.A., Joyce, J., Mazzonetto, M., Piwowarczyk, J. (2016), Systems-thinking social marketing: conceptual extensions and empirical investigations, *Journal of Marketing Management, 32*(11–12), 1123–1144.

Farell, C. (2019), Judicial caning in Singapore, Malaysia and Brunei, *World Corporal Punishment Research*, https://www.corpun.com/singfeat.htm (last accessed: July 10, 2020).

French, J. (2010), STELa Social Marketing Planning Model, *ICE Creates*, http://study.sagepub.com/sites/default/files/Stela.pdf (last accessed: July 10, 2020)

Fry, M.L. (2011), Discourses of consumer's alcohol resistant identities. *Journal of Nonprofit Public Sector Marketing*, *23*(4), 348–366.

Global Initiative to End All Corporal Punishment of Children (2015), Ending legalised violence against children, *Global Initiative to End All Corporal Punishment of Children*, https://endcorporalpunishment.org/ (last accessed: July 10, 2020).

GreenID, (2019), *Air Quality Report 2018, GreenID*, http://en.greenidvietnam.org.vn/view-document/5d35822b6dae2a796f4c26fc (last accessed: July 10, 2020).

Hoek, J., and Jones, S. C. (2011), Regulation, Public Health and Social Marketing: A Behaviour Change Trinity, *Journal of Social Marketing*, *1*(1), 32–44.

HOME. (2019). *Behind Closed Doors: Forced Labour in the Domestic Work Sector in Singapore*. Humanitarian Organization for Migration Economics and Liberty Shared.

Hovell, M. F., Wahlgen, D.R., and Gehrman, C. A. (2002), The behavioral ecological model, in R. J. DiClemente, R. A. Crosby and M. C. Kegler (Eds.), *Emerging Theories in Health Promotion Practice and Research* (1st ed., pp. 347–385), San Francisco, CA: Jossey-Bass.

Hui, K. L., Kim, S. H., & Wang, Q. H. (2017). Cybercrime deterrence and international legislation: Evidence from distributed denial of service attacks. MIS Quarterly, 41(2), 497.

Indramalar, S. (2018, 6 April), Domestic workers continue to be abused until tougher laws can protect them, *Star2*, https://www.thestar.com.my/lifestyle/living/2018/04/06/domestic-workers-will-continue-to-be-abused-until-there-are-tougher-laws-to-protect-them (last accessed: July 10, 2020).

Lee, N. (2019), Planning Work Sheets, *Social Marketing Service*, http://www.socialmarketingservice.com/publications/planning-worksheets (last accessed: July 10, 2020).

Lloyd, B., Matthews, S., Livingston, M., Jayasekara, H., and Smith, K. J. A. (2013), Alcohol intoxication in the context of major public holidays, sporting and social events: a time–series analysis in Melbourne, Australia, 2000–2009, *Addiction*, *108*(4), 701–709.

Manika, D., and Gregory-Smith, D. (2017), Health marketing communications: An integrated conceptual framework of key determinants of health behaviour across the stages of change, *Journal of Marketing Communications*, *23*(1), 22–72.

Maria, A. (2018), Campaign Launched to Change Mindsets about 'Ugly Food' to Save the Environment, *The Independent*, http://theindependent.sg/campaign-launched-to-change-mindsets-about-ugly-food-to-save-the-environment/ (last accessed: July 10, 2020).

Michie, S., Van Stralen, M. M., and West, R. (2011), The behaviour change wheel: a new method for characterising and designing behaviour change interventions, *Implementation Science*, *6*(1), 42.

National Cyber Security Agency (2020), https://www.nacsa.gov.my/ (last accessed July 14, 2020)

National Environment Agency (NEA) (2019), Everyone Urged To Adopt 3 Easy Habits To Reduce Food Waste, *National Environment Agency*, https://www.nea.gov.sg/media/news/news/index/everyone-urged-to-adopt-3-easy-habits-to-reduce-food-waste (last accessed: July 10, 2020).

Parker, L., Brennan, L., and Nguyen, D. (2015), Social marketing: Cambodia, Indonesia, the Phillipines and Vietnam, in B. Nguyen and C. Rowley (Eds.), *Ethical and Social Marketing in Asia* (pp. 161–191), Amsterdam: Elsevier.

PAVE (2020), About Us, https://www.pave.org.sg/ (last accessed: July 14, 2020)

Pettigrew, S., Pescud, M., Jarvis, W., and Webb, D. J. (2013), Teens' blog accounts of the role of adults in youth alcohol consumption, *Journal of Social Marketing*, *3*(1), 28–40.

Pitchan, M. A., Omar, S. Z., Bolong, J., and Ghazal, A. H. A. (2018), Analisis keselamatan siber dari perspektif persekitaran sosial: Kajian terhadap pengguna internet di Lembah Klang, *e-Bangi*, *14*(2), 16–29.

Previte, J., Brennan, L., and Scott, J. (2014), Case study: meso-macro-level theory – DrinkWise: investing in generational social change, in L. Brennan, W. Binney, L. Parker, T. Aleti, and D. Nguyen (Eds.), *Social Marketing and Behaviour Change: Models, Theory and Applications* (pp. 156–175), Cheltenham, UK: Edward Elgar Publishing.

Rimal, R. N., and Real, K. (2005), How behaviors are influenced by perceived norms: A test of the theory of normative social behavior, *Communication Research*, *32*(3), 389–414.

Ringold, D. (2002), Boomerang effects in response to public health interventions: Some unintended consequences in the alcoholic beverage market, *Journal of Consumer Policy*, *25*(1), 27–63.

Singapore Ministry of Manpower (2016), National Approach Against Trafficking in Persons, *Singapore Ministry of Manpower*, https://www.mom.gov.sg/trafficking-in-persons (last accessed: July 10, 2020).

Tan, T. (2017, 18 December), Tenaganita and NGOs draft Bill to protect rights of foreign domestic workers, *The Star Online*. https://www.thestar.com.my/news/nation/2017/12/18/tenaganita-and-ngos-draft-bill-to-protect-rights-of-foreign-domestic-workers/ (last accessed: July 10, 2020).

Tazreiter, C., and Tham, S. (2013), *Globalization and Social Transformation in the Asia-Pacific: The Australian and Malayasian Experience*, London: Springer.

Tenaganita (2020), Our Story, http://www.tenaganita.net/ (last accessed: July 14 2020).

The Project X (2019), The Project X – More than just condom, https://theprojectx.org/ (last accessed: July 10, 2020).

The World Bank (2019), Implementation Completion And Result Report: The Second Northern Mountains Poverty Reduction Project, *The World Bank*, http://projects.worldbank.org/P113493/second-northern-mountains-poverty-reduction-project?lang=enandtab=documentsandsubTab=projectDocuments (last accessed: July 10, 2020)

The World Bank (2019), The World Bank in Malaysia – Overview, https://www.worldbank.org/en/country/malaysia/overview (last accessed: July 10, 2020).

Thomson, L. M., Vandenberg, B., and Fitzgerald, J. (2012), An exploratory study of drinkers views of health information and warning labels on alcohol containers, *Drug and Alcohol Review*, 31(2), 240–247.

TODAY Online (2018, 13 March), Malaysian education minister rubbishes Unicef report on urban poor children, *TODAYOnline*, https://www.todayonline.com/world/malaysian-education-minister-rubbishes-unicef-report-urban-poor-children (last accessed: July 10, 2020).

TWC2 (2017), Migrant workers in Singapore vulnerable to forced labor including debt bondage: Says US TIP report, *TWC2*, https://twc2.org.sg/2017/07/14/migrant-workers-in-singapore-vulnerable-to-forced-labor-including-debt-bondage-says-us-tip-2017-report/ (last accessed: July 10, 2020).

UNICEF Malaysia (2018), Children Without: A study of urban child poverty and deprivation in low-cost flats in Kuala Lumpur, *The United Nations Childrens' Fund, Malaysia*, https://www.unicef.org/malaysia/sites/unicef.org.malaysia/files/2019-04/UNICEF-ChildrenWithout-EnglishVersion-Final%2026.2.18_0.pdf (last accessed: July 10, 2020).

US Department of State (2017), Trafficking in Persons Report 2017, *US Department of State*, https://www.business-humanrights.org/en/us-department-of-state-trafficking-in-persons-report-2017 (last accessed: July 10, 2020).

Vietnam News (2016, 23 September), National Action Plan on Air Quality Management until 2020 launching, *Vietnam News*, https://vietnamnews.vn/print/national-action-plan-on-air-quality-management-until-2020-launching/343281.html (last accessed: July 10, 2020).

Waheed, M. (2018), What's in the Content?: Examining texts of the Klik dengan Bijak (Click Wisely) Campaign Materials, *Human Communication*, *1*(1), 113–122.

Wan, L. (2018), Fighting food waste in Singapore: 'No brainer' tracking tech and rst standard unveiled, *Food Navigator Asi*, https://www.foodnavigator-asia.com/Article/2018/05/16/Fighting-food-waste-in-Singapore-No-brainer-tracking-tech-and-first-standard-unveiled (last accessed: July 10, 2020).

WHO (2018), More than 60 000 deaths in Viet Nam each year linked to air pollution, WHO, https://www.who.int/vietnam/news/detail/02-05-2018-more-than-60-000-deaths-in-viet-nam-each-year-linked-to-air-pollution (last accessed: July 10, 2020).

Wood, M. (2019), Resilience research and social marketing: the route to sustainable behaviour change, *Journal of Social Marketing*, *9*(1), 77–93.

Yazid, Z. (2017, 8 November), SKMM terima 38 kes aduan kes buli siber dalam tempoh 11 bulan tahun ini, *Utusan Online*, https://www.youtube.com/watch?v=yzSAm-hpse4 (last accessed: July 10, 2020).

Gerard Hastings

5 As the Planet and the Climate Breakdown the Last Thing We Need is More Marketing

Introduction

Advertising is as old as human society but it only became a force to be reckoned with just over a century ago with the advent of mass production and the consolidation of business into a small number of powerful corporations. It grew rapidly because there was an urgent need to tell the American people about the new abundance of consumer goods. But despite initial success in encouraging consumption, by the middle of the last century supply was beginning to outstrip demand. This threatened both the new corporations and government: the former risked warehouses full of remaindered stock and reduced profits; the latter faced the dangers of stalled growth and recession – and both feared for their power. The urgent need was for a more effective means to encourage consumption; marketing emerged to meet this need.

Its spectacular success is showing itself today in two ways. First the 'aggregate marketing system' has grown exponentially. By the turn of the millennium, in the US alone, it employed some 30 million people and drove consumer spending worth $5 trillion a year (Wilkie & Moore 1999). To illustrate the magnitude of this figure, the authors explain: 'if we were to try to count it at the rate of $1 per second, it would take more than 150,000 years, or much longer than the history of civilization. Although the aggregate marketing system in the United States may not stretch quite to "eternity" it certainly does stretch a very long way.' The marketing industry has grown further in the 21st century and with the arrival of digital technology become even more powerful.

The second indicator of marketing's success is the woeful state of the planet. We have become so enthralled with consumption that we are despoiling nature, destabilising the climate and threatening our children's survival. Covid 19 is just the latest warning that we need to reduce, not increase our consumption. The aggregate marketing system is bringing us all closer to eternity; it is time for a fundamental rethink.

The Problem is Power, Not Marketing

Ours is a species which survives and flourishes by doing deals; alone we are weak and vulnerable, but in concert we thrive. As Harari (2014) suggests, this need to do business with one another was probably one of the principal drivers of language itself; he points out that the first writers weren't poets but accountants. Without these early bookkeepers there would be no poets – or at least no record of their work.

https://doi.org/10.1515/9783110659566-005

To aid this cooperative project, we long ago developed the ability to tell each other that we had something useful to offer. This was advertising in its original form; it clarified each person's role as a provider to the group and helped everyone to make decisions about how they managed their resources and met their needs. A cobbler would flag up her shoe mending skills and a baker put up a sign saying bread for sale – and potential customers could make informed choices about footwear and food. And yes, we were ever capable of putting an overly positive spin on these offerings (the Ancient Greeks did a great job of selling the wooden horse to Troy) but overt deception was kept in train because there was a reasonable balance of power. The baker needed her customers as much as the customers needed bread – and if the baker became insensitive to this reality, then there were other bakers, or bread could be made at home.

Just over a century ago two phenomena, which emerged in the USA but swiftly globalised, conspired to upset this long-standing balance. First, commerce, which had been dominated by a multiplicity of small businesses, began to coalesce into a much smaller number of bigger companies (Foster et al 2009). The modern business corporation, which has now outgrown most of the world's countries, was born. Hand in glove with this, mass production methods were developed, which concentrated capital and vastly increased the availability of consumer goods. Cars, washing machines and vacuum cleaners could be produced in unprecedented numbers at much reduced cost. The centralisation made mass advertising necessary, and turned its production into an important industry in its own right. Edward Bernays' book, 'Propaganda', appeared in 1928 spelling out the role of this newly professionalised function 'which controls the public mind' and 'is manipulated by the special pleader who seeks to create public acceptance for a particular idea or commodity.' (Bernays 1928). The new order was not lacking in confidence or ambition.

Both were justified: success was stratospheric. Henry Ford could not make his cars fast enough, and such was demand that he could get away with offering only one colour. Other sectors flourished in like fashion, producing a generation of robber barons, massive inequalities and economic upheaval. However, it would be wrong to blame advertising for these ructions; the problem lay not with it per se, but with how it was deployed and by whom – and this, as with so many human dilemmas, was a question of power. Bernays book opens with the observation:

> The conscious and intelligent manipulation of the organized habits and opinions of the masses is an important element in democratic society. Those who manipulate this unseen mechanism of society constitute an invisible government which is the true ruling power of our country.

This is an overt grab for power. Bernays was extremely successful, became an establishment figure and was honoured in 1949 (by which time it might be thought that the word propaganda would have lost some of its allure) by the American Psychological Society for his work on 'engineering consent'.

This consent, however, soon began to flag. Corporate capitalism, despite (or may be because of) its material success, was overly focused on the bottom line, and not good at looking beyond the next AGM. The obvious problem with the 'pile 'em high and sell 'em fast' model is that sooner rather than later you run out of customers. Once everyone has a car, a washing machine and a vacuum cleaner who do you sell to? This inevitable impasse was reached by the middle of the last century in the US – just as Bernays was getting his award.

For the capitalist this presented a disturbing prospect: if there are more things available than needs to satisfy, the buyer becomes more powerful than the seller. They can determine the price, depress sales and dominate the transaction. The market becomes democratic, and capitalists, far from being the 'invisible government' Bernays envisaged, becomes the servants of that democracy. An excess of supply also gives the visible government a head ache: if people don't buy enough goods, the economy stagnates, growth falters and tax revenues decline. Difficult questions then have to be broached about what to do with limited resources – missiles or hospital beds – and voters become much harder to please.

So, both CEOs and Presidents had a difficult circle to square. The obvious solution was too boost demand. A method had to be found to encourage people to buy more, and advertising again offered a solution. As a contemporary text explained, advertising was

> 'waging, on behalf of the producers and sellers of consumer goods, a relentless war against saving and in favour of consumption' to induce 'changes in fashion, create new wants, set new standards of status, enforce new norms of propriety'.   (Baran and Sweezy 1966)

It was time to double down on Bernays' propaganda.

Other choices could have been made. There may have been oversupply in the US, but the global south remained in dire need, not just of vacuum cleaners but enough to eat. As the historian Clive Ponting (2000) points out, by the second half of the last century, there was enough food for everyone, it was just being very unfairly shared out, and many in the global south were suffering from malnutrition. This would have been a good moment at which to rethink the model; to stop chasing yet more profits and start redistributing global resources more fairly. Instead, the advertising war on behalf of the producers and sellers continued unabated and by the end of the century the people of the northern hemisphere were eating their way through double their share of the earth's harvest – even their domestic pets were better fed than the poor of the south. These problems of inequity continue today and not just between hemispheres: witness the rise of foodbanks in the UK, and the Financial Times (Shah R 2018) noting that 15% of US citizens go to bed hungry.

Similarly, 1962 saw the publication of Rachel Carson's 'Silent Spring' and the ecological impact of excessive consumerism was made clear. But nature was also pushed to the back of the queue. The economic illiteracy of the model was highlighted by Fritz Schumacher (1993), and its moral bankruptcy by Vance Packard (2007), each to no avail. There was, then, no shortage of critiques calling for change, but far from rethinking the model, the invisible government went into overdrive.

The Marketing Revolution: Plus ça Change . . .

To be fair, business academics did see the need for the system to change its myopic focus on high-pressure selling (Levitt 1960) – but they were not concerned about the environment or inequalities, just efficiency. Business, it was argued, needed to adopt a 'marketing perspective' which subsumed advertising into a new way of doing business. This inverted existing commercial principles by starting with the consumer rather than the product: successful companies produce what can be sold, rather than trying to sell what has already been (mass) produced (Baker 2003). The new discipline of marketing stressed the importance of market research in providing an understanding of the customer's needs and wants, and tracking a company's success in satisfying these; the watchwords became 'customer defined quality', 'customer satisfaction' and 'consumer sovereignty'; competitive pressures would weed out all those who didn't adapt, and make the market lean and efficient.

Marketing revolutionised business and did bring genuine benefits, as the concept of 'customer defined quality' illustrates (Hastings and Stead 2006). Inventing the world's most effective mouse trap may seem like a guaranteed route to business success. However, sales will depend on your customers agreeing that yours is indeed a great mouse trap, and their opinions on what a good mousetrap is – just as much as its technical performance – will have a fundamental bearing on this. If, for example, your customers can't condone the idea of killing mice, no amount of technological wizardry will convince them to buy a lethal trap. The most ineffective humane alternative will be preferable; will be a better product. Thus, consumer capitalism, the business school argument continues, has been enhanced and genuinely democratised by marketing.

There are three counterarguments to this. First, the fiduciary imperative, which requires every corporation to put their shareholders, not their customers, first shows consumer sovereignty to be no more than sophistry. Second, it is difficult to square a concern for customer needs with harmful products like tobacco and energy dense food and the rise of the 'industrial epidemic' (Jahiel and Babor 2007). Can an industry which knowingly addicts and kills one in two of its customers be said to be delivering 'customer defined quality'? Carbonated drinks companies are masterful marketers, but how can authentic customer satisfaction come complete with diabetes? According to WHO data 90% of Europeans now die of diseases of consumption (WHO 2016).

Third, if the marketing revolution had really resulted in corporations producing exactly what people want, rather than force-feeding them what they don't want, one would expect advertising and other promotional activity to reduce, and resume its historically more modest role of awareness raising about available benefits. But, as Foster et al (op cit) demonstrate, advertising expenditure has increased continuously for over a century, untroubled by the consumers apparent rise to supremacy. The arrival of the new discipline of marketing into 1950s America makes no dent in the steady increase in national adspend – from 25 to 300 billion dollars – between 1920 and the millennium. Furthermore, promotional techniques have multiplied: mass media advertising is now just one of many communications tools which make up the 'integrated marketing communications mix', the planning of which ensures that promotional messages are marshalled and coordinated through every possible channel. The pack, point of sale, bus tickets, clothing, buses – every possible surface is pressed into service. One ad agency even proposed that their cigarette company client should consider using lasers to project its logo onto the moon (Hastings and MacFadyen 2000). The marketing communications mix is tightly knitted into the wider business effort; the promotional P fits neatly into the marketing mix alongside the other three Ps of price, place and product – all focused relentlessly on the consumer. Thus, marketing isn't an isolated function or a separate department, it has entered the corporate DNA.

The underlying task, though, remains unchanged: to boost consumption. To this end, campaigns go way beyond the provision of information: every emotion is tapped, every creative ruse adopted. Despite the proclamation by the UK Advertising Standards Authority that it has ensured that advertising has been 'legal, decent, honest and truthful' for the last fifty years, the reality is very different. At the most obvious level, as noted above, how can the promotion of overtly harmful products – tobacco, junk food, guns, leaded paint – qualify for any of these epithets? However, the problem goes way beyond individual products. Richard Sennett in the Culture of the New Capitalism provides multiple examples of how marketers manipulate our view of products so that minor differences become greatly exaggerated – a process he calls 'gold plating'. Thus, he explains, car manufacturers don't sell us an engine and four wheels but 'the view from the window', and tech firms sell us computing capacity we can never begin to grasp, let alone use, because 'the dramatization of potential leads the spectator-consumer to desire things he cannot fully use' (Sennett 2006). Nothing has changed since the Rosser Reeves, cofounder in 1940 of Ted Bates Advertising, greeted new recruits to the agency by holding up two identical silver dollars and saying: 'Never forget that your job is very simple. It is to make people think the silver dollar in my left hand is much more desirable than the silver dollar in my right hand' (Foster et al op cit). We are back with the robber barons, Edward Bernays and the pursuit of power.

Business academics freely accept this sleight of hand. Product differentiation is essential in a competitive market because it ensures control of the transaction:

> if all products are perceived as being the same then price becomes the distinguishing feature and the supplier becomes a price taker, thus having to relinquish the important managerial function of control.　　　　　　　　　　　　　　　　　　　　　　　　(Baker 2003 p5)

This distinctiveness matters so much, that, if necessary, it has to be concocted:

> preferably this will be achieved through the manufacture of a product that is physically different in some objective way from the competitive offerings but, if this is not possible, then subjective benefits must be created through service, advertising and promotional efforts.
>
> (Baker 2003 p5)

In other words, systematic lying is justified because it ensures that the marketer retains power. The fact that it is subtle, entertaining, even graceful lying only makes matters worse. As John Ruskin observed:

> The essence of lying is in deception, not in words; a lie may be told in silence, by equivocation, by the accent on a syllable, by a glance of the eye attaching a peculiar significance to a sentence; but all of these kinds of lies are worse and baser by many degrees than a lie plainly worded.
>
> (Herrick 2020)

The cowboy would never have got away with saying outright: 'smoke Marlboro because it will make you look independent, tough and cool' – but with hint, association and judicious silence he said it all the same.

Consumer marketing, therefore, has not delivered power to the consumer, but reinforced it in the corporation. Multinational companies are now some of the biggest and most potent entities on earth, dwarfing many countries. Furthermore, with the advent of digital technology, the marketers' power has again been dramatically increased. The warnings from whistle-blowing tech employees and academics are sobering indeed (Einstein 2016 and Seymour 2019). Whether we call it the Psycho-Industrial Complex (Davies 2019) or the Age of Surveillance Capital (Zuboff 2019) it is very apparent that marketers, and through them, corporations, have acquired inordinate power to make the world in their own image. Zuboff goes as far as warning that 'we now face the moment in history when the elemental right to the future tense is endangered'.

But for all this success and power, modern marketers have been even more myopic than their hard-selling predecessors: the robber barons only ran out of customers; the surveillance capitalists have run out of planet. And, rather than face up to this reality, they are again resorting to sleight of hand. Instead of questioning the business model, and the wisdom of a system built on ever-increasing consumption, the response is to cover the cracks in the system with corporate social responsibility and public relations.

CSR Compounds the Problem

CSR rose to prominence in the 1990s when the Shell oil company got into difficulties in the Niger Delta and responded, not by addressing the shortfalls of their business model, but with a wave of PR. Both Amnesty International and Christian Aid bear witness to the lack of any concrete remedial action, and thirty years later the Niger delta is still one of the most polluted places on earth. CSR has continued ever since in the same vein: forever repainting the toilet door when the cistern is broken.

This deception is particularly problematic because it discourages us from thinking critically about the structural problems with our way of life – about the unfair distribution of food; about the Ogoni people of the Niger delta. Without such critical thought, nothing is likely to change. The powerful rarely cede their power voluntarily. This problem can be difficult to see; good deeds – a brewery letting the Red Cross use the sports stadia it sponsors during Covid (Budweiser – One Team 2020); a supermarket giving computers to schools – seem implicitly desirable. As Giridharadas (2020) puts it: 'how can there be anything wrong in trying to do good?'. 'The answer', he points out:

> may be when the good is an accomplice to even greater, if more invisible, harm. In our era that harm is the concentration of money and power among a small few, who reap from that concentration a near monopoly on the benefits of change

There are many such 'greater, more invisible, harms' with corporate marketing; borrowing the 4 Ps rubric, they concern practice, personality, philosophy and the politics. Practice has already been addressed: ubiquitous and sophisticated entrapment made even more powerful by digital technology. The corporate personality was uncovered a generation ago in Joel Bakan's book the Corporation with its diagnosis of psychopathy: they are irresponsible, manipulative, superficial, asocial and lacking in empathy and remorse; all this is camouflaged under a carapace of charm (Bakan 2004).

Marketing's philosophical home is materialism. This again has superficial attractions – consumer orientation; excellent customer service; the perpetual focus on our satisfaction – all have their appeal. Given the resources at the marketer's disposal, which have now risen to $560b per annum globally just for advertising, (Statista 2020) it is perhaps not surprising that we jump for the bate, and in many cases carry loyalty cards to prove our devotion. The more insidious problem is the perpetual reinforcements that stuff will make everything right; that our problems can be solved by shopping. It promotes and perpetuates what Tolstoy (2006) calls 'the eternal error people make in imagining that happiness is the realisation of desires'. In truth, he continues, it is our unsatisfied desires that make us human; without them we have no purpose, no future – anticipating Zuboff's concerns by a hundred years.

Finally, we come to the politics of marketing, and the smell worsens. Consider: the conditions prevailing in extended supply chains: the conflict minerals, the sweat shops, the gig economy; the trash vortex of single use plastic growing each year in different parts of the oceans; the systemically widening inequalities; the collapsing climate; the spreading virus. All in the interests of higher returns for the few and spiralling consumption for those who can afford it. As Patel and Moore (2017) demonstrate, corporate capitalism is a direct descendent of colonialism, and equally repellent.

When spelled out like this, it is astonishing that any of us are willingly do business with corporate marketers, let alone sign up to their loyalty schemes; but we do – and CSR is there to help ease any qualms. Oscar Wilde (1891) pointed out that if you want to abolish slavery the last thing you need is a kindly slave owner:

> Just as the worst slave-owners were those who were kind to their slaves and so prevented the horrors of the system being realised by those who suffered from it, so, in the present state of things in England, the people who do most harm are the people who try to do most good.

Thus, CSR illustrates the awe-inspiring power of marketing: it not only gets us to do appalling things – fund child labour, condone Rana Plaza – but makes us feel ok about continuing to do them. More fundamentally it has blinded us to the inadequacies of an economic system built on ever-increasing consumption.

Why We Need to Reduce Consumption

Even climate scientists have now been drawn into the idea that ever-increasing consumption is a necessary and natural part for human advancement. The key paper supporting the latest IPCC report, written by 21 leading climate scientists, begins: 'The purpose of the global energy system is to provide useful services to end users' (Grubler et al 2018). But despite the fact that 'End-use demand determines the size of the energy system and so the challenges of mitigating climate change', there is no discussion of where this demand comes from; basic needs – for food, for shelter – are naturally occurring; but what about designer handbags? Or Krispy Kreme Donuts? Or SUVs? Even the naturally occurring needs are not necessarily met by shopping: as Philip Kotler observed in his earliest writings on marketing, we can self-provide or barter. And yet the scientists proceed to build their entire model on the assumption that: 'consumer goods continue to proliferate in line with rises in living standards' and devote the rest of the paper to discussing how this contrived and dangerous regime can be maintained.

It is this same commitment to over-consumption that has led the international community to rely into two very dubious ideas: green growth and carbon capture. Green growth posits that consumption can be decoupled from environmental harms by improved efficiency: we can drive twice as many cars, but only cause half the damage if we produce them four times as efficiently. Perhaps unsurprisingly, this promise has not been delivered. Whilst some efficiencies can be made, and relative decoupling is possible in the short term, there is no empirical evidence to support the idea of absolute decoupling: 'Growth in GDP ultimately cannot plausibly be decoupled from growth in material and energy use, demonstrating categorically that GDP growth cannot be sustained indefinitely' (Hickel and Kallis 2019).

Carbon capture and storage (CCS) is also highly controversial, so much so that the IPCC scientists completely exclude it from their modelling, arguing that it is implausible because of likely 'innovation failure, unacceptable investment risks, public opposition, or a combination thereof' (Grubler et al 2018b, p78). And yet, the World Bank, the OECD and the UN's Sustainable Development Goals are all relying on both green growth and CCS, all in the interests of maintaining the bogus idea that there is no need to curtail consumption.

At the same time, the IPCC scientists point out in their technical notes that our consumption behaviour is in fact a key driver of climate breakdown and, if properly addressed, offers much potential for improvement. They give three reasons for this. First, we consumers cause more planetary harm than any other part of the economy: 'the final use of energy has long been identified both as the least efficient part of the global energy system' (Grubler et al 2018b, p3) – we fail to insulate our houses, insist on driving a few hundred metres to the shops and throw away half the food we buy – and consequently 'as having the largest improvement potentials'.

This despite a second technical note showing that our downstream behaviour is much easier and quicker to change than upstream activity: we consumers can switch from cars to bikes overnight, whilst moving from coal to nuclear power generation takes decades.

Finally, meeting our incessant demand for more stuff involves enormous waste:

> the conversion efficiency of total primary energy inputs into services delivered is conservatively estimated at 14% on average for the global energy system in 2020. This means that improving energy efficiency at the service level by 1 unit yields a reduction in primary resource requirements by a factor of 7.　　　　　　　　　　　　　　　　　　　　(Grubler et al 2018b p3)

In other words, every SUV we buy costs the energy equivalent of seven SUVs to produce, and not buying it will produce equally impressive savings.

Conclusion

It is often difficult for fish to see the water in which they swim. Ours is a society suffused in marketing: everywhere we go, online or in life, we are targeted by sophisticated messages, tempting offers, appealing installations and novel opportunities encouraging us to consume. The early proponents of this approach spoke openly of 'conscious and intelligent manipulation', 'invisible government' and 'waging a relentless war . . . in favour of consumption'. Governments are complicit: material plenty makes for more malleable voters. A century of experience, enormous resources and the best of behavioural science have given this marketing immense power, and new technology is raising serious questions about how much free choice we are now exercising in our consumption behaviour.

This marketing power has moved way beyond the individual consumer. It colours our culture; how we think about life; even what it means to be human – which now, it seems, includes an ever-escalating need for more things. CSR and public relations have ensured that stakeholders are drawn into the charade, and struggle to imagine a world where consumption simply decreases. Where we satisfy fewer needs more simply. At the same time, little acknowledgement is given to the role of marketing in this rush to consume, perhaps because politicians, stakeholder and even climates scientists are also consumers – and so, like the rest of us, caught in the consumption trap.

There are exceptions to this collective self-delusion. Some scientists are calling for 'degrowth', and recognising the need to rein in advertising (Degrowth 2015). They are right, but the problem is not just advertising, it is marketing as whole. It is time to completely rethink the way we manage humanity's consumption behaviour, focussing not on the needs of shareholder, or even the consumer, but those of the planet. The first step is to decommission the current failed approach – what might be called the drunken sailor model – of unfettered marketing and boundless consumption. When you are speeding towards a clifftop, a good first step is to take your foot of the accelerator; then you should start to think about the brake.

References

Wilkie W L & Moore E S (1999) *Marketing's Contributions to Society* Journal of Marketing Vol. 63 (Special Issue), 198–216

Harari Y (2014) Sapiens: A Brief History of Humankind, London: Harvill Secker, ISBN 978-006-231-609-7.

Foster JB, Hannah H, McChesney R (2009) The sales effort and monopoly capitalism, *Monthly Review*, vol 6, no 11 New York April.

Bernays E (1928) Propaganda https://bookdepository.live/show/book/493212/propaganda/ 12064225/4252368f/db7ccf8e9609a74/

Baran and Sweezy (1966), Monopoly Capital, New York: Monthly Review Press, p121 quoted in Foster, et al.

Shah R (2018) Rising obesity in Africa reflects a broken global food system, Financial Times, September 17, p 31.

Ponting C (2000) World History – a new perspective Chatto and Windus p790.

Schumacher, E.F. (1993) *Small is Beautiful: A Study of Economics as if People Mattered*. London: Vintage.

Packard, V. (2007) *The Hidden Persuaders*. Brooklyn, New York: IG Publishing.

Levitt T (1960) Marketing Myopia *Harvard Business Review*, July-August, 45–60

Baker, M.J. (2003) 'One More Time – What is Marketing?' in Baker M.J. (Ed.) *The Marketing Book*. (Fifth Edition.) Oxford: Butterworth-Heinemann, p.5.

Hastings GB and Stead M (2006). 'Social Marketing, Origins, Principles and Potential'. in Health Promotion Strategy and Delivery, Open University Press.

Jahiel RI, Babor TF (2007) Industrial epidemics, public health advocacy and the alcohol industry: lessons from other fields. Addiction; 102:1335–9.

WHO (2016) http://apps.who.int/gho/data/view.main.CODREG6EURV?lang=en

Foster op cit.

Hastings, G and MacFadyen L (2000). A day in the life of an advertising man: Review of internal documents from the UK tobacco industry's principal advertising agencies. British Medical Journal, 321(5 August): 366–371

Sennett Richard (2006) The Culture of the New Capitalism, New Haven: Yale University, p.161.

Foster et al p7.

Herrick, S (2020) London Review of Books Vol 42, No 7, April 2 p4.

Einstein M (2016) *Black Ops Advertising*, Or Books.

Seymour R (2019) *The Twittering Machine* Indigo Press.

Davies W (2019) *Let's eat badly: Irrationality and its Other* London Review of Books, 25 November.

Zuboff S (2019) *The Age of Surveillance Capitalism* Profile ISBN 13: 9781781256848.

Budweiser – One Team (2020) https://www.youtube.com/watch?v=3_t9niMNkdg

Giridharadas A (2020) Winners Take All: The Elite Charade of Changing the World 1 Penguin Books
    ISBN: 9780141990910.

Bakan, J. (2004) *The Corporation: The Pathological Pursuit of Profit and Power*. Toronto: The
    Penguin Group (Canada).

Statista (2020) https://www.statista.com/statistics/236943/global-advertising-spending/

Tolstoy L (2006) *Anna Karenina*, Penguin Classics p 465.

Patel R & Moore J (2017) A History of the World in Seven Cheap Things, UC Press ISBN
    9780520293137.

Wilde O (1891) *The soul of man under Socialism* http://struggle.ws/hist_texts/wilde_soul.html

Grubler A, Wilson C, Bento N, et al (2018a), A low energy demand scenario for meeting the 1.5 °C
    target and sustainable development goals without negative emission technologies *Nature
    Energy* 3 June 515–527 www.nature.com/natureenergy p515

Grubler A, Wilson C, Bento N, et al (2018b), A low energy demand scenario for meeting the 1.5 °C
    target and sustainable development goals without negative emission technologies *Nature
    Energy* 3 June 515–527 Supplementary Information.

Hickel J and Kallis G (2019) Is Green Growth Possible? *New Political Economy*, DOI: 10.1080/
    13563467.2019.1598964 p7.

Grubler A, Wilson C, Bento N, et al (2018), op cit Supplementary Information https://doi.org/
    10.1038/s41560-018-0172-6 Supplementary Note 1

Degrowth (2015) https://degrowth.org/2015/05/15/yes-we-can-prosper-without-growth/

Amani Alsalem, Park Thaichon and Scott Weaven

6 What People Actually Know about Posthumous Organ Donation

Introduction

Despite the societal value of organ donation behaviour rates remain low worldwide (Theodosopoulou et al. 2018). Organ shortage is a global problem and the demand for organ transplants has reached a critical stage whereby demand outstrips supply. According to the World Health Organization (WHO), only less than 10% of patients can benefit from transplantation therapies. As a consequence, thousands of patients die or endure a poor quality of life while waiting for the required organ transplantations (González 2019). Therefore, there is an urgent need to bridge the gap between organ supply and demand for transplantation.

This chapter discuss how the community is informed about organ donation and understand the consequences of that exposure. This chapter also discuss the role of objective knowledge in influencing people's attitude towards organ donation. This chapter provides a novel comparison of the level of knowledge between donors (i.e., those who have already signed organ donor cards) and non-donors (i.e., those who have not decided or have refused to sign donor cards). As a result, this study empirically explored certain types of knowledge that distinguish these donors' groups. This chapter provides critical insight for posthumous organ donation, social marketing activities and targeting the attitude-behavior discrepancy relating to low organ donation behaviour. This research assists to develop more audience-oriented programs, which could ultimately help to increase the actual donation behaviour. This research will guide policymakers to target communications toward citizens and promote the expansion of donating.

Organ Donation: Source of Information

The media and personal experience are particularly found to be the key information sources about organ donation that contribute to knowledge (Febrero et al. 2019). In the social marketing and social change literatures, very limited research exists about individual's information sources of organ donation and how this information may influence knowledge, which gives only a fragmented picture on the issue. The existing body of literature needs further exploration of how the community is informed about organ donation and understanding the consequences of that exposure. The following section will discuss the existing body of literature on how the media affects people's knowledge about the issue.

https://doi.org/10.1515/9783110659566-006

The media has a vast reach and, along with accessibility and information exposure, can influence the public's attitudes and behaviours toward organ donation. There is also a range of information sources that are more likely to contribute to the decision to donate, such as; newspapers (Moloney and Walker 2000); television or radio advertisements; movies or television shows (Harrison, Morgan, and Chewning 2008); entertainment television (Morgan, Harrison et al. 2007); the internet; public service announcements; shopping malls; hospitals; medical professionals; family members or friends; personal experience (e.g., knowing a donor or recipient) and government campaigns (e.g., Organ Donor Awareness Week) (Hyde and Chambers 2014); as well as religious institutes (Tumin et al. 2014). Conesa et al. (2004) found that the sources that had a favourable effect on attitudes toward donation included receiving the information about organ donation by health care providers, friends and family. According to Quick et al. (2007) the media and personal experience were found to be the key information sources about organ donation that contribute to knowledge. There is also a positive relationship between coverage of organ donation in television news and actual organ donation rates. When television news coverage of organ donation increases, actual organ donation also increases.

It has been reported that the lack of exposure to the donation and transplantation process probably contributes to a general fear (i.e., fear of the unknown) and negative views toward donating among the general public (Arriola, Perryman and Doldren 2005). This seems to indicate that bringing the issue of organ donation 'into the light' through interpersonal discussions makes people adopt a less fearful stance toward donation. Discussions with friends and family members about organ donation appear to supplement the role of the media in information-gathering about the issue of organ donation. These interpersonal discussions may mitigate the strength of belief in the non-cognitive factors that negatively influence the willingness to become a potential organ donor. Mass media, particularly television exposure, featuring debates or information on the subject of organ donation is the most effective approach to promote repeated discussions with family members (Zouaghi, Chouk and Rieunier 2015). The impact of this coverage is more effective and extensive than the impact of other occasional campaigns carried out by organ donation organisations (Quick et al. 2007). The more organ donation is covered by the media, the less taboo conversations with family about donating organs will seem (Harrison et al. 2008).

Moreover, mass media can also be used to create a culture where the donation is the norm. For example, in Spanish mass media positive stories about organ donation and transplantation are featured regularly (Matesanz 2001). It was suggested that avoiding presenting negative stories on the media because it can create the 'Panorama effect' (Quick et al. 2007). It was found that there is a link between media coverage and organ donation rates (Morgan et al. 2010). Morgan (2009) states that when individuals within communities are exposed to a new organ donation campaign, this will affect their discussions about the topic and could change their existing opinion about donation. In addition, people who signed donor cards were found to be more knowledgeable about organ donation and more primed for pro-donation messages than non-signers. They are also more likely to discuss their donation wishes with family members and significant others in order to confirm their decisions to become organ donors (Feeley 2007). On the other hand, people who did not sign donor cards often had been exposed to negative information in the newspaper or media (Moloney and Walker 2000).

Organ Donation: Knowledge

This chapter will discuss the existing body of literature on how knowledge about the issue affects people's intention to become organ donors. There is also a small but burgeoning body of literature concerning the differences in knowledge about organ donation between donors and non-donors (Morgan and Cannon 2003; Morgan and Miller 2002). This study will provide an opportunity to investigate whether there is a difference between donors (i.e., registered-donors) and non-donors in their level of knowledge. The current study employs only objective knowledge, which is measured by using structured questions with 'true', 'false' or 'not sure' responses (Horton and Horton 1990). The answers to the following research questions are also included '*What organ and tissue donation information sources have the community been exposed to?*', and '*What is the specific knowledge that distinguishes donors and non-donors?*'.

An accepted definition of knowledge about organ donation is 'the understanding of facts about organ donation, whether accurate or inaccurate. This variable includes knowledge about the (non-medical) procedures involved when someone becomes an organ donor as well as the procedures for obtaining an organ donor card and becoming a potential donor . . . ' (Kopfman and Smith 1996, p. 5). The most dominant predictors of the decision to donate include accurate knowledge of the role of next-of-kin, the existing need for transplants, how to make arrangements to donate, the body's normal appearance after donation, as well as donation and transplantation procedures (Nijkamp et al. 2008). The research by Coad, Carter and Ling (2013) found also that most of the people are in favour of organ donation, but only a few sign donor cards, due to the lack of knowledge on how to access and register themselves.

Both qualitative and quantitative studies establish that individuals who have misconceptions about organ donation are far less likely to become organ donors (Morgan and Miller 2002; Morgan, Miller and Arasaratnam 2002; Reubsaet et al. 2001). According to Sellers, McGinnis, Alperin, Sweeney and Dodson (2018), the lack of knowledge about organ donation is likely to increase unfounded fears about the donation process. Most people's existing knowledge has been referred to as erroneous beliefs which are derived from sensationalized portrayals of the transplant process (Morgan et al. 2010). Wakefield, Reid, and Homewood (2011) also suggests that the lack of knowledge about organ donation leads to more negative attitudes towards organ donation. Lack of confidence appears to be exacerbated by poor knowledge, and both contribute towards non-registration behaviours. This limited knowledge and grasp of certain fundamental elements of the organ donation and transplantation procedure by the public is indeed a reflection on the negative attitude towards donating and the low registration rate.

It seems that 'many people still do not understand the relationship of 'brain death' to death: They do not understand, that is, that brain death is simply death' (Mathieu 1988, p. 361). Brain death is in fact real death and the dead person is mechanically maintained only for a short time for the purposes of organ donation, but this does not seem to be understood by the general public. The fear that medical doctors will 'pull the plug' to get a person's organs is likely to be the most prevalent fear among individuals. It appears that brain death is often confused by the public and even by health care professionals with a 'persistent vegetative state' or a 'coma' (Bresnahan and Zhuang 2016; Liu et al. 2019). The concept of brain death poses particular misconceptions due to the following reasons; difficulty to accept the idea that a person with a beating heart is really dead; fear of having pain during the operation and fragments of consciousness might still remain; as well as a concern about the sufficiency of the diagnostic method that was used to pronounce death (Sanner 1994). Death negation and the confusion about the concept of brain death appears to influence the donation decisions (Manuel, Solberg and MacDonald 2010; Siminoff, Burant and Youngner 2004), which contribute to organ donation refusal.

It was found that only certain types of knowledge about organ donation can distinguish between donors and non-donors, and its effect on the way people make their donation decisions (Steenaart, Crutzen and de Vries 2018). For example, they found that registered donors tend to have a higher level of knowledge about organ donation and non-donors tend to have limited information about organ donation. Another belief among non-donors is that people with medical conditions cannot be organ or tissue donors and advanced age alone renders organs undesirable for transplantation (Sander and Miller 2005). It was found that non-registered donors tend to be less aware of organ shortage. Earlier research by Horton and Horton (1990) on the level of knowledge of donors and non-donors found that non-donors have inaccurate knowledge and misconceptions on four topics relating to organ donation and this may be a barrier toward donation. The first barrier deals with the individual's misunderstanding about the religious implications of organ donation, as non-donors tend to be uncertain about the religious perspective regarding donation. Secondly, non-donors also tend to be confused about the nature of brain death. Thirdly, non-donors may be uncertain about ethical policies regarding organ procurement. Finally, they do not have knowledge about the procedure to obtain an organ donor card and the registration process.

Method

The Study Sample

The data were collected from a convenience sample via an online questionnaire distributed to people via Facebook and Twitter. These social media websites were used for collecting the data in order to get a broad and diverse range of participants, for example, different age ranges, genders, educational levels, and geographical areas, as the aim is to achieve a representative sample of the general population. As such, the users of social media platforms are often found to be very influential in contributing to the dissemination of ideas (Albalawi and Sixsmith 2015). A total of 1022 usable surveys were collected. The sample consisted of 1022 participants aged 18 years to over 55 years of age. The sample of respondents is mainly female dominated, with 63% female and 37% males, respectively. Respondents were representative of a wide age range, with 59% (n = 606) between ages of 18–34 years, 35% (n = 357) between ages of 35 and 54, and 5.8% (n = 59) over 55 years of age. In relation to educational level, 18% (n = 184) of the respondents reported completing high school, while a small number 6% (n = 61) had a diploma degree. Also, approximately half 54% (n = 548) of respondents reported that their highest attained education was a bachelor's degree. Also, 14% (n = 149) of the sample had attained a master's degree, while 8% (n = 80) had completed a doctorate degree. Of the 1022 respondents, 190 (18.6%) were working in the health care system. The profile of the respondents is provided in Table 6.1.

Table 6.1: Demographic characteristics.

Characteristics	Registered Donors	Will and Testament	Intend to donate but have not sign	Undecided donors	Refused to donate	Sample Frequency and Percentage
	52 (5.1%)	16 (1.6%)	350 (34.2%)	422 (41.3%)	182 (17.8%)	N = 1022
Gender						
Male	24	5	114	174	61	378 (37%)
Female	28	11	236	248	121	644 (63%)
Age						
18–24	8	7	112	82	31	240 (23.5%)
25–34	16	3	129	158	60	366 (35.8%)
35–44	14	3	56	96	46	215 (21%)
45–54	11	1	35	64	31	142 (13.9%)
55+	3	2	18	22	14	59 (5.8%)

Table 6.1 (continued)

Characteristics	Registered Donors	Will and Testament	Intend to donate but have not sign	Undecided donors	Refused to donate	Sample Frequency and Percentage
Educational level						
High school	8	3	69	66	38	184 (18%)
College graduate	4	0	17	30	10	61 (6%)
Bachelor's degree	23	12	195	169	95	548 (53.6%)
Master's degree	10	1	47	56	18	149 (14.6%)
Doctorate degree	7	0	22	29	21	80 (7.8%)
Profession						
Work in health care	22	5	80	63	20	190 (18.6%)
Do not work in health care	30	11	270	359	162	832 (81.4%)

Source: Developed for this study

The sample of this study was categorised into two categories of donors and non-donors. Donors include 1) those who have signed donor cards or indicated permission by their last will and testament. Non-donors include 2) those who are favourable to organ donation but have not yet signed donor cards, undecided donors or have refused to sign donor cards. The distribution of the data for organ and tissue donor status indicated that 5.1% (n = 52) of respondents were currently registered as an organ donor and 1.6% (n = 16) wrote their donation decision in their will and testament. The majority of the respondents 93.3% (n = 954) (at the present time) were non-registered donors. Of those who stated that they were not currently registered as an organ donor, 34.2% (n = 350) said they intended to become organ donors but had not signed donor cards yet, compared with 41.3% (n = 422) that were still undecided and 17.8% (n = 182) who refused to donate.

Measures

Horton and Horton (1990) established a measure to represent public facts about organ donation. The items that are fact-based were designed to measure aspects of objective knowledge 'what people actually know about organ donation' and include general knowledge about organ donation (i.e., organ shortage and the eligibility requirements to become organ donors). Fact-based knowledge items were also interspersed with myths regarding the process of organ donation in order to best test knowledge accuracy. These scale items were deemed to be appropriate for this study. Accordingly, knowledge was assessed using 15 statements about organ donation that are either true or false. Participants were instructed to choose either 'true', 'false' or 'not sure' in their responses to fifteen statements. Accuracy was determined by the total number of correct answers to items checking factual knowledge about organ donation and transplantation. A 'dummy' code was used across all question scores with the value '1' for a correct answer and '2' if the answer was incorrect ('not sure' was scored as an incorrect response). Chi-square analysis was performed to compare the level of objective knowledge between two groups. Donors include 1) those who have signed donor cards or indicated permission by their last will and testament. Non-donors include 2) those who are favourable to organ donation but have not yet signed donor cards, undecided donors or have refused to sign donor cards.

Data Analysis

Source of Information about Organ Donation

Participants were asked about which methods make the participants aware of organ donation. As shown in Table 6.2, the main source of information was the internet 28% (n = 284), and this was followed by television 26.5% (n = 266). The results also revealed that 14% (n = 149) of the participants heard about organ donation from a family member or friend, or through organ donation campaign in public places 10%

Table 6.2: Information sources about organ donation.

Information sources	%	n
The internet	28	284
Television	26.5	266
A family member or friend	14	149
I have never heard about it before	13	131
Organ Donation campaign in public places	10	107
School or other educational centers	6	65
Health care provider	1.6	17

(n = 107). Furthermore, school and educational centers were cited by 6% of people. A very limited number of people had received information about organ donation from trusted sources. For example, only 1.6% of the respondents had heard about organ donation through healthcare providers. Interestingly, 13% of the participants (n = 131), indicated that they have never heard about posthumous organ donation before.

Comparison between Donors and Non-donors' Level of Knowledge

Understanding an individual's misperceptions is a crucial step towards understanding donation decisions, especially if knowledge is incorrect. Therefore, this section contained questions measuring knowledge aspects of organ donation. This study identifies a number of misconceptions about organ donation that could influence individuals toward posthumous organ donation. The level of factual knowledge among participants was generally poor, and individuals did not display accurate and good knowledge of the topic overall. However, the findings show that certain false information about organ donation differs between donors and non-donors, with non-donors possessing higher levels of misinformation about organ donation in comparison with donors. Non-donor organ donation misconceptions include confusion about the nature of brain death, the religious perspective regarding donation, the eligibility to donate organs, the fairness of organ allocation system, the organ shortage situation, the procedure of obtaining donor cards and also the belief that funeral arrangements have to be postponed in the case of organ donation. The main areas of poor knowledge have been summarised.

Knowledge Regarding the Concept of Brain Death

Non-donors found to be confused about the nature of brain death. For the first item (i.e., brain dead means the person is dead even though his or her heart is still beating) the results indicate that organ donors were significantly more knowledgeable than the non-donors in understanding the nature of brain death 79%. Regarding the second item (i.e., people can't recover when they are brain dead), the results indicate that organ donors were significantly more knowledgeable about non-recovery from brain death 72%.

Knowledge Regarding the Registration Process

It was found that non-registered donors have very limited knowledge about the procedure of obtaining donor cards and the registration process (88%). The study revealed also that only 10% of the non-registered donors were aware of the online registration system.

Knowledge Regarding the Distribution of Organs

Interestingly both donors and non-donors' groups unexpectedly raised concerns about the fairness of organ allocation system and the ethical policies regarding organ procurement. For example, almost half of the participants believed that there is no fair distribution of organs. Also, 83% of people believed that rich or well-connected people can get higher priority on a transplant waiting list and get a transplant faster than others.

Knowledge Regarding Religious Implications of Organ Donation

This domain deals with the individual's misunderstanding about the religious implications of organ donation. A higher number of organ donors answered correctly that organ donation is permitted in nearly all religions. On the other hand, generally, non-donors found to be uncertain about the religious perspective regarding donation. A great number of non-donors also expressed uncertainty about the religious leaders' view about posthumous organ donation 74%.

Knowledge Regarding Donor's Eligibility

This domain includes statements about the donor's health condition requirements, the acceptable donor's age, and smoking history. This study shows that most of the participants (including registered and non-registered donors) had a misunderstanding about organ donation criteria. For example, only 18% of participants were aware that people with medical conditions such as high blood pressure or diabetes can be organ or tissue donors. Another mistaken belief is that smokers cannot donate their organs 75%. Also, 60% of the participants tend to have confusion about the acceptable donor age.

Knowledge Regarding the Shortage of Organs

The results reveal a greater proportion of organ donors answered correctly that there is a shortage of available organs 93%. It was found that non-registered donors tend to be less aware of the shortage of organ.

Donation Process/Timing

The data shows that both donors and non-donors groups have insufficient knowledge about the donation process and timing. For example, 23% of the participants mistakenly think that organ and tissue donation will delay the funeral, therefore, funeral arrangements have to be postponed in the case of organ donation.

Knowledge Related to the Benefits of Donating Organs

Individuals did not display a good knowledge about the benefits of donating organs. For instance, only 31% were aware that a single organ and tissue donor can save up to 8 lives and improve the lives of up to 50 people. All knowledge items, with the total score of correct answers, are provided in Table 6.3.

Table 6.3: Comparison between donors and non-donors on factual knowledge items.

Knowledge Items (correct answer follows question)	Donors correct (n=68)	Non-donors correct (n=954)	Overall correct answer (n=1022)
Do you know how to register to be an organ donor?	80%	12%	16%**
Are you aware of online registration for organ donation?	54%	10%	13%**
Do you feel that there is currently a fair distribution of organs?	50%	25%	48%**
Do you think rich or well-connected people can pay their way for higher priority on a transplant waiting list or 'pull strings' to get a transplant faster (F)	47.1%	14.7%	17%**
Nearly all religions, are in favour of organ donation (T)	87%	45%	48%**
Brain dead means the person is dead even though his or her heart is still beating (T)	79%	63%	64%*
People can't recover when they are brain dead (T)	72%	33%	36%**
People with high blood pressure or diabetes can be organ donors (T)	37%	17%	18%**
People over the age of 40 are still suitable for organ donation (T)	69%	38%	40%**
Smokers can be organ donors (T)	46%	23%	25%**
People on the organ donor waiting list die every day because there are not enough organs available for transplant (T)	93%	60%	62%**
If I die, my family will be asked to grant consent for donation even if I have signed a donor card (T)	62%	29%	31%**
To become an organ donor it is enough to inform your family of your consent (T)	51%	35%	36%*

Table 6.3 (continued)

Knowledge Items (correct answer follows question)	Donors correct (*n*=68)	Non-donors correct (*n*=954)	Overall correct answer (*n*=1022)
Funeral arrangements do not have to be postponed in the case of organ donation (T)	53%	21%	23%**
One organ and tissue donor can save up to 8 lives and improve the lives of up to 50 people (T)	44%	30%	31%*

* Chi square $p < .05$
** Chi square $p < .01$

Discussion of Organ Donation Knowledge

The findings illustrate that knowledge about organ donation was abysmally low, as the participants presented incorrect information about organ donation. Therefore, these identified myths and misconceptions need to be addressed because it has the potential to negatively impact the donation decision. To counter the significant relationship between perceived risks of organ donation and attitudes, it is critical that irrational fears or misconceptions about organ procurement and transplantation are alleviated. In order to increase the number of registered donors, promotion programmes should emphasise positive aspects and focus on reducing fear and negative beliefs (Alsalem, Fry and Thaichon 2020). Additionally, addressing the risks beliefs about donating organs could be done through educational campaign messages as well as extensive formative research (Quick et al. 2014).

Furthermore, addressing specific misinformation and misconceptions about organ donation could to be reinforced by the media (Morgan and Miller 2002), as it can play an essential role by disseminating information to the public, which in turn may influence individuals' behaviour (Kluge 2000). In addition, it was approved that a 60-minute session designed to increase awareness on organ donation was sufficient enough to improve the knowledge of individuals who participated in the interventions (Feeley, Tamburlin and Vincent 2008). It has been acknowledged that formal training can successfully influence individuals' attitude and involvement (Lin et al. 2010; López-Montesinos et al. 2010). For example, it was found that the participants who took part in educational training have also developed a more favourable change in attitude towards organ donation (López-Montesinos et al. 2010).

It seems that most of the educational programs to correct public misconceptions about organ donation may prove successful in increasing consent rates. However, it may not be a 'one size fits all' approach (Callender et al. 1995), as this intervention has not been consistent and sustained, nor the public has been engaged in their continuation. It has been reported that 'simply educating people about the facts of organ donation is not enough' (Weber, Martin and Corrigan 2007, p. 24). Likewise, increasing knowledge about this issue did not necessarily translate into changing individuals' attitudes or behaviours (Morgan et al. 2006). Therefore, campaigns should work harder to understand the nature of the resistance to organ donation and change negative attitudes according to established theories of social influence (Morgan et al. 2002). Furthermore, Parisi and Katz (1986) state that such campaigns tend to overlook the importance of building positive attitudes towards donating, and the messages employed to reduce negative attitudes often do not consider the psychological bases of fear. Lack of information is often the reason for the creation of myths and the cause of unnecessary fear. It was suggested that a fear of the unknown causes people to imagine the worst possible scenario. Campaigns should, therefore, attempt to inform about the procedures involved in organ donation and transplantation, the registration process, help dispel common misconceptions and irrational fears. Furthermore, organ donation campaigns should be linked to social and cultural events in order to increase public awareness and to disseminate information about related matters (Shih et al. 2001). A sophisticated marketing campaign must continue to be employed to ensure appropriate information on all aspects of organ donation and transplantation is uniformly disseminate to the community (Cossé and Weisenberger 2000). Bearing this in mind, a reasonable amount of time should be dedicated to improving knowledge on organ donation and transplantation.

Callender et al. (1995), are pioneers of a successful organ donation program called 'the Minority Organ Tissue and Transplant Education Program'. Community stakeholders were used to plan and implement this education program. Furthermore, Callender, Hall, and Branch (2001) used educational intervention with a sample of Native Americans and Alaskan Natives. It was found that there is a significant improvement in individuals' attitudes, knowledge, beliefs, and intentions towards donation. In a similar vein, Fahrenwald, Belitz and Keckler (2010) recently evaluated the outcome of organ donation educational program for Native Americans called, 'Sharing the Gift of Life'. The intervention strategies derived from the oral tradition of story-telling, as well as written materials and an instructional video which reflected the value of generosity. This intervention approach had great success and the findings indicate a significant positive change in the participant's intention to donate organs.

Building on this approach, community-based interventions have been implemented successfully to target African Americans' attitudes, who generally have less favourable attitudes toward organ donation than Caucasians (Siminoff, Lawrence and Arnold 2003; Siminoff, Traino and Gordon 2011; Wakefield et al. 2010). A project About Choices in Transplantation and Sharing, seeks to increase African Americans positive attitudes toward organ donation and readiness to donate organs. Participants from nine churches received education materials about organ and tissue donation which included mainstream pamphlets and videos. These materials included health messages with religious themes that were informed by African American religious leaders. The results revealed that participants in the intervention group express higher readiness to donate an organ and more positive attitudes towards donating (Traino et al. 2017).

Recommendations for Policy and Practice

Understanding the level of knowledge of an individual's can provide guidance for campaign planners regarding what variables they need to focus on in such campaigns. The study findings provide a framework for social marketers to design and implement relevant strategies to promote the acceptance of posthumous organ donation for the society, therefore bridging the gap between organ supply and demand. This study provides a more complete picture of the target audiences that may be involved in developing persuasive health communication messages. It was suggested that in order to increase the number of actual organ donors, health professionals and organ procurement organisations need to take a more proactive role and provide family and culture-oriented education (Pham and Spigner 2004). This section will discuss some suggestions and recommendations that could assist government policy-makers, social marketing practitioners and educationalists to develop effective educational interventions (Figure 6.1).

Recommendation 1 – Clarifying the Concept of Brain Death

It was found that 'misconceptions regarding the definition of brain death are common, and that most miconceptions entailed a lack of understanding that brain death meant the patient was really dead' (Siminoff, Mercer and Arnold 2003, p. 223). Therefore, a simplified explanation of the brain death concept should be provided with clear terminology. There is a common belief that the person is not certified dead from brain stem death and the family often hope for a 'miracle' that the patient would wake up. Thus, it is also important to clarify that patients diagnosed as brain dead will never recover, therefore downplaying the belief that negatively affects the intention to become organ donors. Furthermore, creating more understanding of the concept of brain-death is needed, as non-donors tend to have considerable confusion between brain death and coma (Siminoff et al. 2004).

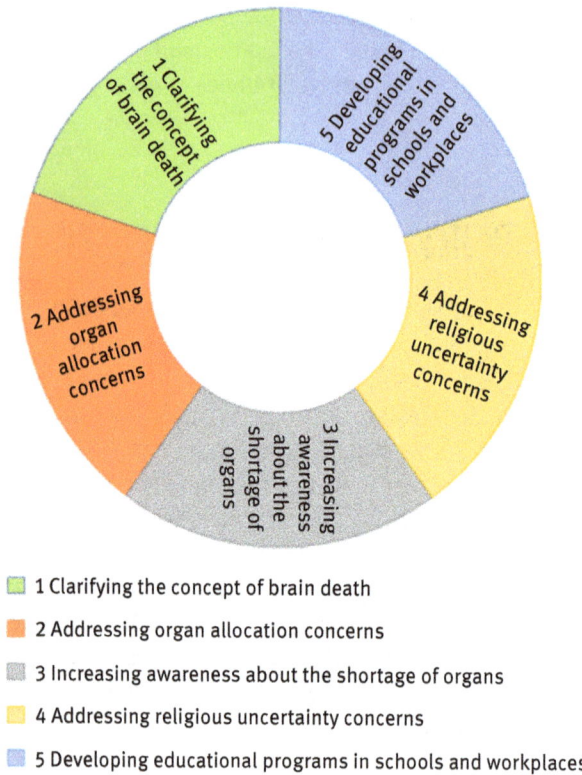

- 1 Clarifying the concept of brain death
- 2 Addressing organ allocation concerns
- 3 Increasing awareness about the shortage of organs
- 4 Addressing religious uncertainty concerns
- 5 Developing educational programs in schools and workplaces

Figure 6.1: The main recommendations to promote an acceptance of organ donation. Source: Developed for this study

Recommendation 2 – Addressing Organ Allocation Concerns

Concerns about the fairness of organ distribution might be addressed far more effectively through explaining the organ allocation system and the checks and balances in the procurement/transplant process which prevents doctors from killing patients for their organs, as well as, prevents the organ allocation system from giving preferential treatment to rich or well-connected people in the society (Morgan et al. 2008). However, despite many rules being in place in allocating organs fairly, individuals still show a significant concern about the allocation process (Boseley 2000). It was found that fairness in the organ allocation system and transparency of the transplantation practice can impact the public's acceptance of it (Boulware et al. 2007; Cohen and Erickson 2006). People are often more attracted to organ donation when they are confident that the allocation system is equitable for all candidates, and is not influenced by other factors such as social standing and usefulness to society (Siegel et al. 2010).

Recommendation 3 – Increasing Awareness about the Shortage of Organs

Both internationally and locally the transplant world is seeking for a solution for the shortage of deceased organ donors. Although most people have heard about organ donation and seem to be aware of the organ shortage, they are fully aware of the negative consequences of this shortage of donor organs because every day people die while waiting for the required organ. Therefore, it is essential to promote awareness of the existing shortage of donors, as some people do not see the urgency to register (Wong 2010). Irving et al. (2012) state that featuring stories of organ transplant recipients, family members of the deceased donors and suffering patients who are receiving dialysis and are still waiting for a transplant have been shown to be effective ways to increase awareness of the organ shortage crisis.

Recommendation 4 – Addressing Religious Uncertainty Concerns

It was suggests that religious beliefs and interpretation had an immense influence on individuals' decision as to whether to donate or not (Clarke-Swaby, Sharp and Randhawa 2011; Morgan et al. 2013; Wong 2010). It was found that the tendency for opposition to organ donation is often based on individuals own understanding and interpretation of their religious beliefs (Oliver et al. 2010). It is not that the religion is blocking people from donating organs, it is the fact that they do not know what their religion's position is. Morgan et al. (2013) found that there is a considerable uncertainty from the religious perspective especially Muslims who commonly required guidance from religious leaders. Rudge, Johnson, Fuggle, and Forsythe (2007) believe that religious objections to posthumous organ donation seem to be a community misconception which is based on ignorance, potentially reinforced by religious leaders or family elders over many years. Therefore, the misunderstanding around religious beliefs and organ donation is a significant barrier.

Recommendation 5 – Developing Educational Programs in Schools and Workplaces

Several researchers recommended taking a grass-roots community-led approach to accessing local social networks in order to increase knowledge and awareness about organ donation (Cantarovich et al. 2000; Cárdenas et al. 2010; Milaniak et al. 2010; Piccoli et al. 2004). According to Siegel (2002), if the campaign messages are 'delivered repeatedly and consistently over a long time period, then the chances of a successful campaign are maximized' (p. 159). Zouaghi et al. (2015) suggest the following approaches to promote organ donation effectively: 1) holding lectures continuously and regularly in order to identify intended donors, and 2) print a regular publication and booklets to educate the public.

Schools Education

A novel approach to increasing high school students' knowledge and improving their attitudes towards organ donation was undertaken by web-based intervention called 'Give Life: The Transplant Journey' (Vinokur et al. 2006). The questionnaires measuring students' knowledge and attitudes towards donation and transplantation were administered pre and post intervention. These researchers randomly assigned classes to an experimental group (n = 152). Students from this group were provided educational material on organ donation in a seven-step story which includes, information about organ shortage, the benefits of organ donation, a series of events from fatal injury to death, followed by transplant donation to a recipient. It also included a persuasive argument for expressing an individual's intention to become a donor, and the need to inform the family members about this. Students (n = 159) were also randomly assigned to a control group (i.e. the control group completed the questionnaire before receiving the educational session). It was found that students in the experimental group displayed a significant increase in knowledge and attitude towards donating as compared to students in the control group.

Workplace Education

It was highly recommended to implement and deliver informal work-site interventions in order to change the employees' attitudes toward organ donation. Quinn et al. (2006) provided a 'Lunch-and-Learn' information and skill-building session to corporate employees who live in Chicago. Testimonials from transplant recipients were provided in the session with the intent of tapping into the affective component of attitudes. Participants were assigned to two educational interventions. The outcome variables included the intention to become a posthumous organ donor, discussion with families about the donation wishes, and registration intention. It was found that both interventions were very effective in changing the participants' intentions to become posthumous organ donors, as a mere 3% of the employees were still in the pre-contemplation stage.

Chapter Summary

This chapter discussed the role of objective knowledge in influencing people's attitude towards organ donation and the information sources contributing to knowledge. Furthermore, a comparison between donors and non-donors in their level of factual knowledge about organ donation was also discussed. The purpose of such an examination is to improve knowledge and foster a deeper understanding of various aspects influencing posthumous organ donation. An understanding of an individual's level of knowledge about organ donation, is critical to gain formative research insights that can be used to design individually focused social marketing campaigns, and ultimately increase participation in organ donation. This study identifies several misconceptions about organ donation that could influence individuals toward posthumous organ donation. The level of factual knowledge among participants was generally poor, and individuals did not display accurate and good knowledge of the topic overall. For example, the most common organ donation misconceptions include confusion about the nature of brain death, the religious perspective regarding donation, the eligibility to donate organs, the fairness of organ allocation system, the organ shortage situation, the procedure of obtaining donor cards and the belief that funeral arrangements have to be postponed in the case of organ donation. Based on these finding, several important suggestions and recommendations was discussed in this chapter.

References

ADDIN EN.REFLIST Albalawi, Y. and Sixsmith, J. (2015). Identifying Twitter influencer profiles for health promotion in Saudi Arabia. *Health promotion international*, dav103.

Alsalem, A., Fry, M.-L. and Thaichon, P. (2020). To donate or to waste it: Understanding posthumous organ donation attitude. *Australasian Marketing Journal (AMJ)*.

Arriola, K. R. J., Perryman, J. P. and Doldren, M. (2005). Moving beyond attitudinal barriers: understanding African Americans' support for organ and tissue donation. *Journal of the National Medical Association*, *97*(3), 339.

Boseley, S. (2000). Transplant chief loses job over racism row. *The Guardian*, *23*, 5.

Boulware, Troll, Wang and Powe. (2007). Perceived transparency and fairness of the organ allocation system and willingness to donate organs: a national study. *American Journal of Transplantation*, *7*(7), 1778–1787.

Bresnahan, M. and Zhuang, J. (2016). Development and validation of the Communicating with Family about Brain Death Scale. *Journal of Health Psychology*, *21*(7), 1207–1215.

Callender, C. O., Bey, A. S., Miles, P. V. and Yeager, C. L. (1995). A national minority organ/tissue transplant education program: the first step in the evolution of a national minority strategy and minority transplant equity in the USA. *Trotter Review*, *9*(1), 8.

Callender, C. O., Hall, M. B. and Branch, D. (2001). *An assessment of the effectiveness of the Mottep model for increasing donation rates and preventing the need for transplantation – adult findings: program years 1998 and 1999*. Paper presented at the Seminars in Nephrology.

Cantarovich, F., Fagundes, E., Biolcalti, D. and Bacque, M. (2000). *School education, a basis for positive attitudes toward organ donation*. Paper presented at the Transplantation Proceedings.

Cárdenas, V., Thornton, J. D., Wong, K. A., Spigner, C. and Allen, M. D. (2010). Effects of classroom education on knowledge and attitudes regarding organ donation in ethnically diverse urban high schools. *Clinical transplantation, 24*(6), 784–793.

Clarke-Swaby, S., Sharp, C. and Randhawa, G. (2011). Attitudes towards organ donation and kidney disease among Black African, Black Caribbean and Asian population in Lambeth, Southwark and Lewisham, London, UK. *Organs, Tissues and Cells.*

Coad, L., Carter, N. and Ling, J. (2013). Attitudes of young adults from the UK towards organ donation and transplantation. *Transplantation research, 2*(1), 9.

Cohen, J. S. and Erickson, J. M. (2006). Ethical dilemmas and moral distress in oncology nursing practice. *Clinical journal of oncology nursing, 10*(6).

Conesa, C., Zambudio, A. R. o., Ramırez, P., Canteras, M., Rodrıguez, M. and Parrilla, P. (2004). *Influence of different sources of information on attitude toward organ donation: a factor analysis*. Paper presented at the Transplantation proceedings.

Cossé, T. J. and Weisenberger, T. M. (2000). Words versus actions about organ donation: A four-year tracking study of attitudes and self-reported behavior. *Journal of Business Research, 50*(3), 297–303.

Fahrenwald, N., Belitz, C. and Keckler, A. (2010). Outcome evaluation of 'sharing the gift of life': an organ and tissue donation educational program for American Indians. *American Journal of Transplantation, 10*(6), 1453–1459.

Febrero, B., Ríos, A., López-Navas, A., Martínez-Alarcón, L., Almela-Baeza, J., Sánchez, J.,. . . Ramírez, P. (2019). Psychological profile of teenagers toward organ donation: a multicentric study in Spain. *European journal of public health.*

Feeley, T. H. (2007). College Students' Knowledge, Attitudes, and Behaviors Regarding Organ Donation: An Integrated Review of the Literature1. *Journal of Applied Social Psychology, 37*(2), 243–271.

Feeley, T. H., Tamburlin, J. and Vincent, D. E. (2008). An educational intervention on organ and tissue donation for first-year medical students. *Progress in Transplantation, 18*(2), 103–108.

González, B. D.-G. (2019). Organ Transplantation: Current Challenges and Solutions. *FarmaJournal, 4*(1), 31–32.

Harrison, Morgan and Chewning. (2008). The challenges of social marketing of organ donation: News and entertainment coverage of donation and transplantation. *Health marketing quarterly, 25*(1–2), 33–65.

Horton and Horton. (1990). Knowledge regarding organ donation: Identifying and overcoming barriers to organ donation. *Social Science & Medicine, 31*(7), 791–800.

Hyde, M. and Chambers, S. (2014). Information sources, donation knowledge, and attitudes toward transplant recipients in Australia. *Progress in Transplantation, 24*(2), 169–177.

Irving, M. J., Tong, A., Jan, S., Cass, A., Rose, J., Chadban, S.,. . . Howard, K. (2012). Factors that influence the decision to be an organ donor: a systematic review of the qualitative literature. *Nephrology Dialysis Transplantation, 27*(6), 2526–2533.

Kluge, E.-H. W. (2000). Improving organ retrieval rates: various proposals and their ethical validity. *Health Care Analysis, 8*(3), 279–295.

Kopfman and Smith, S. W. (1996). Understanding the audiences of a health communication campaign: A discriminant analysis of potential organ donors based on intent to donate.

Lin, L.-M., Lin, C.-C., Lam, H.-D. and Chen, C.-L. (2010). *Increasing the participation of intensive care unit nurses to promote deceased donor organ donation*. Paper presented at the Transplantation Proceedings.

Liu, C. W., Yeo, C., Zhao, B. L., Lai, C. K., Thankavelautham, S., Ho, V. K. and Liu, J. C. (2019). Brain Death in Asia: Do Public Views Still Influence Organ Donation in the 21st Century? *Transplantation*, *103*(4), 755–763.

López-Montesinos, M., Saura, J. M., Mikla, M., Ríos, A., López-Navas, A., Martinez-Alarcon, L.,. . . Ramírez, P. (2010). *Organ donation and transplantation training for future professional nurses as a health and social awareness policy*. Paper presented at the Transplantation Proceedings.

Manuel, A., Solberg, S. and MacDonald, S. (2010). Organ donation experiences of family members. *Nephrol Nurs J*, *37*(3), 229–236.

Matesanz, R. (2001). A decade of continuous improvement in cadaveric organ donation: the Spanish model. *Nefrologia*, *21*(Suppl 5), 59–67.

Mathieu, D. (1988). Organ substitution technology: ethical, legal, and public policy issues.

Milaniak, I., Przybylowski, P., Wierzbicki, K. and Sadowski, J. (2010). *Organ transplant education: the way to form altruistic behaviors among secondary school students toward organ donation*. Paper presented at the Transplantation Proceedings.

Moloney, G. and Walker, I. (2000). Messiahs, pariahs, and donors: The development of social representations of organ transplants. *Journal for the Theory of Social Behaviour*, *30*(2), 203–227.

Morgan and Cannon. (2003). African Americans' knowledge about organ donation: closing the gap with more effective persuasive message strategies. *Journal of the National Medical Association*, *95*(11), 1066.

Morgan, S. E., Harrison, T. R., Chewning, L., Davis, L. and DiCorcia, M. (2007). Entertainment (mis) education: The framing of organ donation in entertainment television. *Health communication*, *22*(2), 143–151.

Morgan and Miller. (2002). Beyond the organ donor card: The effect of knowledge, attitudes, and values on willingness to communicate about organ donation to family members. *Health communication*, *14*(1), 121–134.

Morgan, S., Miller, J. and Arasaratnam, L. (2002). Signing cards, saving lives: An evaluation of the worksite organ donation promotion project. *Communication Monographs*, *69*(3), 253–273.

Morgan, Stephenson, Harrison, Afifi and Long. (2008). Facts versusFeelings' How Rational Is the Decision to Become an Organ Donor? *Journal of Health Psychology*, *13*(5), 644–658.

Morgan, M., Hooper, R., Mayblin, M. and Jones, R. (2006). Attitudes to kidney donation and registering as a donor among ethnic groups in the UK. *Journal of Public Health*, *28*(3), 226–234.

Morgan, M., Kenten, C., Deedat, S. and Team, D. P. (2013). Attitudes to deceased organ donation and registration as a donor among minority ethnic groups in North America and the UK: a synthesis of quantitative and qualitative research. *Ethnicity & health*, *18*(4), 367–390.

Morgan, S. E. (2009). The intersection of conversation, cognitions, and campaigns: The social representation of organ donation. *Communication Theory*, *19*(1), 29–48.

Morgan, S. E., King, A. J., Smith, J. R. and Ivic, R. (2010). A kernel of truth? The impact of television storylines exploiting myths about organ donation on the public's willingness to donate. *Journal of Communication*, *60*(4), 778–796.

Nijkamp, M. D., Hollestelle, M. L., Zeegers, M. P., van den Borne, B. and Reubsaet, A. (2008). To be (come) or not to be (come) an organ donor, that's the question: A meta-analysis of determinant and intervention studies. *Health Psychology Review*, *2*(1), 20–40.

Oliver, M., Woywodt, A., Ahmed, A. and Saif, I. (2010). Organ donation, transplantation and religion: Oxford University Press.

Parisi and Katz. (1986). Attitudes toward posthumous organ donation and commitment to donate. *Health Psychology*, *5*(6), 565.

Pham, H. and Spigner, C. (2004). Knowledge and opinions about organ donation and transplantation among Vietnamese Americans in Seattle, Washington: a pilot study. *Clinical transplantation, 18*(6), 707–715.

Piccoli, G. B., Soragna, G., Putaggio, S., Burdese, M., Longo, P., Rinaldi, D.,. . . Novaresio, C. (2004). *Efficacy of an educational program on dialysis, renal transplantation, and organ donation on the opinions of high school students: a randomized controlled trial.* Paper presented at the Transplantation Proceedings.

Quick, B. L., Meyer, K. R., Kim, D. K., Taylor, D., Kline, J., Apple, T. and Newman, J. D. (2007). Examining the association between media coverage of organ donation and organ transplantation rates. *Clinical transplantation, 21*(2), 219–223.

Quick, B. L., Morgan, S. E., LaVoie, N. R. and Bosch, D. (2014). Grey's Anatomy viewing and organ donation attitude formation: Examining mediators bridging this relationship among African Americans, Caucasians, and Latinos. *Communication Research, 41*(5), 690–716.

Quinn, M. T., Alexander, G. C., Hollingsworth, D., O'Connor, K. G., Meltzer, D. and Consortium, C. C. f. L. (2006). Design and evaluation of a workplace intervention to promote organ donation. *Progress in Transplantation, 16*(3), 253–259.

Reubsaet, van den Borne, Brug, Pruyn and van Hooff. (2001). Determinants of the intention of Dutch adolescents to register as organ donors. *Social science & medicine, 53*(3), 383–392.

Rudge, C., Johnson, R., Fuggle, S. and Forsythe, J. (2007). Kidney, and Pancreas Advisory Group, UKTNHSBT 2007. Renal transplantation in the United Kingdom for patients from ethnic minorities. *Transplantation, 83*(9), 1169–1173.

Sander, S. L. and Miller, B. K. (2005). Public knowledge and attitudes regarding organ and tissue donation: an analysis of the northwest Ohio community. *Patient education and counseling, 58* (2), 154–163.

Sanner, M. (1994). Attitudes toward organ donation and transplantation: A model for understanding reactions to medical procedures after death. *Social science & medicine, 38*(8), 1141–1152.

Sellers, M. T., McGinnis, H. S., Alperin, M., Sweeney, J. F. and Dodson, T. F. (2018). Deterrents to Organ Donation: A Multivariate Analysis of 766 Survey Respondents. *Journal of the American College of Surgeons, 226*(4), 414–422.

Shih, F.-J., Lai, M.-K., Lin, M.-H., Lin, H.-Y., Tsao, C.-I., Duh, B.-R. and Chu, S.-H. (2001). The dilemma of "to-be or not-to-be": needs and expectations of the Taiwanese cadaveric organ donor families during the pre-donation transition. *Social science & medicine, 53*(6), 693–706.

Siegel, J. T., Alvaro, E. M., Crano, W. D., Gonzalez, A. V., Tang, J. C. and Jones, S. P. (2010). Passive-positive organ donor registration behavior: A mixed method assessment of the IIFF Model. *Psychology, health & medicine, 15*(2), 198–209.

Siegel, M. (2002). Antismoking advertising: figuring out what works. *Journal of health communication, 7*(2), 157–162.

Siminoff, L. A., Burant, C. and Youngner, S. J. (2004). Death and organ procurement: public beliefs and attitudes. *Social Science & Medicine, 59*(11), 2325–2334.

Siminoff, L. A., Lawrence, R. H. and Arnold, R. M. (2003). Comparison of black and white families' experiences and perceptions regarding organ donation requests. *Critical Care Medicine, 31*(1), 146–151.

Siminoff, L. A., Mercer, M. B. and Arnold, R. (2003). Families' understanding of brain death. *Progress in Transplantation, 13*(3), 218–224.

Siminoff, L. A., Traino, H. M. and Gordon, N. H. (2011). An exploratory study of relational, persuasive, and nonverbal communication in requests for tissue donation. *Journal of health communication, 16*(9), 955–975.

Steenaart, E., Crutzen, R. and de Vries, N. K. (2018). *The complexity of organ donation registration: Determinants of registration behavior among lower-educated adolescents*. Paper presented at the Transplantation Proceedings.

Theodosopoulou, M., Dor, F. J., Casanova, D., Baskozos, G. and Papalois, V. (2018). Health Literacy: The Way Forward to Increase the Rates of Deceased Organ Donation *Optimizing Health Literacy for Improved Clinical Practices* (pp. 260–273): IGI Global.

Traino, H. M., West, S. M., Nonterah, C. W., Russell, J. and Yuen, E. (2017). Communicating About Choices in Transplantation (COACH) Results of a Pilot Test Using Matched Controls. *Progress in Transplantation*, *27*(1), 31–38.

Tumin, M., Raja, A. R., Mohd, S. N., Abdullah, N., Wan, M. A. W., Ismail, A. Z. and Che, S. M. (2014). Organ Donation among Malaysian Muslims: The Role of Mosques. *Annals of transplantation: quarterly of the Polish Transplantation Society*, *20*, 206–210.

Vinokur, A. D., Merion, R. M., Couper, M. P., Jones, E. G. and Dong, Y. (2006). Educational web-based intervention for high school students to increase knowledge and promote positive attitudes toward organ donation. *Health Education & Behavior*, *33*(6), 773–786.

Wakefield, C. E., Reid, J. and Homewood, J. (2011). Religious and ethnic influences on willingness to donate organs and donor behavior: an Australian perspective. *Progress in Transplantation*, *21* (2), 161–168.

Wakefield, C. E., Watts, K. J., Homewood, J., Meiser, B. and Siminoff, L. A. (2010). Attitudes toward organ donation and donor behavior: a review of the international literature. *Progress in Transplantation*, *20*(4), 380–391.

Weber, K., Martin, M. M. and Corrigan, M. (2007). Real donors, real consent: Testing the theory of reasoned action on organ donor consent. *Journal of Applied Social Psychology*, *37*(10), 2435–2450.

Wong, L. (2010). *Factors limiting deceased organ donation: focus groups' perspective from culturally diverse community*. Paper presented at the Transplantation proceedings.

Zouaghi, S., Chouk, I. and Rieunier, S. (2015). Promoting organ donation through the 'intensity of discussions' with next of kin: role of superstition, taboo of death and personality variables. *Recherche et Applications en Marketing (English Edition)*, 2051570715594132.

Anthony Samuel and Ken Peattie

7 Fairtrade Towns: A Community Based Social Marketing Perspective in Promoting Ethical Consumption

Introduction

Fairtrade is recognised as a major contributor to ethical food and drink consumption, particularly following the successful *mainstreaming* of Fairtrade products and the associated growth in sales volume. Mainstreaming however has created concerns about the potential over-commercialisation of the fairtrade movement and the associated risk of losing its ethical distinctiveness.

This chapter concerns Fairtrade Towns, which have been proposed both as an element of mainstreaming, and as part of a new place-based developmental stage for Fairtrade. It draws on a Grounded Theory based study of Fairtrade Towns to explore them as a form of community-based social marketing that seeks to change consumption behaviours and to influence local social norms and institutions to support Fairtrade, whilst also aiming to preserve its perceived ethical validity. This perspective helps to better understand the marketing dynamics at work through a focus on the downstream and upstream components of efforts to extend Fairtrade consumption and supply within participating towns, and the breadth of the social relationships and interactions that are harnessed to achieve this.

Background

The growth in ethical consumption represents one of the most significant marketing trends of the late 20th and early 21st centuries. The 2017 *UK Ethical Consumer Markets Report* (EC 2017) reveals UK ethical consumption to have passed £80 billion, with food and drink representing the largest element of ethical household spending (at £397 per household in 2016, more than double the 2006 figure). An important component of this growth is accounted for by Fairtrade certified products, of which there are now over 4,000 types available in the UK, generating sales of over £ 1.6 billion (EC 2017). Fairtrade has evolved from an alternative marketing initiative appealing only to the most dedicated ethical consumers of forty years ago, to successfully reach mass market consumers and distribution channels (Doherty et al. 2013; Wilkinson 2007). For the family staple of bananas, Fairtrade now accounts for 25% of UK sales, and retailers such as Marks and Spencer and the Cooperative have developed significant portfolios of own-label Fairtrade products such as tea, coffee and chocolate (Doherty et al. 2013).

https://doi.org/10.1515/9783110659566-007

Even the firmly mass market Greggs bakery chain now uses only Fairtrade coffee across over 1,850 outlets. In addition, some major global brands now carry the Fairtrade label, including Starbucks (for espresso based drinks) and Nestlé (with Kit Kat and their controversial Nescafé Partners' Blend coffee). The growing consumption and availability of Fairtrade products is intertwined with a growth in consumer awareness of Fairtrade. An international 2011 poll of 17,000 consumers found that over 80 percent recognized the Fairtrade mark in the UK, Ireland, Switzerland, Netherlands, Austria and Finland, with 9 out of 10 who recognised the mark expressing trust in it (Globescan 2011).

Fairtrade's successful "mainstreaming" reflects Fairtrade organisations improving their product quality in terms of appearance, taste, aroma, packaging and nutritional characteristics (Lecomte 2003), extending product availability through retail channels (Doherty et al. 2013), and mastering well-established marketing techniques such as labelling and branding (Low and Davenport 2006). These elements are particularly important given that Fairtrade growth is heavily focused on *pleasure* products such as coffee, chocolate, wines, flowers and fruits (Wilkinson 2007).

Another contributor to Fairtrade's mainstreaming success has been the Fairtrade Towns Movement (Lamb 208). This began in Garstang (UK), where a small group of activists lobbied local councils, retailers and other organisations to stock and/or consume Fairtrade products (Alexander andand Nicholls 2006). In November 2001 the Fairtrade Foundation accepted their argument that it should be possible to accredit a place of consumption (rather than production) as Fairtrade, and Garstang became the World's first Fairtrade Town against the agreed criteria of (Fairtrade Towns 2017):

- The local council must pass a resolution supporting Fairtrade, and serve Fairtrade coffee and tea at its meetings and in offices and canteens.
- A range of Fairtrade products must be readily available in the town's (or city's) shops and served in local cafés and catering establishments (with targets set in relation to population).
- Fairtrade products must be used by a number of local work places (estate agents, hairdressers etc) and community organisations (churches, schools etc).
- The council must attract popular support for the campaign.
- A local Fairtrade steering group must be convened to ensure continued commitment to Fairtrade status.

By 2016 there were 612 UK Fairtrade Towns and the movement had internationalised, with 1116 more towns located across a further 25 countries including the USA, Japan and New Zealand (Fairtrade Towns 2017). Despite their growth and prevalence, Fairtrade Towns remain under-researched from a marketing perspective. Nicholls and Opal (2005) provided a pioneering framing of Fairtrade Towns as distinctive and innovative marketing networks combining ethical and place-based marketing perspectives. Following this there have been relatively few studies devoted to Fairtrade Town marketing, beyond Peattie and Samuel's (2016) study of the role of Fairtrade Town steering group members as ethical activists, and Samuel et al.'s (2017) paper exploring brand co-creation processes within Fairtrade Towns.

The success of mainstreaming through the widespread adoption of conventional marketing practices has created two key problems for Fairtrade. Firstly there are concerns that commercial success will be perceived as compromising the ethical distinctiveness of Fairtrade products and producers, potentially weakening Fairtrade's political and developmental message and its core ethical appeal (Golding 2009; Low and Davenport 2005, 2006). Secondly, the success of the mainstreaming strategy has moved the agenda in Fairtrade marketing scholarship away from an emphasis on ethics and Fairtrade as an alternative arena of marketing and consumption, towards more conventional marketing issues and variables relating to branding, pricing, messaging, retail distribution, consumer loyalty and perceived product quality (Low and Davenport 2005 and 2006; Moore et al. 2006).

This chapter focuses on Fairtrade Towns' ability to address these two problems, firstly as vehicles for further mainstreaming of Fairtrade consumption (Lamb 2008), whilst also working to prevent any erosion of trust in the Fairtrade brand; and secondly through Fairtrade Towns' status as highly unconventional marketing networks that invite the use of alternative research lenses to understand the marketing and consumption processes at play. It does this by adopting a previously suggested, but under-developed, perspective on Fairtrade marketing processes by likening them to those of social marketing (Golding and Peattie 2005; Witkowski 2005). It also refines this analogy in a place-based context for Fairtrade Towns by drawing parallels with what McKenzie-Mohr and Smith (1999) conceptualise as community-based social marketing (CBSM).

Fair Trade: From Social Movement to Social Marketing?

Fundamental to Fairtrade is the notion of consumers buying certified products that benefit producer communities through a guaranteed (and generally higher) price than that paid through global commodity markets, complemented by marketing support and community investment. Nicholls and Opal (2005) and Nicholls (2004) argue that the developmental outcome of Fairtrade must be central to all Fairtrade offerings, whilst its marketing should aim to be commercially viable by clearly articulating the social, sustainable and economic connections between producers and consumers. Others, including Low and Davenport (2005 and 2006) and Lamb (2008), similarly argue that ethical virtue should be the starting point of Fairtrade consumption, and central to its promotion should be the altruistic proposition of benefiting distant others. However, this ethical positioning has at times been threatened by mainstreaming, for example through the shift of Café Direct (the UK's largest Fairtrade coffee brand) away from a strongly ethical branding to instead stress product quality with the ethical component reduced to more of a product augmentation (Golding and Peattie 2005). Moore et al. (2006) and Golding (2009) warn that if the social developmental qualities of Fairtrade becomes lost or obscured, it may lead to the Fairtrade message becoming merely a lifestyle choice enacted in the supermarket with no real social meaning or ethical substance resonating with consumers. This may make Fairtrade consumption more vulnerable to changes in lifestyle fashion, and Fridell (2009, p. 92) warns that the logical conclusion of mainstreaming:

> . . . may actually threaten to limit the long-term growth of the network by re-envisioning fair trade as a token project supported by giant TNCs on the sidelines of their larger marketing efforts.

The notion of reframing Fairtrade as social marketing was first put forward by Golding and Peattie, and by Witkowski, both in 2005. Witkowski (2005) explains the potential to frame Fairtrade marketing as social marketing by returning to Kotler and Zaltman's (1971, p. 5) definition:

> Social marketing is the design, implementation and control of programs calculated to influence the acceptability of social ideas and involving considerations of product planning, pricing, communication distribution, and market research . . . It is the explicit use of marketing skills to help translate present social action efforts into more effectively designed and communicated programs that elicit desired audience response.

Witkowski's argument is that Fairtrade's promotion of more socially equitable and sustainable development for producer communities, through the price premium and other benefits that Fairtrade offers, is clearly a social idea that is promoted through the application of marketing skills and processes. As Golding and Peattie (2005, p. 163) put it:

> The suitability of social marketing as a discipline to inform and develop Fairtrade marketing is demonstrated by asking the question 'What is the Fairtrade coffee consumer being asked to buy?' The answer is not the coffee, since that is the means to an end. The consumer is being asked to buy into the idea of a fairer world.

Fairtrade is essentially trying to shift marketing norms beyond a conventional focus on consumers' self-gratification and instead factor into their purchase decisions the potential social and economic benefits to distant others (Barnett et al. 2011).

Golding and Peattie (2005) propose a continuum of marketing approaches, varying from entirely commercially orientated, to entirely socially orientated, but with the potential for hybrid positions, such as social enterprises that seek profit for investment in social causes. Fairtrade represents such a hybrid because, although the marketing processes and profit generating activities resemble conventional commercial marketing, the primary aim, and the underlying purchase motive presented to consumers, is social. Although there is a widespread acceptance that Fairtrade is a form of social enterprise, by adopting primarily commercial means in the pursuit of primarily social ends (Peattie and Morley 2008), equating it with social marketing represents an alternative approach that may yield original insights and suit its social mission. As Golding and Peattie (2005, p. 159) argue:

> An alternative to relying on the principles and practices of conventional marketing to make Fairtrade products more commercial, is to look towards the discipline of social marketing as a means of preserving Fairtrade's social mission while also contributing to its commercial success.

A social marketing perspective can be valuable by refocusing marketers' attention away from elements of the core mix, which is helpful since most Fairtrade producers don't compete on the basis of the tangible product or price, and cannot compete in communications budgets against conventional brands (Golding and Peattie 2005). It is also helpful due to social marketing's emphasis on overcoming barriers to behaviour change, which may be relevant to the challenge of encouraging consumers to follow through on good intentions to purchase more ethical products (Chatzidakis et al. 2007). Finally a social marketing perspective can help to focus attention on the importance of a range of actors within the marketing environment in influencing consumers and retailers. One of the criticisms of existing studies of Fairtrade is that they mostly adopt a commodity chain perspective which focuses narrowly on a direct vertical chain of actors linking producers and consumers (McEwan, Hughes and Bek (2017)). Social marketing contexts often lack such an obvious supply chain, and as a consequence may adopt a more holistic perspective to understand influences on the behaviour of campaign targets. This has been reflected in the growing interest in supporting and complementing "downstream" behaviour change amongst targeted audiences (in this case consumers within Fairtrade Towns), with efforts to change the "upstream" institutional and social environment (Andreasen 2006; Goldberg 1995). This may translate very closely into a Fairtrade context, particularly when promoted through Fairtrade Towns within which a range of stakeholders normally considered to be part of the marketing environment, such as local government, schools and churches, can play an active role in the marketing system (Samuel et al. 2017). This is much more reminiscent of social marketing than conventional commercial marketing and its supply chain focus.

Combing the view of Golding and Peattie (2005) and Witkowski (2005) in considering Fairtrade as a form of social marketing with Nicholls and Opal's (2005) characterisation of Fairtrade Towns as place-based marketing networks logically leads to conceptualising Fairtrade Towns as a form of CBSM. McKenzie-Mohr and Smith (1999) propose CBSM as something of an antidote to conventional social marketing campaigns which they see as often overly-dependent on media advertising and skewed towards creating public awareness rather than achieving actual behaviour change. They argue that particularly for pro-sustainability behaviours "Research on persuasion demonstrates that the major influence upon attitudes and behaviour is not the media, but rather our contact with other people" (p. 95). As Stern and Aronson (1984) identify, many campaigns to foster more sustainable behaviour (such as ethical purchasing) fail as a direct result of paying scant attention to the cultural practices and social interactions that influence human behaviour. CBSM instead draws upon social psychology to develop interventions that are effective because they focus on a community level where interpersonal relationships and a sense of place (Cresswell 2004) are emphasised as catalysts for change (and in the case of Fairtrade Towns this were clearly visible in Wheeler's (2012), sociological exploration of one Fairtrade Town). As McKenzie-Mohr and Smith (1999, p. 16) explain:

> The techniques that are used by CBSM are carried out at a community level and frequently involve direct personal contact. Personal contact is emphasized because social science research indicates that we are most likely to change some behaviour in response to direct appeals or social support from others.

Ethical consumers, like others, rely on an array of information sources about the goods or services they consume, with friends and colleagues'recommendations previously shown to be the strongest influence on their decisions (Arnold, 2009; Walsh et al. 2004). This potentially indicates that information and influence from trusted individuals or groups (McKenzie-Mohr and Smith 1999), originating from local places and social settings, for example, family homes, peer groups and work or community settings, may be vital for the credibility and effectiveness of attempts to market Fairtrade products (Tallontire et al. 2001).

The value of adopting a CBSM perspective to understand and promote sustainability-orientated changes to consumption behaviours at a local level is illustrated by Carrigan et al.'s (2011) consideration of a campaign to promote plastic bag use reduction in the town of Modbury. The value of the CBSM perspective included its emphasis on the relevance of grassroots engagement, its integration of upstream and downstream perspectives, and the provision of structured and practical guidelines for initiatives comprising:

> . . . four key steps: identifying barriers to change through community-based research; outlining a strategy that uses change tools (including the creation of commitment among members, implementation of behavioral prompts, development of new norms, communication of effective messages, creation of incentives, and making it convenient to act); piloting the strategy; and evaluating the outcomes.   (Carrigan et al. 2011, p. 523)

Their study also highlighted the importance of community networks and coalitions and influential "catalytic individuals" in promoting changes to local norms and behaviours.

In our study of Fairtrade Towns, the overarching aim was to understand the marketing processes at work within them. In this chapter we follow the example of Carrigan et al. (2011) in presenting those insights that demonstrate the value of a CBSM perspective in understanding how community-based initiatives and relationships can promote pro-sustainability ethically inspired changes to consumption behaviours at a local level.

Methodology

This study applied the qualitative and interpretive methodology of Grounded Theory pioneered by Glaser and Strauss (1967), which is particularly suitable for phenomena like Fairtrade Towns that lack pre-existing theory or rich data. It applied three core elements of qualitative enquiry to record Fairtrade Town activists' experiences and perceptions. Firstly ethnographic involvement over three years within one Fairtrade Town Steering Group (with permission to record and research), with official minutes and researcher journals acting as data sources. Secondly, semi-structured interviews with twenty nine activitists from eleven Fairtrade Towns across England and Wales. Finally, an in-depth exploration of one Fairtrade Town with three days spent with a founder of the Fairtrade Town movement, learning more about the development of the movement and its application in their hometown. All data was subject to immediate line-by-line coding (by hand), followed by focused and then theoretical coding, from which three core categories emerged (a comprehensive account of the methodology, coding process and codes is available from Samuel and Peattie, 2015). The results presented here synthesise codes that emerged from the data that support a view of Fairtrade Towns as an innovative form of CBSM.

Findings and Discussion

Fairtrade Town activist group strategies and activities were primarily focussed on increasing the volume of Fairtrade sales and consumption within their town, but this was balanced by a strong determination to protect the perceived validity of Fairtrade as providing commercially viable but ethically superior products linked to more sustainable development for producer communities.

    The initiatives and relationships presented here seek to combine conventional downstream social marketing seeking to influence how and why individuals make Fairtrade consumption choices, with upstream social marketing focusing on the social environment factors (Andreasen 2006) that determine how, where and why Fairtrade consumption choices are shaped within Fairtrade Towns. In some cases it revealed marketing contexts, actors and influences that operated upstream and downstream simultaneously. The contexts in which Fairtrade promotion occurred included obvious ones such as the high street, within local councils (whose adoption of Fairtrade consumption is a requirement of accreditation) and within churches who represent longstanding institutional supporters of Fairtrade (Doran and Natale 2011). It also revealed contexts, not necessarily associated with marketing and consumption, that also represent significant channels of influence, including local schools, community groups and events. The key elements of upstream and/or downstream social marketing observed within the study's Fairtrade Towns are discussed below. The full range of codes linking the seven different types of mechanism observed promoting Fairtrade (including consumption opportunities, purchase opportunities, educational initiatives, communications efforts, policy measures and governance mechanisms, the physical and mental resources of local activists and organisations, influences promoting behavioural norms, and particular times and occasions) to the various Fairtrade Town marketing contexts involved are presented in Table 7.1.

Downstream Social Marketing Mechanism: Communication

To complementmore conventional Fairtrade marketing communications such as in-store displays, or Fairtrade Foundation online promotions for Fairtrade Fortnight, a range of place-based media were employed by activists to influence the local population. This included Fairtrade Town supporters actively using personal connections within the social units they belonged to (families, friendship groups, workplaces or organisations) to create opportunities to discuss and promote Fairtrade within their town. More formally it included working with local authorities to integrate Fairtrade information into local newsletters, guides, directories and websites. It also included symbolic consumption acts, such as the display of Fairtrade products in the home by activists, or religious leaders conspicuously consuming Fairtrade in places of worship. Even the local physical environment was enlisted as a promotional medium through displays of signage and banners, and promotional floral displays in some towns.

Upstream Social Marketing Mechanisms

A range of activist-led initiatives sought to expand the demand for, and supply of, Fairtrade products locally through changes to the local institutional, cultural and physical environment:

Education

The intertwining of education in schools and consumption practices within Fairtrade Towns is a theme thoroughly examined by Pykett et al. (2010), and it was visible within the study towns with frequently strong connections between Fairtrade steering groups, local representatives of related civil society organisations (such as Christian Aid, or Amnesty International) and local schools and universities. Although some educational efforts in the classroom or church might be considered as downstream communication aimed at directly inspiring pro- Fairtrade consumer choices, the aim was more commonly to build community understanding of, and support for Fairtrade, and promote it as an element of local place identity and as a local social norm. Educational

Table 7.1: Upstream and Downstream Social Marketing: The How and Where of Volume and Validity in Fairtrade Towns.

Mechanism (How) / Context (Where)	Down and Upstream Social Marketing	Down and Upstream Social Marketing	Upstream Social Marketing	Downstream Social Marketing	Upstream Social Marketing	Upstream Social Marketing	Upstream Social Marketing	Down and Upstream Social Marketing
	Consumption opportunities	Purchase opportunities	Education	Communication	Policy/ Governance	Physical/Mental resources	Normalising behaviour	Time/ occasion
Family and friendship	Giving of gifts; Serving of Fairtrade products in homes;		Ideologically based conversations and social learning;	Symbolic display of Fairtrade in homes; Consumer lead conversations; Word of mouth;		Time taken to engage friends and family in Fairtrade discussions;		Giving of gifts on special occasions eg: birthdays and Christmas; Use in the 'Everyday';
Schools/ Colleges and Universities	Fairtrade served in canteens/ meetings; Use in staff rooms;	Fairtrade sold in school shops and by pupils;	Fairtrade taught in lesson under sustainability and global citizenship; Connecting Fairtrade to younger audiences;	Fairtrade activities such as promotional events like fashion shows, stalls etc;	School Fairtrade policies governing Fairtrade consumption and promotion;	Teachers' time and school resources such as classroom displays;	Via role as supplier and consistent promotion of Fairtrade; Student lead;	Fairtrade Fortnight events; School meal times and meetings;

(continued)

Table 7.1 (continued)

Mechanism (How) / Context (Where)	Down and Upstream Social Marketing — Consumption opportunities	Down and Upstream Social Marketing — Purchase opportunities	Upstream Social Marketing — Education	Downstream Social Marketing — Communication	Upstream Social Marketing — Policy/Governance	Upstream Social Marketing — Physical/Mental resources	Upstream Social Marketing — Normalising behaviour	Down and Upstream Social Marketing — Time/occasion
Civic authority	Fairtrade served in local council meetings as per accreditation criteria;	Fairtrade sold in council canteens;	Linked to promotion of sustainability policies and development aims;	Support for Fairtrade events; Inclusion in newsletters, guides, maps and web pages disseminated to local population;	Fairtrade policies governing consumption and promotion in council offices and other premises;	Support for Fairtrade Towns through resource access including to staff; databases; premises; communication; finance; town locations.	Via role as supplier and consistent promotion of Fairtrade Citizen/council lead;	Fairtrade Fortnight for events; Consumption at meetings and council sponsored events;
Religious Institutions (For this study just Christian Churches)	Fairtrade served in meetings and worship groups; Provision of Fairtrade samples;	Fairtrade sold in church through stalls and TradecraF reps;	Linked to the teaching of the Gospel in sermons and teachings;	Symbolic through consumption by religious leaders; Word of mouth;	Fairtrade policies governing Fairtrade consumption and promotion in places of worship;	Church premises; Church staff time;	Via consistent promotion of Fairtrade; Congregation/Chaplin lead;	Days of worship (Sunday); Fairtrade Fortnight; Church calendar events (e.g. Harvest festival);

Civil Society Organisations (e.g. Christian Aid & Amnesty International)	Fairtrade products/ stock (for promotion and sampling) at events;	Fairtrade products/ stock sold at events;	Presentations to groups and lobbying powers	"Piggy-back" opportunities for Fairtrade for example on leaflets etc; Placing Fairtrade logos and messages into urban landscape;	Influence to keep Fairtrade campaign focus on Fairtrade certified products;	Share experience and knowledge of campaigning; Access to databases of donors and volunteers; Staff & volunteers' engagement; Fairtrade products/ stock (for promotions);	Fairtrade Fortnight; Various other campaigns such as 'Make Poverty History' or child labour awareness;
The High Street	Increased availability in high street catering establishments;	Increased availability in terms of products, and places;	Via point of sale materials (e.g. Co-op stores);	POS displays & literature; Increased in-store visibility;		More floor/ shelf space given;	Increased visibility of Fairtrade produce in local shops and business premises; During Fairtrade Fortnight promotion is increased (e.g. by Co-op);
Community Groups	Fairtrade sampled at meetings & events;	Fairtrade sold at some meetings & events;	Fairtrade can be focus of educational events (e.g. talks or producer visits);	Fairtrade presentations; Use of group media (newsletters, noticeboards);	Consumption policies of group;	Connection of Fairtrade to local groups' agendas;	During meetings;

(continued)

Table 7.1 (continued)

Mechanism (How) / Context (Where)	Down and Upstream Social Marketing	Down and Upstream Social Marketing	Upstream Social Marketing	Downstream Social Marketing	Upstream Social Marketing	Upstream Social Marketing	Upstream Social Marketing	Down and Upstream Social Marketing
	Consumption opportunities	Purchase opportunities	Education	Communication	Policy/ Governance	Physical/Mental resources	Normalising behaviour	Time/ occasion
Community Events	Sampling of Fairtrade products;	Event sales, sometimes for sampling purposes (to then refer interested consumers to retail outlets);	Meeting Fairtrade producers and others; Opportunities to discuss and be presented with the developmental message of Fairtrade;	Fairtrade presence in most Town events (even if unrelated);		Fairtrade producers' time, visits and stories; Civic / Civil Society supported via reduced insurance rates, physical help, stalls etc;		Fairtrade Fortnight; Inclusion in Farmers' markets; Specific events (e.g. town festivals)

efforts could include improving household understanding of Fairtrade through school-children's projects, and also the inclusion of Fairtrade producers at local events where they could enlighten locals about the developmental benefits of Fairtrade consumption through direct contact or reporting via local media.

Policy and Governance

A supportive environment for Fairtrade consumption choices was created in the study towns through policy and governance initiatives enacted through schools, local authorities, churches, retailers and other organisations. The adoption of Fairtrade as a default option in schools, cafes or council premises, effectively edits purchase and consumption choices for workforces, visitors, customers or students, and shifts the conscious support for Fairtrade from the consumer to those organisations (Barnett et al. 2011; Malpass et al. 2007). Such upstream intiatives have the potential to expand Fairtrade consumption, but the removal of active consumer choice risks disconnecting local consumers from the developmental message at the heart of Fairtrade (Golding 2009, Low and Davenport 2005).

Physical and Knowledge-based Resources

Fairtrade Towns'success was significantly dependent on the investment of time and social capital by local activists (Peattie and Samuel 2016). Beyond this,a range of resourceswere supplied by local Fairtrade Town market actors to help shape the local consumption system in favour of Fairtrade. Local councils, schools and civil society organisations provided access to a variety of resources to assist with marketing efforts (such as premises, newsletters, noticeboards and databases) whilst other campaigning organisations shared their experience and knowledge.

Normalising Behaviour

One outcome of Fairtrade Town activists' efforts to expand the consumption and supply of Fairtrade products within their towns is that it normalises Fairtrade consumption as residents see Fairtrade products and messages consistently across local shops, cafes, workplaces, schools, churches and libraries.

Hybrid Down and Upstream Social Marketing Mechanisms

Some activist-led initiatives sought to both encourage greater consumption amongst the local population and to influence the local social environment to support Fairtrade.

Providing Purchase Opportunities

A central marketing function of a Fairtrade Town is to develop distribution outlets and sales opportunities for Fairtrade products, and in the wake of mainstreaming this has often involved extending Fairtrade availability beyond the traditional high street (Low and Davenport 2007). This study found activists negotiating to make Fairtrade products available in places not normally associated with retail commerce including schools, libraries and even churches. It additionally found that Fairtrade products are increasingly available to purchase in public buildings, workplaces, farmers markets and at local events.

Providing Consumption Opportunities

Although often closely related to purchase, separate opportunities to consume Fairtrade products as a promotional strategy were constructed by Fairtrade Town activists. This encompassed serving Fairtrade products to others within their own homes, ensuring they are supplied at meetings within local organisations or groups, churches using Fairtrade communion wine, or sampling opportunities being provided at events. Churches for example were often more comfortable introducing consumers to Fairtrade products through sampling and then encouraging them to purchase else-where, than having a more overtly commercial role in sales.

Specific Times and Occasions

A number of findings emerge from this study showing that place and time are intrinsi-cally linked to some of the marketing dynamics operational in a Fairtrade Town. On an annual basis, Fairtrade Fortnight was frequently mentioned as a focus for organis-ing events or trying to extend the local reach and profile of Fairtrade. On a more day-to-day basis, lunch times and meetings in many businesses, schools or universities create the opportunity to sell or consume Fairtrade products and special occasions such as birthdays and Christmas provide marketing opportunities within private pla-ces for Fairtrade gift giving and consumption. Days of worship such as Harvest Festi-vals or Easter also present times when faith-based organisations disseminate tailored Fairtrade messages.

Preserving Fairtrade's Validity

A further perspective on Fairtrade Towns that this research revealed, is their role as something of an antidote to mainstreaming and the potential loss or dilution of the ethical core of Fairtrade marketing and consumption due to adoption of Fairtrade by highly conventional companies, the reduced differentiation of some Fairtrade suppliers, and the increasing application of choice editing strategies. This was evident in the emphasis Fairtrade Town activists place on the ethical core of Fairtrade when trying to encourage retailers and business to provide Fairtrade products, or members of their social networks to consume them, and when seeking to connect Fairtrade consumption to the values and practices of organisations throughout their local communities. Fairtrade Towns combination of behavioural influence, upstream and downstream focus, community embeddedness, and emphasis on preserving the ethical validity of Fairtrade is encapsulated in a quote from a Keswick Fairtrade Town Group member:

> (Our role) . . . is to promote the buying and the selling of Fairtrade products which means working within our community, working within our community groups as well as working with retailers and wholesalers, so working with the supply side and working on the demand side to promote it. To raise awareness of it and what it does, and therefore to educate the community as a whole, and to make sure also that the profile is maintained so that all of that stays within the context of trade justice . . . so that is what our role is, it's kind of nudging and shoving and talking and singing, if I can put it that way, and also getting others to do the same as well.

This emphasis on ethical validity and community may be important to ensure the continued development of Fairtrade consumption at a time when mainstreaming seems to be losing some momentum, evidenced by the move away from the use of full Fairtrade accreditation by the likes of Sainsburys, Waitrose and Cadbury, and the rise of competing ethical labels, particularly Rainforest Alliance (EC 2017).

What Fairtrade Town marketing reveals, is a quest to expand the volume of Fairtrade sales, whilst protecting the validity of Fairtrade's identity as an ethical and sustainability orientated marketing initiative. As Figure 7.1 summarises, the early solidarity selling era of Fairtrade was limited in its volume and in its validity (from a commercial rather than ethical perspective) by the narrowness of the channels it sought to supply through, and by the compromises inherent in the core marketing mix (Golding and Peattie 2005). The initial growth in Fairtrade by its extension through the alternative high street (Low and Davenport 2007) and the emergence of niche brands, such as Café Direct or Divine Chocolate, brought greater commercial validity without initially attaining mass market impact. A greater volume in Fairtrade sales was achieved through the adoption by mainstream brands and retailers, and the use of choice editing to make Fairtrade the default option in certain consumption contexts, although this may endanger more than enhance Fairtrade's validity due to the threat to the core ethical message (Golding 2009). What Fairtrade Towns offer is a

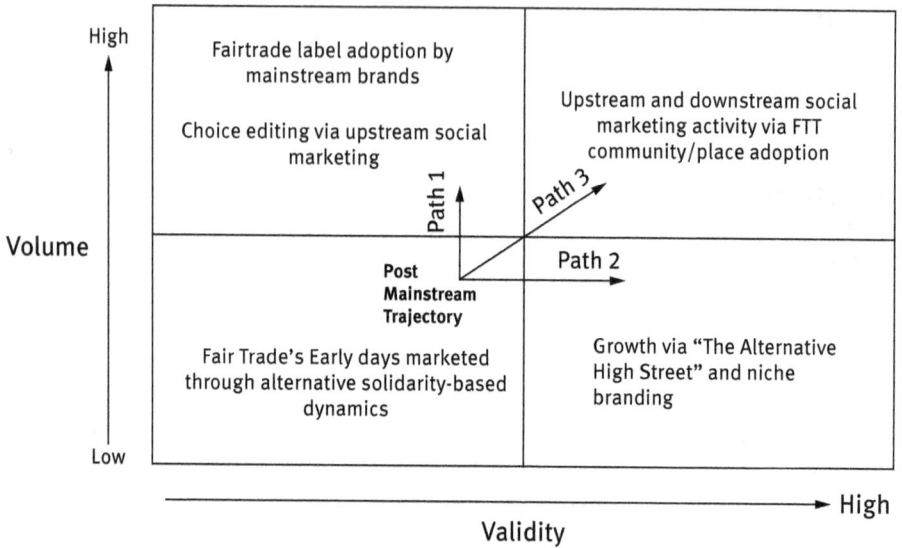

Figure 7.1: Post-Mainstreaming FT Development Trajectories.

third developmental path that integrates Fairtrade consumption into a local community, its organisations, identity and social interactions in a way that can both increase sales volume whilst enhancing commercial and ethical validity. Understood as a CBSM initiative that combines direct downstream appeals to potential consumers with upstream changes to the local institutional and marketing environment that favour Fairtrade consumption, Fairtrade Towns' effectiveness comes from the breadth of social connections and local social capital that are employed to promote local Fairtrade Town consumption.

The Benefits of a CBSM Perspective on Fairtrade Towns

An upstream/downstream CBSM perspective is helpful in understanding Fairtrade Towns' marketing dynamics for several reasons. Firstly it helps to focus attention beyond the usual narrow limits of a commodity chain perspective (Bek et al. 2017) to encompass local organisations and potential contexts for consumption and influence that go beyond those usually considered in commercial marketing. As emphasised by a Bridgnorth Fairtrade Town Group member:

> I do think (our role) is to keep the issues alive in our local community, to promote the issues to as many different groups as we can . . . We think our role is to keep promoting it through

different groups locally and to keep putting on events and just to keep the presence locally and to put pressure on any new organisations that come into the town.

Secondly, it stresses the importance of interpersonal relationships and a sense of place which Fairtrade Town activitists, operating as local catalysts, rely upon in promoting Fairtrade consumption and support. As a member of the Worcester Fairtrade Town Group expressed it: "We're always nudging and pushing. Trying to encourage. It's encouraging through people you know." Thirdly it recognises that Fairtrade Town groups' efforts in promoting Fairtrade are about tackling a behavioural change challenge in respect to local consumers, and the retailers and upstream organisations that can influence them. As a Cardiff Fairtrade Town Group member noted:

> . . . you can push people who might not know about Fairtrade: 'So you know we are now a Fairtrade city, this is what we've agreed to, so could you have a think about introducing more Fairtrade products?' – and we do that in shops. Wherever I go, anywhere, every restaurant I go to, I ask: 'Have you got Fairtrade coffee?' and even if they don't, it raises the question why haven't you got it.

Considering promoting Fairtrade as a behavioural change challenge may be helpful because the activists driving Fairtrade Towns tend to be *believers* in Fairtrade who may not easily appreciate the reasons why people may choose not to consume Fairtrade or why organisations may not already provide Fairtrade products. Finally CBSM provides a structured framework for planning initiatives which encompasses the consideration of the upstream and downstream influences on peoples' behaviour, and focuses on behaviour change barriers and how to overcome them (Carrigan et al. 2011). This is potentially helpful, because once groups moved beyond the focus of achieving initial Fairtrade Town accreditation, the efforts of their volunteer activists, although an important catalyst for local change, were not always that strategic, structured or systematic.

> . . . actually trying to keep the enthusiasm going is always a bit of a pain. Once you've achieved the mark, it's always easy to let it slip . . . Once you've got the status, it's relatively easy to take your foot off the accelerator and think, oh well we're alright now and toddle on for the next so and so.   (Hereford Fairtrade Town Group member)

Groups would use the full range of behaviour change tools associated with CBSM (creation of commitment among members, behavioural prompts, establishing new norms, communication, incentives, and making action convenient), but in using them relied on their existing social networks and social capital, and the particular opportunities that confronted individuals. Embracing a CBSM perspective more formally, including its emphasis on identifying and overcoming change barriers, may help to make Fairtrade Town groups' more strategic and effective in their approach.

Conclusions

Fairtrade Towns have been identified as a contributor to Fairtrade's mainstreaming (Lamb, 2008), and also as a further stage in the development of Fairtrade that goes beyond conventional mainstreaming by broadening Fairtrade s appeal through localisation strategies and strengthing the networking and information flows amongst Fairtrade stakeholders (Alexander and Nicholls 2006). Understanding this process from an upstream/downstream social marketing perspective is helpful because it help to can connect the micro, meso and macro marketing dynamics at play (Goldberg 1995). At a macro level, Fairtrade Towns are effective at connecting citizens' and local organisations' purchasing and consumption habits to their ability to act at a distance and benefit distant others reflecting global ethical concerns (Alexander and Nicholls 2006; Wheeler 2012). At a meso level Fairtrade Towns succeed through upstream social marketing efforts to change local social norms and collective infrastructures of consumption and influence local social institutions (Barnett et al. 2011). At the micro level, Fairtrade Towns seek to encourage behavioural change amongst residents, and although that behaviour mostly involves purchasing and consumption of ethical food and drink products, it resembles CBSM rather than commercial marketing for two reasons. Firstly, due to the emphasis on local social interactions and learning, rather than on conventional commercial marketing communication. Secondly, due to the emphasis on engaging people from a perspective of their multiple identities, not just as abstract consumers, but as members of social groups, communities, congregations or local organisations. As Lamb (2008, p. 42) frames it, Fairtrade Towns succeed through *ordinary people* encouraging other people and organisations to become globally responsible (Barnett et al. 2011) through the act of Fairtrade consumption.

References

Alexander, A. and Nicholls, A. (2006) Rediscovering consumer-producer involvement: A network perspective on fair trade marketing. *European Journal of Marketing*, 40(11/12), 1236–53.
Andreasen, A.R. (2006) *Social Marketing in the 21st Century*. Thousand Oaks, CA: Sage.
Arnold, C. (2009) *Ethical Marketing and the New Consumer*. Wiley, Chichester.
Barnett, C., Cloke, P., Clarke, N. and Malpass, A. (2011) *Globalizing Responsibility: The Political Rationalities of Ethical Consumption*. Chichester: Wiley-Blackwell.
Bek, D., McEwan, C. and Bek, K. (2007) Ethical trading and socioeconomic transformation: Critical reflections on the South African wine industry. *Environment and Planning A*, 39(2), 301–319.
Carrigan, M., Moraes, C. and Leek, S. (2011). Fostering responsible communities: A community social marketing approach to sustainable living. *Journal of Business Ethics*, 100(3), 515–534.
Chatzidakis, A., Hibbert, A. and Smith, A.P. (2007) Why people don't take their concerns about fair trade to the supermarket: The role of neutralisation. *Journal of Business Ethics*, 74(1), 74–89.
Creswell, T. (2004) *Place: A Short Introduction*. Oxford: Blackwell Publishing.

Doran, C. J. and Natale, S.M. (2011) Empatheia and Carita: The role of religion in fair trade consumption. *Journal of Business Ethics*, 98(1), 1–15.

Doherty, B., Davies, I.A. and Tranchell, S. (2013) Where Now for Fairtrade? *Business History*, 55(2), 161–89.

EC (2017) *Ethical Consumer Markets Report 2017*. Manchester: Ethical Consumer.

Fairtrade Towns (2017) *International Fairtrade Towns List*. Available at: http://www.fairtradetowns. org (accessed 10th September 2017).

Fridell, G. (2009) The co-operative and the corporation: Competing visions of the future of fair trade. *Journal of Business Ethics*, 86(1), 81–95.

Glaser, B.G. and Strauss, A. (1967) *The Discovery of Grounded Theory: Strategies for Qualitative Research*. USA: Aldine Transaction.

Globescan (2011) *Shopping Choices Can Make a Positive Difference to Farmers and Workers in Developing Countries: Global Poll*. London: Globescan.

Goldberg, M.E. (1995) Social marketing: Are we fiddling while Rome burns? *Journal of Consumer Psychology*, 4 (4), 347–370.

Golding, K.M. (2009) Fair trade's dual aspect: The communication challenge of fair trade marketing. *Journal of Macromarketing*, 29(2), 160–71.

Golding, K.M. and Peattie, K. (2005) In search of a golden blend: Perspectives on the marketing of fair trade coffee. *Sustainable Development*, 13, 154–165.

Kotler, P. and Zaltman, G. (1971) Social marketing: An approach to planned social change. *Journal of Marketing*, 35(3), 3–12.

Lamb, H. (2008). *Fighting the Banana Wars and other Fairtrade Battles: How We Took on the Corporate Giants to Change the World*. London: Rider.

Low, W. and Davenport, E. (2005) has the medium (roast) become the message? The ethics of marketing fair trade in the mainstream. *International Marketing Review*, 22(5), 494–511.

Low, W. and Davenport, E. (2006) Mainstreaming fair trade: Adoption, assimilation, appropriation. *Journal of Strategic Marketing*, 14, 315–27.

Low, W. and Davenport, E. (2007) To boldly go . . . Exploring ethical spaces to re-politicise ethical consumption and fair trade. *Journal of Consumer Behaviour*, 6(5), 336–48.

Malpass, A., Cloke, P., Barnett, C. and Clarke, N. (2007) Fairtrade urbanism? The politics of place beyond place in the Bristol Fairtrade City Campaign. *International Journal of Urban and Regional Research*, 31(3), 633–45.

McEwan, C., Hugghes, A., and Bek, D. (2017) Fairtrade, place and moral economy: Between abstract ethical discourse and the moral experience of Northern Cape farmers. Environment and Planning A: Economy and Space, 49(3), 572–591.

McKenzie-Mohr, D. and Smith, W. (1999). *Fostering Sustainable Behaviour: An Introduction to Community Based Social Marketing*. Gabriola Island, Canada: New Society Publishers.

Moore, G., Gibbon, J. and Slack, R. (2006) The mainstreaming of Fair Trade: a macromarketing perspective. *Journal of Strategic Marketing*, 14(4), 329–352.

Nicholls, A. J. (2004) Fair trade new product development. *The Service Industries Journal*, 24(2), 102–117.

Nicholls, A. and Opal, C. (2005) *Fair Trade Market Driven Ethical Consumption*. London: Sage.

Lecomte, T. (2003) *Le Pari du Commerce Équitable*. Paris: Éditions d'Organisation.

Peattie, K. and Morley, A. (2008) Eight paradoxes of the social enterprise research agenda. *Social Enterprise Journal*, 4(2), 91–107.

Peattie, K. and Samuel, A. (2016) Fairtrade towns as unconventional networks of ethical activism. *Journal of Business Ethics*, DOI: 10.1007/s10551-016-3392-3

Pykett. J, Cloke, P., Barnett, C., Clarke, N. and Malpass, A. (2010) Learning to be global citizens: The rationalities of fair-trade education. *Environment and Planning D: Society and Space*, 28(3) 487–508.

Samuel, A., and Peattie, K. (2016), Grounded Theory as a Macromarketing Methodology: Critical Insights from Researching the Marketing Dynamics of Fairtrade Towns, *Journal of Macromarketing* 36(1), 11–26.

Samuel, A., Peattie, K. and Doherty, B. (2017) Expanding the boundaries of brand communities: the case of Fairtrade towns. *European Journal of Marketing*, DOI: 10.1108/EJM-03-2016-0124.

Stern, P. and Aronson, E. (1984). Energy Use: The Human Dimension. New York: Freeman.

Tallontire, A., Rentsendorj, E. and Blowfield, M. (2001) *Ethical Consumers and Ethical Trade: A Review of Current Literature*. Policy Series 12, The Natural Resource Institute, University of Greenwich.

Walsh, G., Gwinner, K.P. and Swanson, S.R. (2004) What makes mavens tick? Exploring the motives of market mavens' initiation of information diffusion. *Journal of Consumer Marketing*, 21(2), 109–122.

Wheeler, K. (2012) The practice of fairtrade support. *Sociology*, 46(1), 126–141.

Witkowski, T.H. (2005) Fair trade marketing: An alternative system for globalization and development. *Journal of Marketing Theory and Practice*, 13(4), 22–33

Wilkinson, J. (2007) Fair trade: Dynamic and dilemmas of a market oriented global social movement. *Journal of Consumer Policy*, 30 (3), 219–239.

Ekant Veer and Kseniia Zahrai

8 Wielded by a Different Hand: A Framework for Assessing the Ethicality of Social Marketing Behaviour Change Programs

Introduction

There is little doubt that social marketing's purpose to encourage voluntary behavioural change that benefits the lives of individuals and the society of which they are a part (Andreasen 1994) is a laudable one. Social marketing, health promotion, transformative consumer research and its related fields have collectively saved lives and improved our world (Andreasen 1997; Dutta-Bergman 2004; Harvey 1999; Mick et al. 2011). Social marketing does this by taking a staunch focus on active behavioural change programs that encourage a target audience to make changes to their lives that lead to a betterment in their personal wellbeing or the betterment of society as a whole (Andreasen 1994; Kotler and Zaltman 1971; Lee and Kotler 2011). The manner in which these changes are achieved are wide varied from national campaigns that have wide-reaching implications for a whole society to everyday small changes that can lead to personal growth and developments in one's own life (Thaler and Sunstein 2009).

Again, none of this appears controversial, as long as the goal is to truly lead to a betterment of an individual's life or society as a whole. However, who decides what is 'better' or what is 'right' and on what basis is this change directed for what purpose? Barnett et al. (2005, p. 23) argue that the there is a dual responsibility to engaging in ethical behaviours and that the "governing of consumption and governing of the consuming self" apply. Similarly, Turel and Bechara (2016) highlight the importance of personal responsibility when engaging in health practices. However, how much onus can be placed on consumers when they may not be fully cognizant of the impact and effects of taking on a practice? This chapter explores the ethics of behavioural change programs; especially as these programs become more efficacious and widespread. It is our contention that scrutiny must be placed on any program that has the power to affect change at an individual, community or societal level. Our approach resonates with that of Smith (2001) to say that ethics is not simply about determining right from wrong, but about balancing consequences from actions. However, we extend this to say that the ends achieved by social marketing or behavioural change programs do not necessarily justify the means. Although betterment as an outcome should always be extoled, the manner in which this is achieved should also be carried out in an ethical manner and with the interests of the target population in mind. In this chapter, focus on the power dynamics and transparency of social marketing campaigns. We do this to understand how ethical it is to use the tools at our disposal to change lives. This becomes an important question as the same tools and techniques employed by

https://doi.org/10.1515/9783110659566-008

social marketers to 'do good' are equally usable to cause harm. Ultimately, it comes down to who is wielding the tool, their motivations for change, the manner in which change is made, how covert they are in their actions and what ongoing effects are manifest in society as a result of the changes made.

This chapter aims to discuss the power dynamics associated to social marketing campaigns, identify the areas of ethical concern that social marketers should take into account and from here present a framework that social marketers can use in order to understand whether they are acting in an ethical manner. We offer suggestions for social marketing researchers looking to apply for ethical approval for their interventions and for governmentalities and policymakers seeking behavioural change in a society to understand how their power structures may affect the ethicality of their decisions to determine which behaviours should be valorised and which should be vilified.

Ethicality in Social Marketing

The ethicality of social marketing and behavioural change programs have been debated for some time (c.f. Eagle 2009). Initially, the focus has been on understanding standards of conduct and moral judgement, especially when tensions exist between conflicting standards (Andreasen 2001). This is at the heart of the controversy associated with social marketing, which strives to see 'betterment' in individuals' lives but is tasked with altering behaviour in order to achieve this betterment. This, ultimately, means that an authority must decide that one's behaviour or the behaviour of society does not meet its standards of conduct and should be targeted for change. Some of these changes hold less tension – few would argue that we should reduce the number of people addicted to Class A drugs, such as heroine, during pregnancy. However, controversy often lies when the proposed solution to this behaviour is dealt with through measures that conflict with one's own standards of conduct. Whilst some countries, such as Portugal, have decriminalised drug use and treat addiction cases as a health issue, others continue to treat drug addiction as a criminal offense and seek to change behaviour through criminal action. This tension in enacting the change is at the heart of ethicality of social marketing programs but also the political nature of behaviour change. That is, where an authority is in place to decide a behaviour must change there not only exists a power disparity between the authority and the targeted population but there also exists the potentiality for a political motivation to enact the chosen behavioural change. The end goal to improve lives may be laudable, but if this end goal is politically motivated, ill-informed or leads to downstream unintended consequences then the ethicality of such a program must be questioned. Table 8.1 shows Cho & Salmon's (2007) typology of unintended consequences of health communication campaigns (p. 300). These unintended consequences or downstream effects show how powerful social marketing campaigns and behavioural change programs can be in influencing behaviour but also causing potential damage in the future. These effects must be considered when carrying out social marketing campaigns so as to not only be aware of what impact one's own campaign can have on a target population but also be aware of the impact the current campaign may have on the efficacy of future campaigns or its influence on future ideologies and behaviour.

Table 8.1: Unintended Consequences of Health Communication Campaigns.

Effects	Definitions
Obfuscation	Confusion and misunderstanding of health risk and risk prevention methods
Dissonance	Psychological discomfort and distress provoked by the incongruence between the recommended health states and the audiences' actual states
Boomerang	The reaction by an audience that is opposite to the intended response of persuasion messages
Epidemic of apprehension	Unnecessarily high consciousness and concern over health produced by the pervasiveness of risk messages over the long term
Desensitization	Repeated exposure to messages about a health risk may over the long term render the public apathetic
Culpability	The phenomenon of locating the causes of public health problems in the individual rather than in social conditions
Opportunity cost	The choice of communication campaigns as the solution for a public health problem and the selection of certain health issues over others may diminish the probability of improving public health through other choices
Social reproduction	The phenomenon in which campaigns reinforce existing social distributions of knowledge, attitudes, and behaviors
Social norming	Social cohesion and control and accompanying marginalization of unhealthy minorities brought about by campaigns
Enabling	Campaigns inadvertently improve the power of individuals and institution and promote the images and finances of industries
System activation	Campaigns influence various unintended sectors of society, and their actions mediate or moderate the effect of campaigns on the intended audience

Source: Cho and Salmon (2007, p. 300)

Behaviour change, in its essence, can be argued as a form of social engineering. The purposeful creation of a society that fits a frame of being and behaviour that is acceptable to an authoritarian power (Kocowski 1971; Larsson, Letell, and Thörn 2012). Again, many would not argue that murder is immoral. However, these same societies may both rally against euthanasia reforms and whilst equally supporting the death penalty for violent criminals. Social engineering has been a force for good, such as societal rejection of tobacco smoking as being 'cool', whilst the same methods have been used to cause harm. In this way, politically motivated social engineering practices that influence the social fabric and social norms of a culture need to been done in a manner that maintains a level of ethicality and limits the reach of such influences. In Bristow's (1996) book on 'Making Men Moral' she describes the role that the American Commission on Training Camp Activities (CTCA) was initially tasked with developing a program to protect American soldiers fighting in the Great War from venereal diseases. However, as they saw the success of these behaviour change programs their reach continued to stretch and influence behavioural norms that it has not initially been tasked with. As such, when Americans who did not share the same values of those being afforded to the CTCA caught wind of their social engineering programs the CTCA had to defend their activities and the moral justification of the norms they were instilling into those serving at war. Indeed, Bristow comments that "Reform has been at its best when it has promoted equality, justice, and fairness. Yet the reforming impulse has promoted inequality as commonly as it has equality, injustice as commonly as justice, and discrimination as commonly as fairness" (Bristow 1996, p. xx). Behaviour change holds a neutral power to do what its wielder wishes and it is the morality, ethicality and motivation of the person wielding that power that must be questioned when it comes to influencing behaviour.

Valorisation and Vilification of Behaviour

Social marketers usually take guidance from an authority to determine what issues to tackle. One such authority is the United Nation's Sustainable Development Goals (UN Sustainable Development Goals 2019). These goals outline 17 broad reaching targets that the UN has agreed needs to be addressed. These goals give UN member nations targets to achieve to address what the UN has decided are undesirable behaviours or societal norms that should be eliminated. Common criticisms of these SDGs is that they are difficult to quantify and measure progress (Liverman 2018) but also that they take a cultural and geo-political lens that is not easily afforded to many countries that do not share the hegemonic values of many industrialised nations (Sultana 2018). Sultana (2018, p. 189) states that:

> International development, aid monies, and all development goals are effectively about power. Thus, deconstructing and demonstrating the ways power relations operate, the kinds of powers that exist, and asking questions of what, who, why, and where, become critical in assessing these large international interventions that impact peoples and places. Development monies, policies, and projects will be modified in the pursuit of these goals, whether they are preset or to be determined, and thus these discourses and prescriptions play important roles in the ways societies will be impacted for quite some time.

Where development monies are directed and controlled by powerful authorities, so are behavioural change programs that seek to provide alterations to consumption patterns, choices and behavioural standards. In order to achieve this then an authority must exist with the substantive power to enact control over a less powerful target population. As controversial as this may sound it can be reasoned that behaviour change programs are only effective because the program's effects are stronger than a target population's existing behaviour. This may be in the form of social advertising campaigns that educate a population about health risks associated with a specific behaviour or a legislative intervention that seeks to eliminate a behaviour from society. The means may be different, but the end goal is still ultimately a change in behaviour to align with the authority's positive behavioural standard.

In order to do this, someone needs to determine what is a positive behavioural standard that they wish to see promulgated across their society and what is considered a negative behavioural standard that they would like to see targeted by social marketing campaigns and behaviour change programs. Already, we reach another key ethical issue with social marketing: the notion that 'right or wrong' is somehow a shared collective norm that is shared between the powerful authority and persons in a target population. Social norms vary from family to family, from society to society and change over time. Where once tobacco smoking was not only considered 'cool' but also promoted by physicians as being healthy (Gardner and Brandt 2006) there is almost unanimous agreement today that tobacco smoking is deleterious to our health. Where some may valorise the advancement of science and the right of scientists to make changes in health information as new data is made available others may see these changes as indicative of the untrustworthiness of such authorities. Common rhetoric used by anti-vaccination supporters is that they mistrust the information being presented to them and the authorities presenting the information (Schuster, Eskola, and Duclos 2015). As such, we are placed in a situation whereby the target audience is not only unlikely to change their own behaviour, but this mistrust may compromise future behavioural change programs.

In order to bridge such a tension many social marketers employ 'social contracts' in order to facilitate behavioural change (Dunfee, Smith, and Ross 1999). These contracts act as *quid pro quo* whereby a behaviour is changed in return for a reward of perceived equal or greater value. For example, a 'payment' of 30 minutes of cardio exercise a day will be rewarded with a significantly reduced risk of heart disease and hypertension. Where these contracts are seen as equitable and transparent there is evidence to suggest that behaviour change can be sustained (Torres, Sierra, and Heiser 2007). However, as with any contract, the equity of such an agreement, as abstract as it may be, relies upon the realisation of the return for the behaviour change enacted. If the target population changes their behaviour but does not realise a return for their change, for whatever reason, then the social contract is not only broken but the trust of future social contractual agreements is broken. This presents a further ethical contention with social marketing in that the knowledge and transparency associated with a program may be either not present or not accessible to the target population.

A Framework for Assessing the Ethicality of Behavioural Change Programs

Ultimately, understanding what constitutes an 'ethical' social marketing program is far more complex an issue than can be expressed in a single chapter. However, to draw upon the key frames of *power,* and *transparency* we argue that many behavioural change programs can be created and delivered in a more ethical fashion. Firstly, to notions of power and agency, where a target population has no influence or ability to fight against a change in their behaviour there exists a level of power distance that is authoritarian in nature. This is not to say that, on its own, authoritarian change is immoral, but rather than change that is mandated without any support or buy-in from a population is contrary to the ideals of a democratised society. In 2018 the New Zealand government announced with very little warning that single-use plastic bags were to be banned (Saxton 2019). This was not a policy that was held by the Labour-led government with some claiming it was an opinion led decision by the government's partners, the Green Party, rather than one based on scientific evidence (Newman 2018). To this day, single-use plastic bags are not allowed to be used or sold in New Zealand leading to a cultural shift towards reusing multi-use bags at a greater level that was not evident prior to the policy change. The policy has reduced the demand for single-use plastic bags, reduced wastage and made a marginal contribution to the country's carbon footprint. Again, with very little public input or agency to fight against the policy. Such authoritarian approaches are particularly necessary when organic, socially driven change is either too hard to manage or too slow to make any real difference. Does the laudable outcome make the authoritarian approach immoral or unethical? In this case, perhaps not, because the end result is a true betterment of a society without any real harm caused (except when we forget to carry our linen bags to the supermarket to get groceries, but this is more a frustration rather than harm). However, the *potential* for harm to be caused in an authoritarian society versus a democratised society is far greater and so the level of authoritarianism being wielded should be considered when planning a social marketing behavioural change campaign.

Secondly, the notion of transparency must be considered when determining the ethicality of a social marketing program. Where covert actions are being used to influence social norms and drive behavioural change without the knowledge and agency of the target population we erode the democratisation of a society, individual agentic power and, arguably, the ethicality of a program. A very commonly used example in this realm is the role that Cambridge Analytica played in collecting, collating and analysing user data to influence the stories seen by American voters on their social media feeds prior to the 2016 election campaign (Beck 2018). This covert action with little agentic power from the users meant that when it was discovered that such actions we being taken by Cambridge Analytica it not only made

Facebook users distrust Cambridge Analytica's practices but also the practices of Facebook, as they felt that Facebook helped to facilitate Cambridge Analytica's covert practices (Herhold 2019).

This is not just the level of covert actions being used to drive behavioural change, but also the transparency of the motivations behind the chosen behavioural change. If the motivation is not the betterment of the individuals or society but rather to achieve a person or political goal then the level of ethicality associated with the behaviour change program must be questioned. In this way, full transparency associated with behavioural change programs and social marketing campaigns can aid in not only sharing the ethicality of the change but also in developing engagement and adoption through capacity building in a target population (Whitelaw et al. 2011). This capacity building approach not only allows for a target population to feel as if there is a stronger understanding of the purpose behind a change but also that they have greater agency to feel empowered as part of the change (Eger, Miller, and Scarles 2018).

Associated with understanding the rationale and motivation for implementing a behavioural change program there should be transparency associated with the downstream consequences of a behavioural change program. Do we fully understand and appreciate the ongoing impact of such a social engineering practice and what processes are put in place to mitigate any unintended consequences, as described in Table 8.1, which may arise? Does the target population have full knowledge of these potential effects and do they have full agency to reverse the behavioural change program if they feel that the downstream impact is more harmful than the benefits provided by the change? If a target population is trapped with the negative consequences associated with a change and little ability to change to an alternative system the ethicality of the behavioural change program should be questioned.

Both power and transparency are interwoven in their relationship with one another but overarching both of these concepts is still, at the heart, the purpose of social marketing and that is the betterment of the target population (Andreasen 1994; 2001). Without this focus on wellbeing and betterment the ethicality and morality of a behavioural change program is compromised. Figure 8.1 shows this intersectionality of power and transparency encompassed within betterment to help understand where ethical questions can arise. We argue that the further a program is from a democratised transparent system the more important the betterment value must be to ensure that morality is maintained. That is, where an authoritarian covert program is put in place it *must* be for the greater betterment of the society and that *must* be evidenced and rigorously maintained. In reality, it may be impossible to determine the true betterment realised from a behavioural change program, so a democratised and transparent practice is often more likely to be argued as being more ethical. However, any program that breaches the bounds of betterment for the target population, regardless of how transparent or democratised should have its morality and ethicality questioned.

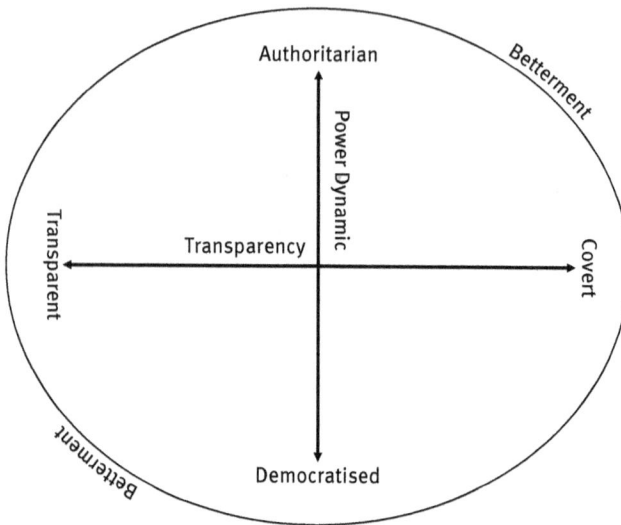

Figure 8.1: Factors to consider when developing and implementing social marketing campaigns.

Conclusion

In this chapter we have shown the importance of three key considerations when developing and implementing social marketing and behavioural change programs. Central to all social marketing should still be the betterment of a target population's welfare and wellbeing. Programs that fall outside of this boundary should not be called social marketing and should not be treated as such. Conflating social engineering for political or personal gain at the expense of betterment can have ongoing downstream effects that hinder future social marketing campaigns that have a true betterment motivation. From here, issues associated with the power dynamics and transparency associated with a social marketing campaign should be considered. Where coversion and authoritarianism is prevalent in a behaviour change program there is the potential for decreased agentic power by a target population a greater likelihood that the ethicality of such a program can be questioned. There may be situations where a democratised approach does exist for the behaviour change program but the underlying rationale for the change is not transparent and not well explained. This lack of transparency, despite a democratised approach to achieving the change, can also call into question the ethicality of a behaviour change program. When it comes to transparent change programs the campaigns that have a greater level of authoritarianism may face resistance from a target population as the change may feel forced upon them without the buy-in from those who are affected by the change. Many colonial social engineering practices would fall into this category whereby the authority is transparent about the changes and the motivations and feel their actions are for the betterment of the target population but without the capacity building associated with a democratised effect it can be seen as unethical. Finally, a democratised and transparent approach that is truly for the betterment of the target population is likely to be considered to be the least unethical, but this is not to say that all programs that fall into this camp are devoid of scrutiny, especially when the downstream effects of such actions are not well understood or catered for. The unintended consequences should always be kept in mind and protections put in place to ensure that the target population are well supported.

This chapter in no way attempts to relieve all the concerns associated with ethicality in behaviour change programs. Rather, we seek to find ways in which social marketers can be more assured in their practices and more confident in the way in which their campaigns can both truly lead to consumer betterment; can avoid downstream unintended consequences; be as transparent as possible in both the rationale being used to initiate the change and the practices employed to achieve the change, and ensure that the target population has some agentic power to own the changes being made and reverse them if betterment is not achieved. From here, we seek to support ethics boards and review panels to judge social marketing programs against the concerns raised over transparency and power dynamics and not just on the eventual betterment for the target population. We argue that it is both the means and the ends that must justify a behavioural change program and that any form of social engineering should be aware of the negative impacts of its implementation, especially the unintended downstream impact from behavioural change.

References

Andreasen, Alan R. 1994. "Social Marketing: Its Definition and Domain." *Journal of Public Policy and Marketing* 13 (1): 108–14.

Andreasen, Alan R. 1997. "From Ghetto Marketing to Social Marketing: Bringing Social Relevance to Mainstream Marketing." *Journal of Public Policy and Marketing* 16 (1): 129–31.

Andreasen, Alan R. 2001. *Ethics in Social Marketing.* Georgetown University Press.

Barnett, Clive, Paul Cloke, Nick Clarke, and Alice Malpass. 2005. Consuming ethics: Articulating the subjects and spaces of ethical consumption. *Antipode, 37*(1), 23–45.

Beck, Julie. 2018. "Did Cambridge Analytica Change Facebook Users' Behavior?" The Atlantic. June 7, 2018. https://www.theatlantic.com/technology/archive/2018/06/did-cambridge-analytica-actually-change-facebook-users-behavior/562154/.

Bristow, Nancy K. 1996. *Making Men Moral: Social Engineering During the Great War.* NYU Press.

Cho, Hyunyi, and Charles T. Salmon. 2007. "Unintended Effects of Health Communication Campaigns." *Journal of Communication* 57 (2): 293–317. https://doi.org/10.1111/j.1460-2466.2007.00344.x.

Dunfee, Thomas W., N. Craig Smith, and William T. Ross. 1999. "Social Contracts and Marketing Ethics." *Journal of Marketing* 63 (3): 14–32. https://doi.org/10.1177/002224299906300302.

Dutta-Bergman, Mohar J. 2004. "A Descriptive Narrative of Healthy Eating: A Social Marketing Approach Using Psychographics in Conjunction with Interpersonal, Community, Mass Media and New Media Activities." *Health Marketing Quarterly* 20 (3): 81–101.

Eagle, Lynne. 2009. "Social Marketing Ethics: Report Prepared for the National Social Marketing Centre." In.

Eger, Claudia, Graham Miller, and Caroline Scarles. 2018. "Gender and Capacity Building: A Multi-Layered Study of Empowerment." *World Development* 106 (June): 207–19. https://doi.org/10.1016/j.worlddev.2018.01.024.

Gardner, Martha N., and Allan M. Brandt. 2006. ""The Doctors' Choice Is America's Choice"." *American Journal of Public Health* 96 (2): 222–32. https://doi.org/10.2105/AJPH.2005.066654.

Harvey, Philip D. 1999. *Let Every Child Be Wanted: How Social Marketing Is Revolutionizing Contraceptive Use Around the World*. Westport, Connecticut: Auburn House.

Herhold, Kristen. 2019. "How People View Facebook After the Cambridge Analytica Data Breach." Medium. March 29, 2019. https://medium.com/swlh/how-people-view-facebook-after-the-cambridge-analytica-data-breach-4dc1261a0249.

Kocowski, Tomaz. 1971. "Social Engineering Methods of Motivation Shaping." *The Polish Sociological Bulletin*, no. 23: 29–45.

Kotler, Phillip, and Gerald Zaltman. 1971. "Social Marketing: An Approach to Planned Social Change." *Journal of Marketing* 35 (July): 3–12.

Larsson, Bengt, Martin Letell, and Håkan Thörn. 2012. "Transformations of the Swedish Welfare State: Social Engineering,Governance and Governmentality." In *Transformations of the Swedish Welfare State: From Social Engineering to Governance?*, edited by Bengt Larsson, Martin Letell, and Håkan Thörn, 3–22. London: Palgrave Macmillan UK. https://doi.org/10.1057/9780230363953_1.

Lee, Nancy R., and Philip Kotler. 2011. *Social Marketing: Influencing Behaviors for Good*. SAGE Publications.

Liverman, Diana M. 2018. "Geographic Perspectives on Development Goals: Constructive Engagements and Critical Perspectives on the MDGs and the SDGs." *Dialogues in Human Geography* 8 (2): 168–85. https://doi.org/10.1177/2043820618780787.

Mick, David Glen, Simone Pettigrew, Cornelia Pechmann, and Julie L. Ozanne. 2011. *Transformative Consumer Research for Personal and Collective Well-Being*. New York, NY: Routledge.

Newman, Dr Muriel. 2018. "Plastic Bags – a Matter of Perception Not Science." November 18, 2018. https://www.nzcpr.com/plastic-bags-a-matter-of-perception-not-science/.

Saxton, Amanda. 2019. "NZ Plastic Bag Ban: The Exemptions and the Rules Explained." *Stuff*, June 28, 2019. https://www.stuff.co.nz/national/113845919/nz-plastic-bag-ban-the-exemptions-and-the-rules-explained.

Schuster, Melanie, Juhani Eskola, and Philippe Duclos. 2015. "Review of Vaccine Hesitancy: Rationale, Remit and Methods." *Vaccine*, WHO Recommendations Regarding Vaccine Hesitancy, 33 (34): 4157–60. https://doi.org/10.1016/j.vaccine.2015.04.035.

Smith, William A. 2001. "Ethics and the Social Marketer: A Framework for Practitioners." In *Ethics in Social Marketing*, edited by Alan R. Andreasen, 1–16. Washington, D. C.: Georgetown University Press.

Sultana, Farhana. 2018. "An(Other) Geographical Critique of Development and SDGs." *Dialogues in Human Geography* 8 (2): 186–90. https://doi.org/10.1177/2043820618780788.

UN Sustainable Development Goals. 2019. Sustainable Development Knowledge Platform. Accessed December 9, 2019.https://sustainabledevelopment.un.org/?menu=1300.

Thaler, Richard H., and Cass R. Sunstein. 2009. *Nudge: Improving Decisions About Health, Wealth, and Happiness*. Revised&Expanded edition. New York: Penguin Books.

Turel, Ofir, and Antoine Bechara. 2016. A Triadic Reflective-Impulsive-Interoceptive Awareness
    Model of General and Impulsive Information System Use: Behavioral Tests of Neuro-Cognitive
    Theory. *Frontiers in Psychology*, *7*, 601.
Torres, Ivonne M., Jeremy J. Sierra, and Robert S. Heiser. 2007. "The Effects of Warning-Label
    Placement in Print ADS: A Social Contract Perspective." *Journal of Advertising* 36 (2): 49–62.
    https://doi.org/10.2753/JOA0091-3367360203.
Whitelaw, S., E. Smart, J. Kopela, T. Gibson, and V. King. 2011. "Developing Social Marketing
    Capacity to Address Health Issues." *Health Education* 111 (4): 319–31. https://doi.org/10.1108/
    09654281111144274.

Erin Hurley, Timo Dietrich and Sharyn Rundle-Thiele

9 Blurred Minds Parent Program: Applying Marketing to Start Teenage Conversations

Introduction

Parents play a key role in preventing and reducing alcohol related risks in adolescents. Literature demonstrates a strong link between parenting specific behaviours and adolescent alcohol attitudes, expectations and drinking behaviours (Mynttinen et al. 2017; Yap et al. 2017). Parent alcohol programs which aim to influence specific parenting behaviours are an important strategy in reducing risks associated with underage drinking (Kuntsche and Kuntsche 2016). Examination of the evidence base indicates alcohol programs targeting parents have previously demonstrated mixed effects (Adolfsen et al. 2017; Brown et al. 2014). In addition, alcohol related programs have been found to be largely expert-driven, taking a top-down approach in which the target audience provide little, if any, contribution to program design (Dietrich et al. 2016a). With its consumer orientated philosophy to program design (Andreasen 2002) social marketing may offer an innovative approach that can be implemented to design and deliver an engaging and effective parent program.

A largely expert driven, top down approach in which the target audience provide little, if any, contribution to program design typifies alcohol programs (Dietrich et al. 2016a). Expert dominated approaches fail to recognise that the target audience are experts of their own worlds who can contribute to program design (Sanders and Stappers 2008; Hurley, Trischler and Dietrich 2018). As a consequence, programs that are designed for and not with the target audience often result in solutions that do not engage, which severely limits program effectiveness (Buyucek et al. 2016). Current social marketing programs have a narrow methodological focus with focus groups and surveys dominating formative research methods (Carins et al. 2016; Kubacki et al. 2015). While focus groups and surveys may be beneficial for uncovering participants' perspectives and opinions on current prospective ideas (Kubacki and Rundle-Thiele 2016), they might not sufficiently capture insights on latent user needs and preferences (Witell et al. 2011). Additionally, these formative methods do not provide the freedom for program users to initiate program design concepts or to introduce novel ideas.

Shifting consumer roles and recent practices in research and design increasingly emphasise the importance of actively engaging end users during the development of new market offerings (Ostrom et al. 2015). Participatory design empowers end users to take on a more active role in the design process (Sanders and Stappers 2008). The approach acknowledges that those who are affected by a design should ultimately have a say in the design process and is in stark contrast to traditional market research where researchers 'listen in' to explore new combinations of customer needs

https://doi.org/10.1515/9783110659566-009

(Poetz and Schreier 2012). Through participatory design, end users are invited into idea generation and concept development stages and in doing so they are given the opportunity to directly contribute to the outcome of the design (Goodyear-Smith, Jackson and Greenhalgh 2015). From a design theory perspective participatory design represents the basis for the concept of co-design (Sanders and Stappers 2008).

Co-design refers to the collective creativity of designers and participants during the design process (Sanders and Stappers 2008). During the co-design process, expert's (i.e., researchers and/or designers) facilitate and participants are given a 'voice' sharing their insights and experiences while generating and developing program ideas (Dietrich et al. 2017). To date, the role of co-design has been widely discussed and differences between user generated ideas and expert driven ideas have been observed (Dietrich et al. 2016b, Rundle-Thiele et al. 2019b). Active user involvement through co-design can have important benefits for the innovating organisation (Steen, Manschot and De Koning 2011). Specifically, user generated ideas are generally found to be more creative and useful than those developed by experts (Magnusson et al. 2003; Poetz and Schreier 2012; Witell et al., 2011). Active forms of user involvement, such as co-design may be more effective than traditional market research techniques (e.g. focus groups and interviews) (Witell et al. 2011), while identifying and capturing key elements that are valued ultimately affecting the user experience (Trischler et al. 2018b).

Essential for the active and creative user contribution is the application of appropriate co-design tools (Ind and Coates 2013). Co-design tools enable facilitators to sensitise participants to the topic (Dietrich et al. 2017), provide meaningful ways to integrate insights from existing literature (Villalba et al. 2019), and help to uncover participants latent needs (Sanders and Dandavate 1999) and new ideas (Rundle-Thiele et al. 2019b). In addition, specific processes and procedures for implementing a co-design approach are required to effectively plan and conduct sessions as well as evaluate generated ideas (Dietrich et al. 2017). Co-design can be approached in a variety of ways with numerous approaches being explored by researchers over the years (Mattelmäki and Visser 2011). For example, Dietrich et al. (2017) outlined a sequential six-step process that researchers and practitioners can apply to facilitate co-design sessions. This framework was later refined by Trischler, Dietrich and Rundle-Thiele (2019) to reflect a collaborative and iterative process allowing for multiple iterations and close stakeholder consultation following the initial co-design stage.

These insights across numerous studies suggest that co-design might help to increase the likelihood of program success through greater user participation, satisfaction and an improved program experience. This case study aims to extend understanding showcasing how co-design insights can be used to inform the build of a social marketing program that changes parent's attitudes to alcohol supply to their children and increases parental monitoring.

Program Build

The pilot social marketing program targeting parents of adolescent was developed to be implemented alongside an existing social marketing program named Blurred Minds, which is delivered to adolescents aged between 14 and 16 years. Blurred Minds is a five-module social marketing program that has been designed following the eight social marketing benchmark criteria (The National Social Marketing Centre 2010). The Blurred Minds social marketing program was delivered in 2017 via a comprehensive stratified randomised controlled trial in more than a dozen schools. The program delivered positive changes for adolescent participants across a number of outcome variables including increasing knowledge about alcohol and its effects, and delivering more negative attitudes towards excessive drinking while maintaining low intentions to drink excessively (Dietrich et al. 2019). The newly co-designed pilot parent alcohol social marketing program was designed as a standalone program for parents to complement the existing Blurred Minds program. The specific components of the program for parents of adolescents is detailed next.

Program Components

Parent (user) generated ideas for the pilot program are described in detail in Hurley et al. (2018). Analysis of parent-designed ideas led to the identification of three overarching strategies for program design, namely a) usability means flexibility, b) meaningful content, c) time is money (Hurley, Trischler and Dietrich 2018) and d) community connectedness (see Table 9.1).

Table 9.1: Co-design insights mapped to program design.

Theme	Key co-design insights	Program features
Usability means flexibility	Online and postal are good supporting components but require prior knowledge and advice.	Online materials and text message conversation starters delivered as supporting components. Face to face session includes an overview of supporting components available.
	Face to face session with facilitator is important to engage parents with program and allow for questions and feedback.	Core program component requires parents to attend face to face session with facilitator.
	Interactive learning methods over static power point presentation.	Online quiz platform used to increase interactivity and parents engaged in discussions as opposed to didactic methods of learning.

Table 9.1 (continued)

Theme	Key co-design insights	Program features
Meaningful content	Provide up to date knowledge on adolescents and alcohol.	Myth busters activity: Evidence based facts on adolescents and alcohol presented to parents.
	Practical tips on how to monitor adolescents.	Advising and guiding your teen activity: Parents provided with practical tips on how to monitor their adolescents.
	Provide prompts to encourage parent-child communication.	Text message conversation starters: Follow up text messages sent to parents which provide a conversation cue to promote parent-child communication.
Time is money	Multiple face to face sessions are a deterrent for parents.	Program requires parents to attend only one face to face session with facilitator.
	Under 1 hour is an ideal time frame.	Face to face session runs for 45 minutes.
	Parents favour the addition of components that can be completed in their own time.	An option for parents to sign up for a series of follow up text messages delivering communication cues.
Community connectedness	Opportunities for parents to get to know other parents in the community are valuable.	Face to face session delivered within schools allowing parents to attend program session with parents in the same school community
	Allow for interaction between parents for support and feedback.	Program activity 'advising and guiding your teen' designed to encourage communication and collaboration, providing an opportunity for parents to share strategies and tips related to monitoring practices.
		Closed Facebook Group 'Blurred Minds for Parents' created for parents to join.

During co-design sessions parents mentioned being time poor while still wanting face-to-face interaction with experts. As a result, the Blurred Minds pilot program targeting parents was designed as a one off 45-minute session delivered face-to-face by the research team and supported by follow up text messages. In addition, the co-design outcomes generated by parents highlighted alcohol specific knowledge acquisition, parental monitoring and parent-child communication as meaningful topics to cover in program delivery. Leveraging off these co-design insights, the pilot program was organised around three core objectives which included; 1) provide best practice monitoring advice and guidance to assist parents, 2) raise awareness about the roles that parents play in adolescent alcohol use, and 3) increase parent-child communication. Additionally, during co-design parents highlighted the importance of communication and collaboration with other parents in order to gain insights and knowledge. Therefore, the parent program was developed to be relevant, interactive and engaging. The session was designed to allow parents to participate in group discussion in an informal and relaxed atmosphere while giving them time to reflect on their specific circumstances. The program featured an ice breaker activity, myth buster session, advising and guiding your teen session as well as an overview of the supporting materials which are presented next.

Ice Breaker Activity

The purpose of the ice breaker activity was to introduce parents to the topic of underage drinking and the role parents play while creating an informal and relaxed atmosphere. Following a brief overview of the session's activities, parents were presented with a short video clip which used humour to portray a key message about parents and their influence on their adolescent's alcohol initiation and subsequent drinking. Following the ice breaker activity, parents were introduced to the 'myth busters' activity.

Myth Busters

The myth buster activity aimed to build knowledge and confidence on the topic of parents and their influence on adolescent drinking. Understanding current issues that are relevant to adolescents was a specific benefit that parents described as valuable during co-design (Hurley, Trischler and Dietrich 2018). Using Kahoot (an online quiz platform), parents were presented with multiple choice questions which they could individually answer using their mobile devices. Parent answers appeared in a de-identified manner as a poll on the screen (see Figure 9.1). The questions were based on evidence-based facts (Kaynak et al. 2014; Berends, Jones and Andrews 2016) that were interesting and relevant to parents.

The aim of the use of the online quiz format was to ensure that parents could think about the question on their own and answer each question anonymously without fear of judgement. Next, a guided discussion with parents was facilitated by the lead researcher. For example, parents were asked; 'Can you teach 'responsible drinking' through controlled exposure to alcohol?'. With little to no research that supports the notion of teaching 'responsible drinking' parents were presented with two or more facts which state that parents who supply alcohol; 1) undermine important messages about the unacceptability of underage drinking as teens who perceive that their parents disapprove are less likely to drink (Berends, Jones and Andrews 2016), and 2) are likely to accelerate their adolescents drinking as parental provision of alcohol is

Figure 9.1: Example question asked of parents using Kahoot.

associated with increased alcohol use by adolescents (Kaynak et al. 2014). Next followed the 'advising and guiding your teen' activity.

Advising and Guiding your Teen

Advising and guiding your teen aimed to provide parents with practical examples on how they could effectively monitor their adolescent. During the co-design sessions parents deemed content on monitoring as highly relevant and noted that practical tips specifically for parents to implement in their household were of value (Hurley, Trischler and Dietrich 2018). In groups, parents were allowed time to discuss what monitoring strategies did or did not work in their household. Specifically, they were asked to consider behaviour expectations, how they keep in touch with their adolescent and how rules and consequences are implemented, communicated and enforced in their household. Following the small group discussions, parents had the opportunity to share their effective strategies with the larger group and additional best practice examples were provided by the facilitator. Next, the supporting components of the program were presented to the parents.

Supporting Components

Parents were offered the opportunity to sign up for weekly SMS conversation starters with the aim to promote parent-child communication post program completion. During co-design sessions parents highlighted the importance of utilising multiple

platforms (i.e. face to face, online, and text messages) to add versatility and continuity of the program and therefore provide a more holistic form of program delivery
(Hurley, Trischler and Dietrich 2018). The conversation starters consisted of one
message a week for eight weeks. Each message presented a conversation cue to promote communication with their adolescent (see Figure 9.2). Each point discussed
was selected in line with both the materials addressed in the parent program and
the materials presented to the adolescent during the Blurred Minds student program. For example; 'The pressure for your teen to drink may be intense and sometimes simply saying 'no thanks' is not enough. Has your teen heard of a good
excuse to avoid alcohol? Help them come up with an answer they feel comfortable
with when people ask them why they are not getting drunk. E.g. I'm driving, I have
a big day tomorrow, my parents are waiting up for me, I'd rather dance.'

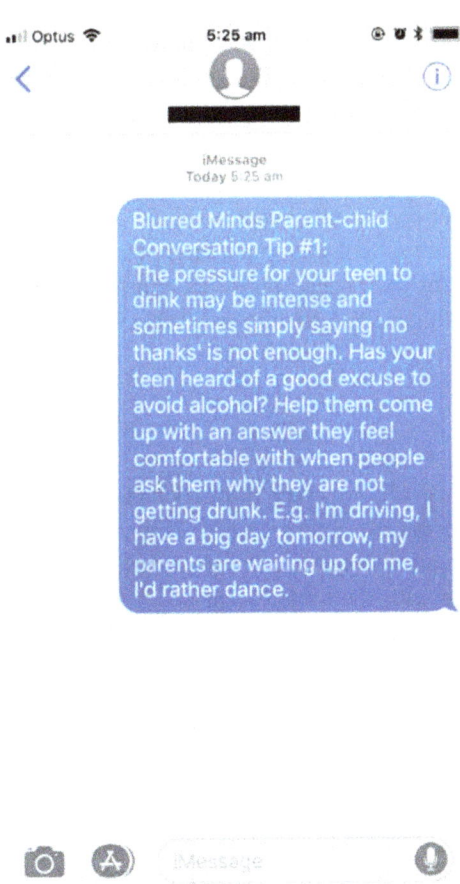

Figure 9.2: Conversation starter text message.

In addition, the Blurred Minds website featured a webpage dedicated for the parents. On this page parents could find a series of infographics which were related to the content that was delivered during the session. The four infographics included were; 1) an overview of the facts presented during the myth busters activity, 2) a checklist for monitoring social media, 3) practical examples to monitor adolescents, and 4) conversation tips which detailed practical tips on how and when to start the conversation with their adolescent (see Figure 9.3).

Program Evaluation: Method and Outcomes

Recruitment and Participants

The co-designed parent alcohol social marketing program was piloted in four Australian schools. Schools in which the adolescent Blurred Minds program was being implemented were approached to offer the pilot parent program. Out of the eleven schools that were approached, five were willing to organise the parent program and invite parents to attend. However, in one of the schools no parents attended the session due to a scheduling conflict – another community event was held on the same evening. To assist in recruiting parents, each school was sent a brief overview of the program as well as promotion messages for their social networks and email newsletters. In total 65 parents participated in the parent program (see Table 9.2).

Measures

A repeated measure research design was used for outcome evaluation (see Table 9.3 for outcome evaluation items) and two process evaluation items were included in the post survey to gain parent feedback on the pilot program to inform program improvement. Parents confidence to communicate with their adolescent about alcohol was measured using 7-point scales adapted and adjusted for the context following Bandura's (2006) self-efficacy measures. Parents permissive attitudes towards adolescent alcohol use was measured using scales derived from the Community Readiness Survey, which was designed to measure attitudes towards substance use (Beebe et al. 2001). This scale has been used in a previous study evaluating the efficacy of a parent based alcohol education program (see Brown, Dunn and Budney 2014). Parental monitoring was measured using two selected items from the Bandura (2006) parental self-efficacy 5-point scale to understand parents efficacy in monitoring their adolescent and their efficacy to exercise control over their adolescents drinking behaviour. The scale has previously been used to gain a better understanding of parents influence on their adolescent's activities (Bandura et al. 2001; Caprara et al. 2003).

SOCIAL MEDIA CHECKLIST

get to know the **technology** and its **features**

establish ground rules:
- no checking social media during meal times
- only add friends who you have a connection with in real life

discuss online dangers
- sharing persona information
- cyberbullying

don't post hurtful comments
- put your phone **away** at dinner time

check privacy **settings** (e.g. limit who can see your teens posts)

monitor pictures posted online

limit when wireless internet connections and/or mobile devices will be available

be a **good** example of how to use social media for example.

teach teenagers about **Online Reputation:** what goes online, stays online

know social media age limits: Facebook, Snapchat, Twitter, Instagram, Reddit & Pinterest are limited to users aged **13** and **over**, anyone younger must **lie** about their age if they want to set up an account

encourage your teen to engage in **outside** activities and **value** time with friends

CONSIDER THE CONVERSATION

make it a **conversation**, not a **lecture**. give your teen **uninterrupted** time to talk while you listen

choose an **appropriate** time and place. e.g.

around the dinner table or driving home from weekend sports

don't start a discussion when your teen is about to go out with friends or right before bedtime

be **open** and honest

empower your teenagers to make decisions for themselves

bring up the topic **informally**

encourage your teenagers to **express** their feelings, thoughts and opinions

check out our text **messages** for **cues** to get the conversation **started**

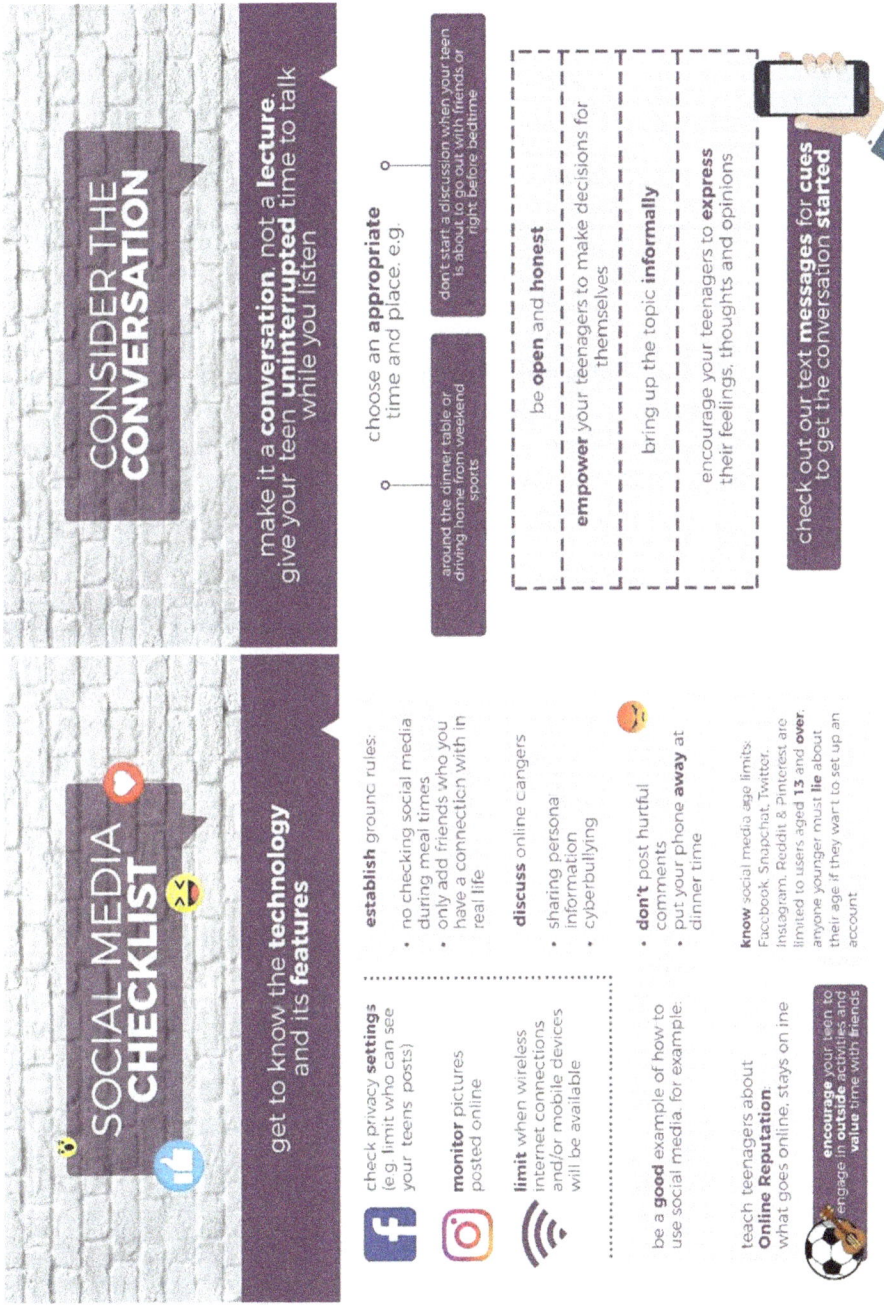

Figure 9.3: Online infographics for parents.

Table 9.2: Program delivery overview.

School	Location	Delivery date	N
A	Toowoomba	August 2017	8
B	Brisbane	August 2017	33
C	Mount Isa	August 2017	13
D	Toowoomba	October 2017	11

Reliability tests for constructs were performed using Cronbach's alpha. All measures exceeded the threshold of 0.70 demonstrating acceptable reliability (Hair et al. 2006). In addition, two open ended questions were included to measure satisfaction with the pilot program by asking how the program was perceived and how it could be improved moving forward. Socio-demographic (i.e., gender, yearly income and employment status) data was also collected. Finally, data on parents drinking behaviour was collected.

Table 9.3: Constructs, item wording and response anchors for survey measures.

Constructs and item wording	Response anchors
Self-efficacy ($a = 0.90$) How confident do you feel about talking to your teen about alcohol? I believe I have the ability to talking to my teen about alcohol How confident are you that you could talk to your teen about alcohol?	(−3) Not at all confident – (3) completely confident
Attitudes ($a = 0.80$) In my opinion it is acceptable for teenagers under the age of 18 to drink alcohol at parties if they don't get drunk In my opinion it is acceptable for teenagers under the age of 18 to drink as long as they don't drive afterward In my opinion it's okay for parents to offer their children under the age of 18 alcoholic drinks in their own home	(1) Strongly disagree – (4) strongly agree
Monitoring ($a = 0.70$) How much can you do to keep track of what your adolescents are doing when they are outside the home? How much can you do to prevent your adolescent from becoming involved in drugs or alcohol?	(1) Nothing – (5) a great deal
Program satisfaction Overall, how satisfied were you with todays Blurred Minds Parent Session?	(1) Very dissatisfied – (5) very satisfied

Data Analysis

Parents filled out a survey prior to their participation in the program and immediately post completion of the face to face component of program delivery. All responses were entered in SPSS and a unique identifier code was used to match parent data across the two collection points. Data was analysed using paired sample t-tests.

Demographic and Sample Characteristics

The overall sample (N = 65) was 68% female with 43% of parents reporting they worked full time. Sixty five percent of parents reported they consumed on average one or two standard drinks containing alcohol on a typical day when they were drinking. Only 3.4% of parents reported consuming five to nine drinks in one sitting. No parents reported drinking 10 or more alcoholic drinks in one sitting or consuming six or more alcoholic drinks daily (see Table 9.4). Overall parents were very satisfied (49.2%) or satisfied (49.2%) with the program. Only 1.6% of parents were neither satisfied nor dissatisfied with the program. Aspects of the program that parents favoured were the short time frame, group discussions involving interactions with other parents, learning practical tips and strategies, and the presentation of evidence-based facts.

Table 9.4: Summary of parents drinking behaviours.

Drinking behaviour	Percentage
Frequency of alcohol consumption	
Never	12.9
Monthly or less	22.6
2 to 4 times a month	32.3
2 to 3 times a week	21
4 or more times a week	11.3
Standards drinks in one sitting	
0	13.3
1 or 2	65
3 or 4	18.3
5 or 6	1.7
7, 8 or 9	1.7
10+	0
Frequency of heavy drinking (6 or more drinks in one sitting)	
Never	50
Less than monthly	40.3
Monthly	8.1
Weekly	1.6
Daily or almost daily	0

Changes in Parents' Confidence, Attitudes and Monitoring

A significant increase in parents confidence to communicate with their adolescent was observed pre (M = 2.6, SD = 0.5) and post (M = 2.9, SD = 0.3) program. A significant decrease in parents permissive attitudes towards underage drinking was observed pre (M = 1.9, SD = 0.7) and post (M = 1.5, SD = 0.6) program. Finally, a significant increase was also seen in parents ability to monitor their adolescent pre (M = 3.7, SD = 0.7) and post (M = 4.1, SD = 0.5) program.

While positive effects were observed for parents participating in this program, room for improvement is noted with only four out of eleven approached schools adopting the pilot program and a total of 65 parents participating. The research team noted several factors that contributed to the lack of program acceptance and implementation from schools approached. Notably, time and scheduling limitations inhibited the acceptance of programs within schools. Due to scheduling limitations, the research team only offered to deliver the program in schools on the evening the adolescent program was delivered. This lack of flexibility with delivery date options resulted in scheduling conflicts within some schools which ultimately meant they declined to participate in the program. Similarly, as some schools were approached to deliver the program at the end of a school semester, school staff did not consider it an optimal time for engaging with parents and therefore declined to participate.

Lessons Learnt and Path Forward

The purpose of this case study was to demonstrate how key co-design insights were built into program design and to report on program outcomes for the co-designed program. The application of a co-design method provided rich audience driven insights that were translated into workable design solutions. A co-design method offers the potential to design and implement more effective and engaging programs that are grounded in the target audience's real world experiences.

The parent alcohol program was designed incorporating key insights generated by parents participating in previous co-design sessions (Hurley, Trischler and Dietrich 2018). Specifically, parent preferences regarding program duration, content and delivery format were included. Hence, the program was designed to be delivered within a workshop setting in a short time frame, provide parents with opportunities to collaborate and interact with other each other and focus on content associated with parental communication and monitoring practices. Several studies highlight concerns regarding the meaningful contributions of user ideas, suggesting that user generated design outcomes lack feasibility for implementation (Magnusson, Matthing and Kristensson 2003; Poetz and Schreier 2012). The current case study demonstrates that parents successfully generated co-design insights that were converted into viable

program concepts, thus increasing the extent to which the program is user cen-
tred. Importantly, program evaluation demonstrated effectiveness of the final co-
designed program.

The pilot parent program showed significant positive program effects on all three
constructs. In addition, according to Cohen (1988) the effect size for each construct suggested a 'moderate' to 'large' practical significance. Post program, parents were more
confident in their ability to communicate to their adolescents about alcohol. Frequent
and open alcohol specific communication between parents and adolescents can reduce
adolescents' alcohol usage, while also increasing their perceptions of the negative consequences associated with alcohol use (Miller-Day and Kam 2010). In addition, post
program parents had less permissive attitudes regarding underage drinking. A change
in parental attitudes is an important step towards ultimately influencing parenting specific behaviours as influencing attitudes has shown to increase the likelihood of changing behaviour intentions and ultimately behaviour (Fishbein 2008). Finally, parents felt
significantly more capable of monitoring their adolescent. Operating as one of the strongest protective factors for adolescent alcohol use (Mynttinen, Pietilä and Kangasniemi
2017), parental monitoring has been found to both minimise (McCann et al. 2016) and
prevent adolescent alcohol use (Mynttinen, Pietilä and Kangasniemi 2017). Preliminary
findings demonstrate that a social marketing program that was co-designed by parents
can deliver positive outcomes for parents, which in turn may further assist to support
adolescents. This is a first study to examine parents and alcohol from a social marketing
perspective and demonstrates promising results.

Implications

A co-designed social marketing pilot program was evaluated to gain an understanding as to co-designs effectiveness. The focus thereby was on integrating co-design
insights into program design and outcome measures to examine the effectiveness of
the pilot program. The findings resulting from this evaluation have a number of important implications for social marketing theory and practice.

This case study demonstrates how insights derived through a co-design process
can be developed into feasible program design concepts to produce more audience
orientated programs that ultimately influence outcome change. The current case
study suggests that given the right procedures a co-design process that involves the
creative collaboration between parents can produce feasible ideas that are successfully translated into program design concepts and deliver desired outcome change.

This study provides a method that can be applied to develop audience orientated
programs. Co-design allows for user insights to be derived through close collabora-
tions with the target audience during the span of the design process (Sanders and
Stappers 2008). The benefits of co-design are evident in the literature (Steen et al.
2011; Ward et al. 2018), however the implementation and evaluation of co-designed

programs is lacking. The current program co-designed by parents represents a radical shift from the existing expert driven programs that largely make up the alcohol education space (Dietrich et al. 2016a). Through co-design, the complexities of the parent's individual circumstances are taken into account, in a process that focuses on designing programs from participant's everyday reality as opposed to traditional expert driven approaches (Ward et al. 2018). This results of this study provide pilot evidence that a program designed from audience generated insights can in fact lead to a positive change in program participants.

Finally, this case shows how social marketing can be used for alcohol education program design. Existing parent based alcohol programs demonstrate mixed effects (Adolfsen et al. 2017; Brown et al., 2014) and are largely developed in the prevention science space (Koutakis et al. 2008; Adolfsen et al. 2017). Social marketing is a credible behaviour change discipline that has demonstrated success in various contexts including alcohol education (Kubacki et al. 2015), food choice behaviour (Baranowski et al. 2002), and physical activity (Kadir, Kubacki and Rundle-Thiele 2019). An audience focus is an essential feature of social marketing and sways from traditional, expert driven or top down approaches (Grier and Bryant 2005) which typify current alcohol programs (Dietrich et al. 2016a). Through the integration of co-design this study demonstrates how social marketing techniques can be applied in the context of alcohol education to positively influence alcohol specific parenting factors.

Finally, for practitioners this study provides insights into how program acceptance and implementation can be improved in order to maximise program exposure. Reflecting on the challenges identified during program recruitment and implementation it becomes clear that strong networks are needed in order to successfully achieve the investment needed to facilitate program delivery within schools. When implementing a program within a school setting it is dependent upon the commitment of a faculty member to invest time and effort into organising program aspects such as venue arrangements and parent recruitment. In schools where the program was implemented the research team liaised with a dedicated staff member who was enthusiastic to be a part of the project. Building relationships with school staff may therefore help to increase acceptance of the program. Additionally, involving key stakeholders such as teachers and school administrators in the co-design process may have fostered a sense of ownership of the program, resulting in increased program acceptance. Therefore, co-design approaches should not be limited to collaborating with end users. We need to move beyond co-designing with those who will participate in the programs and involve other key stakeholders who will support, promote, facilitate and endorse program delivery.

Conclusions, Limitations and Future Research

This study demonstrates how insights from co-design sessions informed the build of a pilot program targeting parents. Several limitations prevent generalisability beyond the current study. First, outcomes in the present study are limited to self-report data and as such are subject to response bias. Furthermore, it is recognised that due to self-selection bias the parents who chose to attend may not be representative of the target population. Programs which reach only those already equipped with the desired skills are not enough to see the desired social change. Second, this study is limited by a lack of theory integration. In social marketing and other behavioural change fields, theories are used in the development of programs to effect better outcome change (Michie and Prestwich 2010), through influencing constructs that are known to cause specific behaviour (Hardeman et al. 2005) and behavioural change (Rundle-Thiele et al. 2019a). Thus, future research is needed to design and evaluate social marketing programs which incorporate theory during the co-design process. Third, due to difficulties in recruiting parents, the study is limited to a small sample size. Consequently, future research should aim to increase parent attendance by offering the program outside of school settings. Next, as the program was co-designed with parents only, other important stakeholders (e.g. teachers, addiction experts, industry professionals) were not considered. Co-design teams representing a mix of users and experts can produce outcomes higher in novelty and greater in user benefits than those produced by user only co-design teams (Trischler et al. 2018a). As such, future research should aim to capture knowledge and insights from a range of stakeholders in order to further assist in improving the outcomes observed through co-design. Finally, as a pre and post evaluation method was utilised, understanding of program effectiveness is limited to the face to face component. The authors acknowledge that future research is needed that allows for evaluation of the multiple components of the parent program (i.e. online and SMS conversation starters).

References

Adolfsen, Strøm, Martinussen, Handegård, Natvig, Eisemann and Koposov., (2017). Parent participation in alcohol prevention: Evaluation of an alcohol prevention programme. *Nordic Studies on Alcohol and Drugs.* **34**(6), 456–470.

Andreasen., (2002). Marketing social marketing in the social change marketplace. *Journal of Public Policy and Marketing.* **21**(1), 3–13.

Bandura., (2006). Guide for constructing self-efficacy scales. In: T. Urdan and F. Pajares, ed. *Self-efficacy beliefs of adolescents.* Connecticut: Information Age publishing. 307–337.

Bandura, Barbaranelli, Caprara and Pastorelli., (2001). Self-efficacy beliefs as shapers of children's aspirations and career trajectories. *Child Development.* **72**(1), 187–206.

Baranowski, Baranowski, Cullen, Demoor, Rittenberry, Hebert and Jones., (2002). 5 a day achievement badge for african-american boy scouts: pilot outcome results. *Preventive Medicine.* **34**(3), 353–363.

Beebe, Harrison, Sharma and Hedger., (2001). The community readiness survey: Development and initial validation. *Evaluation Review.* **25**(1), 55–71.

Berends, Jones and Andrews., (2016). Adolescent drinking, social identity, and parenting for safety: Perspectives from Australian adolescents and parents. *Health and Place.* **38**, 22–29.

Birrell, Deen, Champion, Newton, Stapinski, Kay-Lambkin, Teesson and Chapman., (2018). A mobile app to provide evidence-based information about crystal methamphetamine (ice) to the community (Cracks in the Ice): Co-Design and beta testing. *JMIR mHealth and uHealth.* **6** (12),e11107.

Brown, Dunn and Budney., (2014). Development and initial evaluation of a web-based program to increase parental awareness and monitoring of underage alcohol use: A brief report. *Journal of Child and Adolescent Substance Abuse.* **23**(2), 109–115.

Buyucek, Kubacki, Rundle-Thiele and Pang., (2016). "A systematic review of stakeholder involvement in social marketing interventions. *Australasian Marketing Journal (AMJ).* **24**(1), 8–19.

Caprara, Barbaranelli, Borgogni, Petitta and Rubinacci., (2003). Teachers', school staff's and parents' efficacy beliefs as determinants of attitudes toward school. *European Journal of Psychology of Education.* **18**(1), 15.

Carins, Rundle-Thiele and Fidock., (2016). Seeing through a Glass Onion: broadening and deepening formative research in social marketing through a mixed methods approach. *Journal of Marketing Management.* **32**(11–12), 1083–1083.

Cohen J. (1988) Statistical power analysis for the behavioral sciences, 2nd edn. L. Erlbaum Associates, Hillsdale, N.J.

David, Rundle-Thiele, Pang, Knox, Parkinson and Hussenoeder., (2019). Engaging the dog owner community in the design of an effective koala aversion program. *Social Marketing Quarterly.* **25**(1), 55–68.

Dietrich, Rundle-Thiele, Kubacki, Durl, Gullo, Arli and Connor., (2019). Virtual reality in social marketing: a process evaluation. *Marketing Intelligence and Planning.* **37**(7), 806–820.

Dietrich, Rundle-Thiele, Schuster and Connor., (2016b). Co-designing social marketing programs. *Journal of Social Marketing.* **6**(1), 41–61.

Dietrich, Rundle-Thiele, Schuster and Connor., (2016a). A systematic literature review of alcohol education programmes in middle and high school settings (2000–2014). *Health Education.* **116** (1), 50–68.

Dietrich, Trischler, Schuster and Rundle-Thiele., (2017). Co-designing services with vulnerable consumers. *Journal of Service Theory and Practice.* **27**(3), 663–668.

Eyles, Jull, Dobson, Firestone, Whittaker, Te Morenga, Goodwin and Mhurchu., (2016). Co-design of mHealth delivered interventions: a systematic review to assess key methods and processes. *Current Nutrition Reports.* **5**(3), 160–167.

Fishbein., (2008). A reasoned action approach to health promotion. *Medical Decision Making,* **28** (6), 834–844.

Goodyear-Smith, Jackson and Greenhalgh., (2015). Co-design and implementation research: challenges and solutions for ethics committees. *BMC Medical Ethics.* **16**(1), 78.

Grier and Bryant., (2005). Social marketing in public health. *Annual Review of Public Health.* **26**, 319–339.

Hair, Black, Babin, Anderson and Tatham., (2006). *Multivariate data analysis.* Uppersaddle River, NJ: Pearson Prentice Hall.

Hardeman, Sutton, Griffin, Johnston, White, Wareham and Kinmonth., (2005). A causal modelling approach to the development of theory-based behaviour change programmes for trial evaluation. *Health Education Research.* **20**(6), 676–687.

Hurley, Trischler and Dietrich., (2018). Exploring the application of co-design to transformative service research. *Journal of Services Marketing.* **32**(6), 715–727.

Ind, N. and Coates, N. (2013), "The meanings of co-creation ", *European Business Review*, Vol. 25 No. 1, pp. 86–95.

Kaynak, Winters, Cacciola, Kirby and Arria., (2014). Providing alcohol for underage youth: what messages should we be sending parents? *Journal of Studies On Alcohol And Drugs.* **75**(4), 590–605.

Koutakis, Stattin and Kerr., (2008). Reducing youth alcohol drinking through a parent-targeted intervention: the Örebro Prevention Program. *Addiction.* **103**(10), 1629–1637.

Kubacki and Rundle-Thiele., (2016). *Formative Research in Social Marketing: Innovative Methods to Gain Consumer Insights.* Singapore: Springer.

Kubacki, Rundle-Thiele, Pang and Buyucek., (2015). Minimizing alcohol harm: A systematic social marketing review (2000–2014). *Journal Of Business Research.* **68**(10), 2214–2222.

Kuntsche and Kuntsche., (2016). Parent-based interventions for preventing or reducing adolescent substance use – A systematic literature review. *Clinical Psychology Review.* **45**, 89–101.

Lefebvre., (2013). *Social marketing and social change: Strategies and tools for improving health, well-being, and the environment.* Chichester, UK: John Wiley and Sons.

Lefebvre and Flora., (1988). Social marketing and public health intervention. *Health Education Quarterly.* **15**(3), 299–315.

Lipson-Smith, White, White, Serong, Cooper, Price-Bell and Hyatt., (2019). Co-design of a consultation audio-recording mobile app for people with cancer: The Secondears app. *JMIR Formative Research.* **3**(1), e11111.

Lowe, Horne, Tapper, Bowdery and Egerton., (2004). Effects of a peer modelling and rewards-based intervention to increase fruit and vegetable consumption in children. *European Journal Of Clinical Nutrition.* **58**(3), 510–522.

Magnusson, Matthing and Kristensson., (2003). Managing user involvement in service innovation: Experiments with innovating end users. *Journal of Service Research.* **6**(2), 111–124.

Mattelmäki and Visser., (2011). *Lost in Co-X: Interpretations of Co-design and Co-creation.* 4th World Conference on Design Research (IASDR 2011). Delft, The Netherlands.

McCann, Perra, McLaughlin, McCartan and Higgins., (2016). Assessing elements of a family approach to reduce adolescent drinking frequency: parent–adolescent relationship, knowledge management and keeping secrets. *Addiction.* **111**(5), 843–853.

Michie and Prestwich., (2010). Are interventions theory-based? Development of a theory coding scheme. *Health Psychology.* **29**(1), 1–8.

Miller-Day and Kam., (2010). More than just openness: Developing and validating a measure of targeted parent–child communication about alcohol. *Health communication* **25**(4), 293–302.

Mynttinen, Pietilä and Kangasniemi., (2017). What does parental involvement mean in preventing adolescents' use of alcohol? An integrative review. *Journal of Child and Adolescent Substance Abuse.* **26**(4), 338–351.

Ostrom, Parasuraman, Bowen, Patricio and Voss., (2015). Service research priorities in a rapidly changing context. *Journal of Service Research.* **18**(2),127–159.

Poetz and Schreier., (2012). The value of crowdsourcing: can users really compete with professionals in generating new product ideas? *Journal of Product Innovation Management.* **29**(2), 245–256.

Rangelov and Suggs., (2015). Using strategic social marketing to promote healthy nutrition and physical activity behaviors to parents and children in Switzerland: the development of FAN. *Cases in Public Health Communication and Marketing.* **8**, 27–50.

Rundle-Thiele., (2015). Looking back and moving forwards: An agenda for social marketing research. *Recherche et Applications en Marketing (English Edition).* **30**(3), 128–133.

Rundle-Thiele, David, Willmott, Pang, Eagle and Hay., (2019a). Social marketing theory development goals: an agenda to drive change. *Journal of Marketing Management.* **35**(1–2), 160–181.

Rundle-Thiele, Pang, Knox, David, Parkinson and Hussenoeder., (2019b). Generating new directions for reducing dog and koala interactions: a social marketing formative research study. *Australasian Journal of Environmental Management* **26**(2), 173–187.

Sanders and Dandavate., (1999). *Design for Experiencing: New Tools.* First International Conference on Design and Emotion, TU Delft.

Sanders and Stappers., (2008). Co-creation and the new landscapes of design. *Co-design.* **4**(1), 5–18.

Steen, Manschot and De Koning., (2011). Benefits of co-design in service design projects. *International Journal of Design.* **5**(2), 53–60.

Suggs, Rots, Jacques, Vong, Mui and Reardon., (2011). I'm allergic to stupid decisions": An m-Health campaign to reduce youth alcohol consumption. *Cases in Public Health Communication and Marketing.* **5**, 111–135.

Tael-Oeren, Naughton and Sutton., (2019). A parent-oriented alcohol prevention program "Effekt" had no impact on adolescents' alcohol use: Findings from a cluster-randomized controlled trial in Estonia. *Drug and Alcohol Dependence.* **194**, 279–287.

The National Social Marketing Centre., (2010). Social Marketing Benchmark Criteria. [online]. The NSMC. [Viewed January 2020]. Available from: https://www.thensmc.com/sites/default/files/benchmark-criteria-090910.pdf.

Trischler, Dietrich and Rundle-Thiele., (2019). Co-design: From expert to user driven design ideas in public service design. *Public Management Review.* **21**(11), 1595–1619.

Trischler, Pervan, Kelly and Scott., (2018a). The value of codesign: The effect of customer involvement in service design teams. *Journal of Service Research.* **21**(1), 75–100.

Trischler, Zehrer and Westman., (2018b). A designerly way of analyzing the customer experience. *Journal of Services Marketing.* **32**(7), 805–819.

Villalba, Jaiprakash, Donovan, Roberts and Crawford., (2019). Testing literature-based health experience insight cards in a healthcare service co-design workshop. *CoDesign.* 1–13.

Ward, De Brun, Beirne, Conway, Cunningham, English, Fitzsimons, Furlong, Kane, Kelly, McDonnell, McGinley, Monaghan, Myler, Nolan, O'Donovan, O'Shea, Shuhaiber and McAuliffe., (2018). Using co-design to develop a collective leadership intervention for healthcare teams to improve safety culture. *International Journal Of Environmental Research And Public Health.* **15** (6),1182.

Witell, Kristensson, Gustafsson and Löfgren., (2011). Idea generation: customer co-creation versus traditional market research techniques. *Journal of Service Management.* **22**(2), 140–159.

Yap, Cheong, Zaravinos-Tsakos, Lubman and Jorm., (2017). Modifiable parenting factors associated with adolescent alcohol misuse: a systematic review and meta-analysis of longitudinal studies: Parenting and adolescent alcohol misuse. *Addiction.* **112**(7), 1142–1162.

Giuseppe Fattori
10 Social Media and Health Promotion

Introduction

The digital revolution has brought innovations and transformations across many fields and the galaxy of health is no exception. The digital platforms have transformed the way citizens and healthcare professionals interact on a daily basis; used effectively they can bring new opportunities to build a sustainable community and reorientate behaviours.

Billions of users through Instagram, Facebook, Twitter and YouTube interact, share their contributions, create exchanges among people and groups and build a new form of communication called Web 2.0 (Hesse 2011, p. 10). Internet, apps and mobile phones, together with the tools of Web 2.0, enable both a rapid and widespread dissemination of these achievements in *Health Promotion*, with constant evolution and daily progress.

It is very difficult to crystallise these dynamic and continuously updated realities such as Web 2.0 and the new technologies; it is even more so if we want to shed light on their implications in a complex and delicate field such as health and its promotion. Thanks to Web 2.0, patients also claim an active role and ask to participate in decisions regarding their health 'Citizen included' (De Bronkart 2019). The new protagonists of the world of health will therefore be the citizens, as their access to technologies and information will change the way they interact with healthcare professionals and access clinical research. The way to meet people's needs is however through citizens participation: their involvement is fundamental for effective health promotion, going beyond simply reaching the target audience, to influence changes in a sustainable manner and facilitate the co-creation of new behaviours (Kite 2016).

By reaching a wide audience *social media* can reduce social inequalities (Ramanadhan 2013, p. 1129) and increase the effectiveness of health promotion programs aiming at changing behaviours (Laranjo 2015, p. 243). Social networking platforms have increased peer support (Farmer 2009, p. 455) and helped marginalized and disadvantaged populations with low literacy levels (Veinot 2011, p. 1146). Citizen participation in health promotion programs is far from easy, their engagement however greatly increases the chances of success (Evans 2016).

Health promotion uses three levers to change behaviour:
- social marketing;
- social media;
- the laws.

We will discuss the relationships between these tools and their impact on people's behaviours and lifestyles.

https://doi.org/10.1515/9783110659566-010

Health Promotion and Social Marketing

Health promotion is a global process which goes beyond the generic safeguard of health, but refers to a specific strategy with references at an international level. Following this direction, the Ottawa Charter, the final act of the First International Conference on health promotion, represents a starting point: on this occasion the concept of *health promotion* was recognized for the first time as a process allowing people to gain greater control over their own health and to improve on it.

Follows the 1988 Adelaide conference and the 1997 Jakarta declaration developed on the indications provided at the Ottawa conference, supporting the importance of shared decisions and the need for wider participation in health processes. Fostering citizens participation is recognized as key component to empower the individuals and their community to take action in promoting the health of the entire population. A new and difficult challenge considering that most health promotion activities have had, and continue to have, the objective of acting on each single individual (Raphael 2006, p. 236). Informed and aware citizens today are at a lower risk of becoming patients tomorrow.

Furthermore, the concept of health promotion cannot be fully understood if it is not considered in a broader perspective, as a *program*: this means to radically review both the strategy for its development and the means for its implementation. Designing and implementing a health promotion program involves putting together scientific evidence, intervention strategies and sustainability of the results achieved.

Health promotion, defined as the science and art to help people change their lifestyles towards an optimal state of health, is an extremely inclusive discipline. It is this flexibility that makes health promotion suitable for facing the challenges that new technologies set every day. A clear path is however required, together with the understanding of how technologies are integrated, shared and implemented in the field of health.

Health promotion began to develop as early as the eighteenth century, in order to reduce the complications that plagued workers employed in unhealthy environments. The most effective promoters of health were the parish priests and teachers who used the language of ordinary people to spread awareness for the prevention of certain diseases. The need to live in health is confronted with the need of trade and profit: the conviction to do away with smoking contrasts with the interests of cigarette manufacturers, as when centuries ago the closure of a city's gates stemmed an epidemic but halted commercial trade.

A plurality of disciplines, among which it is possible to include medicine, sociology, psychology, anthropology, communication sciences and social marketing, have explored different aspects of communication campaigns on sustainable lifestyles. These campaigns have the fundamental purpose of providing individuals with tools to gain greater control over their condition, acting on the determinants of health, namely the living conditions of a cultural, social, economic and environmental nature and, finally, on personal and social behaviour.

At the end of the twentieth century we started to consider health as physical, social and psychological well-being, as well as a resource for human life (Nutbeam 1988, p. 27). This approach also underlines how societies founded on principles of social equity, that develop health promotion as a value to defend, are the most successful and offer those who are part of it, better life prospects. However, health policies need means to achieve their goals and, fundamentally, also coordination within the different levels of planning and operations, in an organizational model in which managerial and production responsibilities are defined and assessable.

Social marketing is one of these levers and is rapidly becoming an integral part of health promotion strategies. Even today the definitions of 'health promotion' and 'social marketing' are being dynamically adapted to take account of the inevitable differences between the different communities and between the different segments of the population (Griffiths 2008): a *work in progress* which perhaps will never come to an end, as the point of arrival of the theoretical discussions is in contradiction with the perpetually evolutionary character of society.

The logical models used in planning and evaluating health promotion and marketing initiatives have been described in the different phases of the planning, development, implementation and evaluation process (Griffiths 2008):

- Logical model of explanatory factors: on the nature and origin of a question;
- Logical model of change processes: on understanding behaviour change processes;
- Logical model of program/action: on the formation of the practical program;
- Logical model of outcome/evaluation: on expected results.

Positioning of Social Marketing

Social marketing is a discipline in itself, distinct from communication, education, commercial marketing and other economic and social sciences, from which however it draws approaches and contributions. Specifically, it began to take shape from an article by Kotler and Zaltman in the early 1970s.

> Social marketing is the use of marketing principles and techniques to influence a target group to accept, reject, modify or abandon a behaviour voluntarily, in order to gain an advantage for individuals, groups or society in its complex. (Kotler 1971, p. 3)

It starts from the fundamental definition of social marketing's analysis of the terminology adopted to indicate the currents of thought and actions aimed at promoting a more correct behaviour towards one's own body and towards the determinants of individual and collective health. Various authors have also paid particular attention to the concept of *societal marketing* as also being the commitment that a private company undertakes to assure good environmental or social behaviour.

> The concept of societal marketing states that the task of a company is to determine the needs, desires and interests of the target markets and to fulfil them more effectively and efficiently than their competitors, in ways that preserve and strengthen the well-being of the consumer and the society.
>
> (Adel 1974, p. 316)

The attention of the private sector towards its own social responsibility can extend beyond the mere sale of the product and involves quality assurance, health and safety compliancy, acceptable costs, a production chain that does not excessively damage the environment, the elimination of harmful materials, the non-exploitation of child labour and energy savings. The extent in which these elements are adopted can greatly impact on the long-term positioning of a company in the market as they reflect its social role and responsibility.

In social marketing, therefore, the systematic application of the concepts of marketing and its techniques has as its goal the improvement of the general quality of life, paying particular attention to the most vulnerable sections of the population: strategies that are not 'random', but attentive to the Weak in terms of economic, social and cultural capital to promote greater health equality among people.

It is opportune to highlight the role of *the partners* during the process: local authorities, institutions, the world of health, the environment, sport, volunteers, entrepreneurs, trade associations, trade unions, individual citizens who contribute together, if involved, to the definition and the realization of the concept of 'well-being', also through the modification of behaviours and of the established health objectives.

Social marketing aimed at the adoption of healthy lifestyles therefore intends to encourage the concept of sharing between citizens and the community within the territory in which the promoter organization operates, of a wider range of alternative behaviours that guarantee more appropriate, free and mindful choices that affect their state of health and which is defined as community empowerment (Freire 2018). Empowerment means a social process that promotes the participation of individuals, organizations and communities with the aim of increasing individual, social and political control over health, improving the quality of life and social equity (Griffiths 2008).

Health promotion and social marketing can guarantee strategies and practices to improve community health in an effective way through the empowerment of citizens (bottom-up); however, empowerment interventions must be compared with the objectives defined by the institutions for issues such as health and the environment that arise from top-down policies.

Laverack et al make the two modes of intervention coexist by integrating in a sustainable manner the programs and the top-down objectives with the bottom-up requests and needs in the field of *parallel tracking* (Laverack 2019). Parallel tracking shifts our focus from the top-down / bottom-up dichotomy by linking public health and empowerment in all phases of the programming cycle: goal setting, strategic approach, management, implementation and evaluation.

The pathway for the definition of social marketing and its strong characterization in the field of health promotion (understood, as already underlined, as the outcome of a plurality of physical, environmental and cultural determinants) can be facilitated by its positioning (Maibach 2002, p. 437) in a 'Behaviour Management Continuum' that consists of three levers, alternative or integrated: communication, social marketing and laws, all aimed at proposing a healthy lifestyle.

The levers of influence on the proposed lifestyles (social media, social marketing, regulatory interventions) can be distinguished with respect to the attitude of the recipients:

–   in the case of willing recipients motivated towards a specific behaviour, coupled with weak competition, communication through *social media* may be sufficient to perceive the advantages and motivate action;
–   when obstacles to change present themselves, in a situation that can be defined as intermediate between propensity and resistance, as well as with present and active competition, it is useful to resort to *social marketing*, a more refined development of the system, to help highlight the advantages of adopting a specific action and reducing its barriers to adoption. Consider that the interventions can be structural: if the consumption of fruit and vegetables is low, it is certainly important to communicate the advantages of a more varied and balanced nutrition, but it may be necessary to increase the possibilities of access to such foods through, for example, the diversification of the offer of vending machines, widely present in places of life and work (Fattori 2009, p. 149);
–   in cases of greater resistance on the part of the recipients and of a situation in which competition is unmanageable the choice falls on a *regulatory approach* to reduce the social costs of a behaviour that is being repressed. The more difficult it is to induce change, the more the legislative sanctions will be used: a smoking campaign will be accompanied by penalties for failure to comply with the rules, while violence against women or sexual or ethnic minorities may lead to imprisonment of the offender.

In support of this reflection it is opportune to point out that the different levels of change can be:

–   *cognitive* (information campaigns that increase the degree of awareness on a specific issue, such as racism, nutritional values, etc.);
–   *action* (initiatives that aim to have concrete action taken in a certain period of time, favouring an amortization of the costs that the reference population will face; for example, in the field of vaccination, or blood and organ donation);
–   *behavioural* (to which social marketing projects aim, in search of stable changes in individual and collective health behaviours that benefit the individual, society and the environment. Consider the application on topics such as drugs, alcohol, smoking, contraception, waste recycling, violence against women);

- *values* (changes in moral opinions, such as racial, sexual, religious prejudices) depending on the level of penetration that one wants to achieve in the conscience of the recipients (Lee 2019).

The fields in which social marketing has the greatest use are (Hastings 2018) above all environmental ones (air and water quality, nature protection, recycling, renewable energy sources, sustainable urban planning), those of purely social initiatives (going to the polls, prevention of domestic violence, volunteering, facilitating access to information and services for the weakest sections of the population), public health (HIV/AIDS, alcohol, smoking, obesity, tuberculosis, unwanted pregnancies) and accident prevention (road accidents, accidents in the workplace).

Health and Web 2.0

With the birth of second-generation web services, commonly known as Web 2.0, a virtually unlimited possibility of interaction and sharing was provided, especially thanks to the use of social networks (Instagram, Facebook, Twitter, Forum and Blog) and of mobile technologies. This technological and information revolution has also largely involved the field of health and its promotion: the method of transmission of knowledge between users and professionals has radically changed (McDaid 2011).

The innovations cited have contributed to the spread of social media in health promotion. Social media significantly facilitate the exchange of data and experiences regarding one's health. It is at this level of the process that the promotion should be inserted: informative change dictated by technological innovations and by the network cannot fail to correspond to a different way of promoting health which takes into account the new scenario.

If the goal of a health promotion campaign is to inform and raise awareness in individuals about a specific problem in order to create the necessary conditions to change ideas and behaviours, it is necessary not only to use the most suitable messages, but also to choose the most appropriate and effective channels and means. Until now, health promotion campaigns have been based on traditional tools and have used very few new high-involvement technologies such as social media and mobile applications.

It is unlikely however that the same message can effectively reach a heterogeneous target which increasingly requires targeted and engaging content. The use of new media, in particular of Web 2.0 tools, can significantly help to effectively reach the target audience; it is therefore necessary to favour a new idea of promotion that takes into account and valorises synergistically the great potential that technology offers us. It is necessary to reaffirm that innovation is the only way to redesign an organized health system based on the citizens' new request for health and well-being.

New paradigms in the field of health enter the scene; public and private innovators connect and consult with each other, giving a concrete demonstration of how the citizens and their needs must be placed at the centre of the system.

The introduction of the internet in the field of health has had a disruptive effect as it has created a veritable divide between the concept of classic health and what we could call Health 2.0 today: health promotion must also take this revolution into account. As early as 2006 Kerry E. Evers was one of the first authors in literature to address this interesting subject matter. In the article *'eHealth promotion: the use of the Internet for health promotion'* the use of the Internet for the promotion of health and, in particular, the reproducibility, and the evaluation strategies for online interventions are analysed (Evers 2006, p. 1).

Evers' work laid the foundations for what would have become the evolution of health promotion in the following years: shifting more and more towards e-health promotion interventions. Peter Korp also supported Evers' ideas in 2006 in the study *'Health on the Internet: Implication for Health Promotion'* which focuses in particular on the concept of empowerment (Korp 2006, p. 78).

Thanks to the advent of the Internet, information is easier to access, more social contacts and networks are created, the citizens are more informed about their health. However, there is no shortage of problematic aspects such as the digital divide, the assessment and reliability of sources, the strong control of technicians and experts, an excessive increase in medicalization and health. The task of a good health promoter, therefore, is to design strategies that are able to strengthen the users' ability to evaluate the various sources of information in relation to their interests and needs, rather than in relation to scientific and / or professional standards.

With the spread of the internet, therefore, eHealth enters the scene with eHealth Promotion. Programs based on eHealth promotion automate data collections and ensure greater interactivity and flexibility. Efforts must therefore be focused on combining health promotion with eHealth. In a recent report by the European Community Commission, eHealth is described as a useful tool for both health professionals and patients.

In reference to interactive communication technologies (Ratzan 2011, p.1) we are experiencing an era of opportunities never before experienced. So-called *participatory technologies*, such as Web 2.0 and its extensions, must be well exploited and used by both potential patients and stakeholders. Thanks to the ever-increasing *digital health*, we are now able to develop effective communication strategies for health in preventing, helping and supporting patients wherever they live.

Of all the tools introduced in recent years, undoubtedly apps and social media are the ones that have had the most significant impact in healthcare. So much so that we can talk about a pre and post Web 2.0, as well as a pre and post and -Health. Lee Aase, in the text 'Bringing the Social Media Revolution to Health Care', is one of the first to believe in the power of social media in health care (Aase 2016).

Hospitals must face and manage this radical change by learning to use these tools of dialogue with communities, redesigning their organization, encouraging participation, building a network of professionals, sharing ideas. A pioneer in the use of social media in medicine is Bertalan Meskò, founder of *Webicina* and author of 'Social Media in Clinical Practice' (Meskò 2013). According to Meskò, social media have changed the world of health care. Web 2.0, internet, social media are representations of the same concept: digital communication.

Social media can facilitate communication, doctor / patient interaction. The ultimate goal is not that every healthcare professional becomes a blogger or a Twitter expert but that each of them can choose the platforms, tools, solutions that facilitate their own and personal communication flow with patients, with communities.

An important medical association like the ASCO (American Society of Clinical Oncology), through its portal helps oncologists to understand and use Twitter, supporting mutual enrichment for those specialists who, thanks to social media, can better confer with colleagues, patients and caregivers.

The theme is therefore very current, especially if mobile applications, which have of late become protagonists in the eHealth field, come into play. Flexibility, innovativeness and easy integration with all portable devices (smartphones, tablets) have made them the cornerstones of the new concept of electronic health. In the same app we find prevention and health; *mobile health* is no longer simply a phenomenon, but a reality with which we must confront ourselves in a society that has discovered the incredible potential of smartphones and tablets and does not want (and perhaps cannot) do without them anymore.

The apps available today in the health area are divided mainly into five macro-areas: diet, exercise, health and personal care, sexuality and sleep disorders. All the applications allow a greater diffusion of information among the population and make users prone to the implementation of certain behaviours. Alongside research that suggests the use of apps and looks upon them positively, there are still studies that show criticism. An article published by the Journal of Medical Internet Research 'There's an app for that: content analysis of paid health and fitness apps' analysed some smartphone applications dedicated to health, in particular fitness, assessing the potential impact of each in behavioural change. A critical look that underlines how few applications are developed respecting the most consolidated theories of health promotion (West 2012, p.12).

Currently academic literature presents little analysis on the use of apps in health promotion (Hasman 2011, p. 322). The potential of the Internet began to be understood at the end of the nineties; today, healthcare companies, hospitals, research institutes, should preside over the places in which patients exchange information and support each other, while embracing and facing the social revolution. At this further level the strategy becomes a focal point.

Social media are Internet-based tools that are created and exploit the ideological and technical premises of Web 2.0 and allow the production and exchange of '*user generated content*' (Kaplan 2010, p. 59). Adapting to these changes becomes essential, especially if we talk about health. The complexity of the communication, the interactions and the implications that can be generated through the direct contact of health professionals with the user/patient must be recognized.

With the union between Web 2.0 and health, a new research sector is created, in which health promotion plays a central role.

Given the complexity of the topic, the intent is to trace and describe a path that starts from the concept of health promotion and ends in eHealth, passing through Web 2.0 and social media.

It would be useless to talk about Health Promotion and its developments if the competences shared at international level were not established and possessed by all those who wish to operate in the sector. In this direction, the project *Developing Competencies and Professional Standards for Health Promotion Capacity in Europe* (CompHP) which sees the participation of 24 countries around the world coordinated by the European Office of International Union for Health Promotion and Education (IUPHE), aims to identify the basic competences of operators (health and non-health) for health promotion (Speller 2012). The project proposes some relevant objectives for the professional development of the Health Promotion sector and presents its professional standards. The document describes the programs, policies and other health promotion interventions.

Ethical values are fundamental for actions in Health promotion and form the context in which all other skills are practiced. They include: equity, social justice, respect for autonomy and the choice of individual and group work processes based on collaboration and consultation. The nine standards identified by the CompHP Project are:
- *Promote* behaviour change through *empowerment* and citizen participation;
- *Improve* health and well-being by facilitating communities and groups to articulate their needs and support the development of policies and procedures in all sectors which have a positive impact on health;
- *Mediate* through partnership, build successful partnerships through collaborative work and facilitate the development and sustainability of coalitions and networks for health promotion action;
- *Communicate* health promotion actions through techniques and technologies suitable for a heterogeneous public;
- *Leadership*, through work with stakeholders to agree on a shared vision and strategic direction;
- *Analyse* the needs and resources in collaboration with stakeholders, within the framework of political, economic, social, cultural, environmental, behavioural and biological determinants;
- *Plan* through the development of health promotion objectives that are both measurable and based on the assessment of needs and activities in collaboration with stakeholders. Mobilize, support and involve the participation of stakeholders in the planning of health promotion actions;

- *Implement* effective and efficient actions in collaboration with interested parties;
- *Evaluate* the impact and effectiveness of health promotion actions.

In health promotion, social media can be used as a medium to promote citizen empowerment, improve health and well-being, mediate through partnerships, communicate, analyse/collect data, implement, evaluate and research.

From Social Networks to Social Media

The history of social networks begins long before the internet, Euler's work and his graph theory that underlies the entire theory of networks of today dates back to 1736. The social network is made up of a group of people connected to each other through different kinds of relationships (personal, professional, religious, etc.). Since these early studies, social networks have never stopped developing; in the early 2000s, the first collaborative services such as Wikipedia, YouTube and Facebook appeared on the scene.

Web 2.0 was rising from the ashes of the 2001 crisis. Starting from the early years of the new millennium, the social network timeline has been accelerating very fast: in 2003 LinkedIn was introduced, in 2004 Facebook went online, in 2005 YouTube, in 2006 a minimalist microblogging service like Twitter was launched, Instagram in 2010.

The network interaction mode (profile, connection or friendship, message, status, comment, etc.) has quickly established itself, becoming the standard with which people have become accustomed to interact. Taking a step forward, Social Networks are one of the key elements of a broader 'revolution' that should be pigeonholed under the name of Social Media. This term means a group of techniques and rules for creating and sharing online content. It is a change of roles: the users also become producers of content.

Better managing social media means developing multi-channel digital campaigns with social media, websites, apps, mobile, wearable technology where social media is integrated with traditional communication tools. Now we will try to define the scope of action and learn about the social media most in use today.

Social Media

Social media is a constellation of tools and technologies that enable peer-to-peer conversations and co-creation. Each of these tools has different characteristics and finds different applications with respect to health promotion. To this end, social media have been divided into (De Angelis 2018, p. 1):

- collaborative projects such as *Wikipedia*: these are websites that allow users to add, remove and modify text-based content and enable the joint and simultaneous creation of content by many end users;
- content communities such as *Youtube, Instagram* and *Podcast*: these allow users to share multimedia content such as videos, photos and audio;
- blog and microblogging such as *Twitter*: these are specific websites that provide information in different formats, particularly appreciated by professional networks;
- social network such as *Facebook*: these are applications that allow users to connect by creating personal information profiles, inviting friends and colleagues to access these profiles and exchanging e-mails and instant messages;
- virtual worlds such as *Second life*: these are platforms that replicate a three-dimensional environment in which users can appear in the form of personalized avatars and interact with each other as in real life;
- discussion *forums*: these allow participants to converse using posted messages; they have been considered a form of social media as they incorporate user-generated content.

Social media is not just a means of entertainment, it is now part of our lives. It is therefore necessary to adopt a professional approach to social media and adopt a social media strategy.

Social media strategies can be traced back to some more common types:
- *Monitoring strategies* aim to establish as much as possible a broad and solid participation of the company in terms of content and without a predefined deadline. These are costly strategies both in terms of economics and resources (dedicated staff, etc.). Once adopted, such strategies require an innovative and precise metric system to calculate the ROI (Return on Investment). A service like Facebook lends itself well to developing such a strategy;
- *Promotion* strategies are those undertaken by companies to support the launch of a campaign or initiative. Often these strategies are supported by a significant investment on average. They are targeted strategies and have time limits
- *Project* strategies are always of a temporary character but are less limited to a specific subject / topic. The organization tends to work on the specific objective to be achieved. Such strategies can only succeed if they are addressed to the appropriate community.
- *Listening* strategies are the way for those companies that have, by choice or by waiting-and-seeing, decided to only confront social media 'passively'. The limits of listening-only strategies are obvious because they do not use social media for communication. In any case, they do not preclude the possibility of intervening at a later time and represent an option that, if managed well, can be useful.

In health promotion, precise indications to determine strategic objectives cannot be ignored. The importance of establishing priorities and objectives is also emphasized

by Lee Aase of the Mayo Clinic Center for Social Media in the seven points to be considered for a social media strategy (Aase 2016):
- Start from priorities and goals;
- Become familiar with the tools;
- Start a strategy from observation and listening;
- Ask for help;
- Pay attention to the community rules;
- Don't be overwhelmed by purists;
- Remember that planning is more important than plans.

Social media changes the way people communicate and organizational goals need to be redesigned to engage people. Furthermore, the choice of the reference target will influence the choice of the channel. Spending time developing and maintaining social media presence will be unproductive if we do not decide how to use the chosen channel.

In particular, we must define the objectives (for example, promote the company or create a personal online presence) and design a good strategy based on our needs: Twitter, for example, can be used for brief conversations, while blogs are preferable for sharing opinions, essays and presentations.

Some important indications (Meskò 2013):
- Do not mix professional and personal life online;
- Be open to discussions;
- Communicate as you would in real life;
- Be consistent;
- Always show intellectual rigor and be committed.

Social Media and Health Promotion

The guidelines of the Centers for Disease Control and Prevention of Atlanta (CDC 2011) propose the innovative use of Social Media in health promotion. In this direction, social media and mobile communication technologies favour:
- the immediacy of information;
- sharing content with partners;
- personalization of messages;
- facilitating the integration between different organizations and institutions;
- support toward the choice to adopt healthy behaviours.

Social media do not eliminate the disparities between groups but due to the low cost and the growing spread of the Internet they can reduce the inequalities caused by the digital divide and the different levels of health literacy (Bodie 2008, p. 175). Popular platforms like Facebook Instagram or Twitter have allowed a myriad of new voices to emerge in the social media sphere where individuals can be equally as present as big companies, researchers and governments.

The evolution of the media introduces new problems due to the truthfulness of the data, to fake news and to privacy issues. Health promoters can no longer base their authority only on social position as social media offers the public equal or greater means than professionals to act on controversial issues such as vaccinations or alternative medicine.

By integrating Web 2.0 into health promotion dynamics, the aspect of evaluation is relevant. In the planning phase, the reason for which you intend to use that particular social network and to recognize the contribution that the latter can offer in the adoption of healthy lifestyles should be established.

Despite the increasing use of social media, we still have a long way to go regarding the appropriateness of their use to promote health and on their evaluation. In order to examine this dimension in depth, the following have been evaluated (Neiger 2012, p. 159):

– the purpose of social media in health promotion;
– the potential KPI (Key Performance Index) associated with these purposes;
– evaluation metrics for social media related to KPI.

Experiences

Social media are extremely widespread, but the rapidity in which they change makes it difficult to evaluate them within complex public health issues. We have selected various projects, each one for its distinctive features, that have chosen different platforms of social media for health promotion but are always linked to shared public health objectives.

Social Networking Technologies as an Emerging Tool for HIV Prevention

Addressing at-risk populations among Internet users is particularly important because those seeking sex on the Internet may be more susceptible to HIV. This 12-week intervention showed that participants who received information on HIV prevention via Facebook were more likely to require HIV testing than those who had received general health information. These interventions, through the peer figure of the online community, have allowed the use of condoms to increase and the number of unprotected sexual relations to decrease. Communities on social networks are considered effective tools to increase the request for HIV testing among at-risk populations (Young 2013, p. 318).

Obesity in the New Media: A Content Analysis of Obesity Videos in YouTube

On the subject of obesity, as of March 2010, more than 12,000 videos have been found and the most popular of these have been viewed more than 9 million times by YouTube users. The search on the YouTube site was done in March 2010 using the key words 'obesity' and 'obese'. Research through the key word 'obesity' produced 38,000 results, while those with the word 'obese' 37,500.

Obese people are associated with negative characteristics much more than normal-weight ones and are subject to many more negative judgments and/or stigmatizations. In every single video category of YouTube, unhealthy nutrition and a sedentary lifestyle have been portrayed as the main causes of obesity.

The videos themselves, in all the different formats, have therefore recommended that the best solution to combat obesity is to modify individual behaviours doing physical activity or having a healthy diet (Yoo 2012, p. 86).

Remote and Web 2.0 Interventions for Promoting Physical Activity

Doing an insufficient amount of physical activity leads to an increased risk of chronic diseases and both physical and mental problems. Regular physical activity can produce social, physical and emotional benefits and as such should be a goal for all adults. From a total of 11 studies, 5,862 apparently healthy adults were recruited, and it emerged that the use of technology is appreciated when supporting adults to become more active, follow a weekly recommended fitness plan or be in better shape. Changes can be obtained with the help from a professional and through personal support by phone, e-mail or written information (Foster 2013).

An Online Community Improves Adherence in an Internet-Mediated Walking Program. Results of a Randomized Controlled Trial

Traditional health promotion interventions cannot produce improvements in the lifestyles of the population as much as interventions based on the use of the Internet, which instead can be widely disseminated at a reduced cost.

Online communities, like those for walking programs, allow participants to communicate with each other by sending and reading messages. All participants (n = 324) wore the pedometer for the 16 weeks and uploaded the data online. The recourse to the online community for a walking program using the Internet has not increased the number of steps counted on average, but has reduced the abandonment by the participants.

Online communities can be a promising approach to reducing the abandonment of health activities, particularly in populations with low social support (Richardson 2010).

Web 2.0 and Beyond: Risks for Sexually Transmitted Infections and Opportunities for Prevention

The continual growth of the Internet as a means of communication has also had important implications for the transmission and prevention of sexually transmitted infections (STIs). The purpose of this review is to describe recent developments in a rapidly evolving field.

The meeting point between the Internet and sexually transmitted diseases (STDs) is described in three perspectives: the Internet as a risk environment, a place where sexual partners can be recruited; Internet as a place where public health prevention interventions can be performed aimed at preventing sexually transmitted diseases and HIV; Internet as an increasingly important work environment for all MST prevention disciplines.

The review highlights recent developments and identifies potential avenues for future research. The growing interactivity of the Internet, in particular the social networking sites that allow users to closely share unlimited amounts of personal information with their peers on the net, increases the potential of the Internet as an environment both for STIs risk and for its prevention (Rietmeijer 2009, p. 67).

Smoking Cessation Support Delivered via Mobile Phone Text Messaging (txt2stop): A Single-Blind, Randomized Trial

Smoking cessation programs based on text messages from mobile phones can increase smoking cessation in the short term. Smokers willing to make an attempt to quit (5800) were randomly assigned to a control group, using an independent telephone randomization system: the smoking cessation program was called *txt2stop*. The messages sent were motivational and behavioural.

On the basis of the results obtained, it is clear that the tobacco cessation program txt2stop has significantly improved the divestment rates over a period of 6 months and can be included in the services aimed at tobacco cessation (Free 2011, p. 49).

Youth Drinking Cultures, Social Networking and Alcohol Marketing: Implications for Public Health

Millions of posts on notice-boards, profiles and photos that go around about alcohol play an important role in the normalization of drinking alcohol within the life and culture of young people. Social Networks can be used positively in healthcare to encourage young drinkers to responsibly change their habits.

Users of Social Networks on the one hand can benefit from the creation and sharing of content, on the other they represent an easy target to be reached by alcohol sellers. The unregulated and probably uncontrollable characteristics of Social Networks make them popular with alcohol producers as they increasingly bring them in closer contact with consumers (McCreanor 2013, p. 110).

Social Media and Organ Donor Registration: The Facebook Effect

A study published in the American Journal of Transplantation by researchers at Johns Hopkins University in Baltimore showed that Facebook has effectively made citizens aware of organ donation. On May 1, 2012, the social network, Facebook, changed its platform to allow members to specify Organ Donor status on their profile. This choice was shared on the friends' page via notification and was further enhanced by sending educational links on the themes of the donation.

On the first day of the 'Organ Donor' initiative on Facebook, there was an increase in the actual number of new donors of 21.1 times, going from an average of 616 daily registrations to 13,054. Overall in the observation period (the study lasted 13 days) there were 39,818 registrations, of which 32,958 attributable to the Facebook effect.

New applications through social media can therefore prove to be effective in increasing organ donation rates and similarly could be used in other public health fields where communication and education are essential (Cameron 2013, p. 2059).

'Too Young To Drink'. An International Communication Campaign to Raise Public Awareness of Fetal Alcohol Spectrum Disorders

Prenatal exposure to alcohol can cause a range of lifelong physical, behavioural, and intellectual disabilities, collectively known as fetal alcohol spectrum disorders (FASD). FASD is recognized to be an international public health problem. Increasing awareness about the risks of drinking during pregnancy is considered the first step towards FASD prevention. An international awareness campaign was organized, called 'Too Young to Drink' (Figure 10.1).

Figure 10.1: Too Young to Drink – Fabrica.
Source: Available from: https://web2salute.com/tytd/ (Viewed 3 July 2020)

The campaign used theoretical models of social marketing applied to health promotion. The approach aimed to spread information among the general population, sharing ideas and using the power of the Internet and social media. The launch followed the methods of 'guerrilla marketing'. Social media, mainly Facebook and Twitter, were the driving force to the diffusion of the campaign.

Findings from the campaign 'Too Young to Drink' showed that it was possible to develop and carry out an international action plan to raise public awareness of FASD, using social marketing strategies and social media to spread materials and information on the issue among different cultures with a low budget (Bazzo 2017, 111).

Breastfeeding with Start4Life on Amazon Alexa

In England, breastfeeding rates are among the lowest in the world. 75% of women start breast-feeding when their baby is born, unfortunately between the sixth and eighth week this drops to 44%. Expectant mothers who are supported properly breastfeed longer. England's Public Health Start4Life program provides support for parents to adopt healthy behaviours.

For the first time the Amazon Alexa voice service is also available. Mothers can ask Alexa (Figure 10.2) a series of questions about breastfeeding and the answers will be tailored to their child. This means that they can receive useful advice also through voice commands (Public Health England 2018).

A survey showed that 24-hour access 7 days a week to breastfeeding support via a phone line, website or chatbot may more likely result in:
– having a positive breastfeeding experience;
– deciding to try breastfeeding (59%);
– breastfeeding longer (58%).

Figure 10.2: Start4Life Breastfeeding.
Source: Available from: https://twitter.com/PHE_uk/status/970628333665968128?s=20
(Viewed 3 July 2020)

#FridaysForFuture 'Our House is on Fire'

#FridaysForFuture is a very present topic on social media, young people have used Instagram, Facebook, Twitter and YouTube to support their cause. Social media have facilitated knowledge of climate change and mobilization of activists by providing platforms for discussion and sharing (Thunberg 2019).

The ability of these platforms to spread videos, images and text and to be online have enabled the creation of a worldwide movement. Young people asked to step up actions to tackle global climate change and used social media to promote offline activities.

Social media can give visibility to social issues and have a real effect on public opinion. The Global Strike For Future took place on Friday, 15 March 2019, with the participation of 1.5 million students in more than 2,083 cities in 125 countries (Figure 10.3).

The Technological (and Social) Revolution

Through social media, human relationships, conversations and information overcome space-time barriers: in addition to the technology revolution, we are facing a

Figure 10.3: School students go on strike over the lack of action on climate change.
Source: Available from: https://twitter.com/GretaThunberg/status/1106638130290049024?s=20
(Viewed 3 July 2020)

social revolution. A new world to know and to interpret; beyond the obstacles to innovation, we see enormous opportunities for social media and health promotion.

The new health professional is witnessing the most important revolution of all time; rules, hierarchies, skills change. All at a surprising speed. 'Dr. Google' is changing the patient medical relationship and the relationships between citizens. Social media promoters can develop strategies to engage the public and encourage learning (Norman 2009).

Even when social media is effective in producing positive health outcomes we must continually follow its evolution and change the approach of operators and policy makers to adapt to these new realities. All sectors of society are involved and we have also seen that health promoters are defining which skills and values to adopt internationally.

In the previous stories we have described social media experiences for health promotion. Today we have a new ally, a protagonist who wants to sit at the table of 'rules' to help define his future, *Patient Dave* who tells us 'nothing about me without me'; the competent citizen is interested in participating in 'Citizen included' research and prevention.

References

Aase, L., Goldman, D., (2016). *Bringing the Social media Revolution to Health Care* [online]. Mayo Foundation for Medical Education And Research. [Viewed 3 July 2020]. Available from: https://cdn.prod-carehubs.net/n1/73faa102fe023137/uploads/2015/05/Bringing-the-Social-Media-Revolution-to-Health-Care.pdf

Adel, I., Ansary, E., (1974). Towards a Definition of Social and Societal Marketing. *Journal of the Academy of Marketing Science.* **2**(1–4), 316–321.

Bazzo, S., Black, D., Mitchell, K., Marini, F., Moino, G., Riscica, P., Fattori, G., (2017). Too Young To Drink. An international communication campaign to raise public awareness of fetal alcohol spectrum disorders. *Public Health.* **142**, 111–115.

Bodie, G., Dutta, M.J., (2008). Understanding health literacy for strategic health marketing: ehealth literacy, health disparities, and the digital divide. *Health Marketing Quarterly.* **25**, 175–203.

Cameron, A. M., Massie, A. B., Alexander, C.E., Stewart, B., Montgomery, A. R., Benavides, N. R., Fleming, G. D., Segev, D. L., (2013). Social Media and Organ Donor Registration: The Facebook Effect. American Journal of Transplantation, 13: 2059–2065.

Centers for Disease Control and Prevention (CDC). (2011). *The Health Communicator's Social Media Toolkit.* [Viewed 3 July 2020]. Available from: https://www.cdc.gov/socialmedia/tools/guide lines/socialmediatoolkit.html

De Angelis, G., Wells, G.A., Davies, B., King, J., Shallwani, S.M., McEwan, J., Cavallo, S., Brosseau, L., (2018). The use of social media among health professionals to facilitate chronic disease self-management with their patients: a systematic review. *Digit Health.* **4**, 1–13.

DeBronkart, D., (2019). Remember the patients. *BMJ* [online]. **18**, 365: l1545. [Viewed 3 July 2020]. Available from: doi: https://doi.org/10.1136/bmj.l1545

Evans, W.D., (2016). *Social Marketing Research for Global Public Health: Methods and Technologies.* London: Oxford University Press.

Evers, K.E., (2006). eHealth Promotion: The Use of the Internet for Health Promotion. *American Journal of Health Promotion.* **4**(20), 1–7.

Farmer, A.D., Bruckner Holt, C.E., Cook, M.J., Hearing, S.D., (2009). Social networking sites: a novel portal for communication. *Postgraduate Medical Journal.* **85**(1007), 455–459.

Fattori, G., Artoni, P., Tedeschi, M., (2009). Choose Health in Food Vending Machines: Obesity Prevention and Healthy Lifestyle Promotion in Italy. In: H. Cheng, P. Kotler, N. Lee (Eds). *Social Marketing for Public Health: Global Trends and Success Stories.* Jones and Bartlett Publishers. pp. 149–170.

Foster, C., Richards, J., Thorogood, M., Hillsdon, M., (2013). Remote and Web 2.0 interventions for promoting physical activity. *Cochrane Database of Systematic Reviews.* [Viewed 3 July 2020]. Available from: https://www.cochranelibrary.com/cdsr/doi/10.1002/14651858.CD010395. pub2/full

Free, C., Knight, R., Robertson, S., Whittaker, R., Edwards, P., Zhou, W., Rodgers, A., (2011). Smoking cessation support delivered via mobile phone text messaging (txt2stop): a single-blind, randomised trial. *The Lancet.* **378**, 49–55.

Freire, P., (2018). *Pedagogy of the Oppressed: 50th Anniversary Edition.* Bloomsbury Academic.

Griffiths, J., Blair-Stevens, C., Thorpe, A., (2008). *Social marketing for health and specialised health promotion.* London: National Social Marketing Centre.

Hasman, L., (2011). An Introduction to Consumer Health Apps for the iPhone. *Journal of Consumer Health on the Internet.* **15**(4), 322–329.

Hastings, G., Domegan, C., (2018). *Social Marketing: Rebels with a Cause.* Oxford: Routledge.

Hesse, B.W., O'Connell, M., Augustson, E.M., Chou, W-Y.S., Shaikh, A.R., Rutten, F., (2011). Realizing the promise of Web 2.0: engaging community intelligence. *Journal of Health Communication* **16**, Suppl 1, 10–31.

Kaplan, A.M., Haenlein, M., (2010). Users of the world, unite! The challenges and opportunities of Social Media. *Business Horizons*. **53**(1), 59–68.

Kite, J., Foley, B.C., Grunseit, A.C., Freeman, B., (2016). Please like me: Facebook and public health communication. *PLoS One [online]*. [Viewed 3 July 2020]. Available from: https://dx.plos.org/10.1371/journal.pone.0162765

Korp, P., (2006). Health on the Internet: implications for health promotion. *Health Education Research*. **21**, 78–86.

Kotler, P., Zaltman, G., (1971). Social marketing: an approach to planned social change. *Journal of Marketing*. **35**, 3–12.

Laranjo, L., Arguel, A., Neves, A.L., Gallagher, A.M., Kaplan, R., Mortimer, N., (2015). The influence of social networking sites on health behavior change: a systematic review and meta-analysis. *Journal of the American Medical Informatics Association*. **22**(1), 243–256.

Laverack, G., (2019). *Public Health: Power, Empowerment and Professional Practice*. Red Globe Press.

Lee, N.R., Kotler, P., (2019). *Social Marketing: Behavior Change for Social Good*. SAGE Editor.

Maibach, E. W., Rothschild, M. L., Novelli, W. D., (2002). Social Marketing. In: K. Glanz, F. M. Lewis, B. Rimer (Eds). *Health Behavior and Health Education*. 3rd ed. San Francisco: Jossey-Bass. pp. 437–461.

McCreanor, T., Lyons, A., Griffin, C., Goodwin, I., Moewaka Barnes, H., Hutton, F., (2013). Youth drinking cultures, social networking and alcohol marketing: implications for public health. *Critical Public Health*. **23**, 110–120.

McDaid, David., Park, A., (2011). Online health: untangling the web. *London School of Economics*. [Viewed 3 July 2020]. Available from: https://www.researchgate.net/publication/232041614_Online_Health_Untangling_the_Web

Mesko, B., (2013). *Social media in clinical practice*. London: Springer-Verlag.

Neiger, B.L., Thackeray, R., Van Wagenen, S.A., West, J.H., Barnes, M.D., Fagen, M.C., (2012). Use of Social Media in Health Promotion: Purposes, Key Performance Indicators, and Evaluation Metrics. *Health promotion practice*. **3**, 159–64.

Nutbeam, D., (1988). Evaluating health promotion: progress, problems and solutions. *Health Promotion International*. **13**, 27–44.

Norman, C.D., (2009). Health promotion as a systems science and practice. *Journal of evaluation in clinical practice*. **15**, 868–872.

Public Health England (2018). Latest technology supports new mums to breastfeed. [Viewed 3 July 2020]. Available from: https://www.gov.uk/government/news/new-technology-supports-new-mums-to-breastfeed

Ramanadhan, S., Mendez, S.R., Rao, M., Viswanath, K., (2013). Social media use by community-based organizations conducting health promotion: a content analysis. *BMC Public Health*. **13** (1): 1129.

Raphael, D., Bryant, T., (2006). Maintaining population health in a period of welfare state decline: political economy as the missing dimension in health promotion theory and practice. *Promotion & Education*. **13**, 236–42.

Ratzan, S.C., (2011). Web 2.0 and Health Communication. *Journal of Health Communication*. **16**, 1–2.

Richardson, C.R., Buis, L.R., Janney, A.W., Goodrich, D.E., Sen, A., Hess, M.L., Mehari, K., (2010). An online community improves adherence in an internet-mediated walking program. Part 1: results of a randomized controlled trial. *Journal of Medical Internet Research*. **12**(4), e71.

Rietmeijer, C.A., McFarlane, M., (2009). Web 2.0 and beyond: risks for sexually transmitted infections and opportunities for prevention. *Current Opinion in Infectious Diseases*. **22**, 67–71.

Speller, V., Parish, R., Davison, H., Zilnyk, A., (2012). *The CompHP Professional Standards for Health Promotion Handbook*. Paris: IUHPE. [Viewed 3 July 2020]. Available from: https://www.iuhpe.org/images/PROJECTS/ACCREDITATION/CompHP_standards_handbook_final.pdf

Veinot, T.C., Campbell, T.R., Kruger, D., Grodzinski, A., Franzen, S., (2011). Drama and danger: the opportunities and challenges of promoting youth sexual health through online social networks. *AMIA Annual Symposium proceedings*. 1436–1445.

West, J.H., Hall, P.C., Hanson, C.L., Barnes, M.D., Giraud-Carrier, C., Barrett, J., (2012). There's an app for that: content analysis of paid health and fitness apps. *Journal of Medical Internet Research*. **14**(3), e72.

Thumberg, G., (2019). #SchoolStrike4Climate. [Viewed 3 July 2020]. Available from: https://www.facebook.com/732846497083173/posts/793441724356983?sfns=mo

Yoo, J.H., Kim, J., (2012). Obesity in the new media: a content analysis of obesity videos on YouTube. *Health Communication*. **27**, 86–97.

Young, S.D., Cumberland, W.G., Lee, S.J., Jaganath, D., Szekeres, G., Coates, T., (2013). Social networking technologies as an emerging tool for HIV prevention: a cluster randomized trial. *Annals of internal medicine*. **159**, 318–24.

Amy Yau

11 Chinese Consumers' Values and Perspectives of Sustainable Consumption

Introduction

The field of sustainable consumption has received increased attention over recent decades with the realisation that those in the developed world are living beyond the means of our planet (Creyer and Ross 1997; Harrison et al. 2008; Hendarwan 2002; Freestone and McGoldrick 2008; Sen and Bhattacharya 2001). However this is also becoming true for many economies such as China where consumers are adopting a more consumerist lifestyle, with seemingly little exploration of the negative effects caused as a result (Devinney et al. 2010; Martinsons et al. 1996). China is the second largest economy in the world (Crossley and Yao, 2021) but at the price of having the world's worst environmental standards (Wang and Duce 2010; Gamso 2018), and has been labelled as the 'smelliest, dirtiest, most ecologically unsound place in the world' (Martinsons et al. 1997, p. 278). China is reaching a tipping point of using an unsustainable level of resources, driven by rapid economic growth and mass consumption (Anderlini 2010). This goes hand-in-hand with an increase in disposable income and higher standards of living for many in Chinese society and shifts more Chinese consumers into the socio-demographic middle class, ironically most associated with sustainable consumption behaviour (Harrison et al. 2008). All of this makes China an especially pertinent context in which to study sustainability in consumption.

This chapter aims to address the scarcity of research on sustainability in Asia (Chan et al. 2008; Woods and Lamond 2011) and specifically China (Piron 2006). Research in this field typically retests Western scales of ethicality (Chan et al. 1998; 2008; Zhoa and Xu 2013) or responses to corporate social responsibility (Ramaswamy and Yeung 2009; Tian et al. 2011) amongst Chinese consumers at the expense of sensitivity to local cultural traditions (Piron, 2006; Wang and Lin 2009). Thus, previous research tends to view sustainability with Western-dominant hegemonic discourse, rather than from the ideology of those involved in the marketplace context. This sentiment has been reflected in work dealing with sustainability in China (e.g. Piron et al. 2006; Chan et al. 2008) as well as in mainstream consumer research (Arnould and Thompson 2005; Belk, 1988; Kozinets 2002) in which they have highlighted the potential misunderstandings and the ramifications of excluding cultural dimensions from the study of consumption habits. This danger is only exacerbated in a country as culturally distant from Western culture as China.

https://doi.org/10.1515/9783110659566-011

This chapter therefore explores the perspective of the Chinese consumer, their position as consumers and the cultural contexts in which behavioural patterns have formed and manifested, which in turn contributes to the socio-historical programming of their consumer lifestyle (Arnould and Thompson 2005). This research therefore addresses the scarcity of qualitative cultural studies in Chinese sustainability consumption, with the aim of providing a more culturally sensitive backdrop for future research into Chinese sustainable consumption.

Cultural Values and Sustainable Consumption

Culture is widely accepted by theorists as one of the underlying determinants of consumer behaviour (e.g. McCracken 1972; Boyd and Massey, 1972; Mooij 2003). Increasingly, as more research is undertaken, culture is seen to have a monumental influence on the values and lifestyle of individuals. Thus culture is ever changing in order to reflect movement as well as to maintain harmony within the society. Due to this connection and dynamism, individuals' psychological constructs change, and therefore, their consumption patterns (Triandis 1989). With this in mind, a need for cultural understanding of consumption and the effect of change is pertinent. Most Chinese cultural research has been conducted in the organisational environment (e.g. Ralston 1999) looking at ethical business values, (e.g. Lam 2003; Ip 2009) or business relationships (e.g. Hwang et al. 2009; Fan 2002). Some research has been undertaken regarding Chinese consumption and Confucian values, for example how Chinese Confucian values affect the consumption patterns of pirated CDs (Wan et al. 2009), travel and tourism (Mok and DeFrankco 2000), gift giving (Qian et al. 2007; Yau et al. 1999), luxury consumption (Wong and Ahuvia 1998), and compulsive buying (Jiang et al. 2009). Through these studies there emerges a new stream of research suggesting changes in the dominant Traditional Confucian Values (TVC) which have dominated Chinese behaviour for thousands of years (e.g. Wang and Lin 2009) to what we now term as Modern Confucian Values (MCV).

Sustainable consumption is an underdeveloped specialism of business and marketing ethics (Auger et al. 2003) with most research focusing on bad rather than good ethics; on customer dishonesty and unethical behaviour rather than on the potential of sustainable behaviour, consumer idealism and responsibility (Brinkmann and Peattie 2008). Schaefer and Crane (2005) and Brinkmann and Peattie (2008) both highlight that most of the sustainable consumption literature is limited to rational, psychological models of consumer behaviour and advocate the need to harness a more radical, holistic approach to exploring sustainable consumption. Amongst others, Foxall (1993) and Fukukawa (2003) criticise rational cognition approaches for isolating consumers from a wider socio-cultural context of consumption, leaving an often limited and overly sanitised body of theory around sustainable consumption that lacks practical significance and explanatory power.

Globalisation brings together consumers and businesses from around the world and an individual's culture has a profound effect on how they interpret ethics (Pitta et al. 1999). As Belk et al. (2005) assert, to study ethical choices without explicitly considering cultural context is not realistic. Therefore we see a compelling need to acknowledge that different regional/cultural values will dramatically effect what information is considered relevant in making sustainable consumption decisions. However, this is an area almost entirely explored from a Western moral perspective, with little exploration of what ethical or sustainable consumption means to the rest of the world.

There is a need to acknowledge relative differences in ethical dilemmas and mindsets from different cultures, because an individual's culture affects his/her ethical perspectives and decision-making (e.g. Ferrell and Gresham 1985; Hunt and Vitell 1986). Phau and Kea (2007) assert that certain values, ethical behaviours or moral principles considered to be conducive to the economic development for one country may not be for another. Thus, understanding the relationship between culture and ethics is seen as vital in order to better understand consumers and for managers to operate effectively and efficiently in the global market. Deng et al. (2006) purport that understanding sustainable consumption is directly related to the concept of culture. 'What life is and what life should be has set the standards for what is right and what is wrong, what is good and what is bad, what one can be and what one could be' (Christie et al. 2003, p. 264). These become unconscious or subconsciously accepted as 'right' and 'correct' by people who identify themselves as members of society (Leung and Rice 2002; Hofstede et al. 1990). The notion that different populations with specific social practices and cultural traits are likely to hold different values towards nature and the environment is therefore asserted by many (e.g. Bartels 1967; Singhapadki et al. 2001). Therefore different populations with diverse social practices and cultural traits are likely to hold different values or attitudes towards sustainability (Bartels 1967; Singhapadki et al. 2001). This means that data collection vehicles on sustainable consumption from a non-Chinese cultural perspective are highly circumspect and information aimed at increasing sustainable consumption is often unreliable when extrapolated from 'Western' viewpoints.

Traditional Chinese Confucian Values

Traditional Chinese cultural values are based on notions of interpersonal relationship and social orientation. These values are highly influenced by the work of Confucius (Fan 2000; Yau 1988; Wang and Lin 2009). Thus this study uses the term

'Traditional Confucian Values' (TCV) to account for this. Woods and Lamond (2011) outline six TCV prerequisites for being human, which are (1) benevolence (*ren*); the most vital in Confucian philosophy and means to 'love your people' and that one loves his people and helps others to take their stand in that he himself wishes to take his stand (Lin and Ho 2009). (2) Righteousness (*yi*); the opposite of the word 'profit' or 'gain' (*li*) (Lin and Ho 2009). (3) Ritual propriety (*li*); to follow the ancient rituals and sacrifices that were a part of life in the time of Confucius; however, to broaden the idea, it includes the importance of following the social norms of polite conduct when interacting with others (Woods and Lamond, 2011), which was believed to build self-regulation (Cheng 2004). (4) Wisdom (*zhi*); the learning and ability to perceive situations accurately and make correct judgments (Romar 2002), wherein it is part of self-regulation. (5) Trustworthiness (*xin*); loyalty to moral principles and to ritual and social rules. In addition to that, it also refers to loyalty to one's superiors in hierarchical relationships; however, the emphasis is on standing by one's word, or being a dependable support for others (Woods and Lamond 2011), and lastly (6) Filial Piety (*xiao*); to serve and obey parents and respect ancestors with all of one's capacity (Zhang 2000) and serves as foundational among virtues of human relationships (Yao 2000). The values in various literatures are defined with nuanced meanings and of varying importance. For instance, Fan (2000) provided a list of 71 values within eight broad categories. However, the ones most related to this consumption study are referred to in Table 11.1.

Table 11.1: Relevant Confucian Values Discussed in Literature.

Important Values	
Self-regulation	Directs the degree of moral self-control, which is the key to most of the values and within that, social consciousness, face and moderation directs this self-control (Kindle 1985).
Face (*Mianzi*)	*Mianzi* is the embodiment of prestige, achieved through success in life and ostentatious acts (Ang and Leong 2000; Ho 1976; Hu 1944) also known as '*materialistic face*' (Durvasala and Lysonski 2010).
Face (*Lien*)	*Lien* is society's confidence in the integrity of the individual's moral character (Ho 1976), which is also seen as the '*moral face*' (Durvasala and Lysonski 2010). This moral control leads to the process of governing one's behaviour towards the self-cultivation and refinement of one's character (Tu 1998).
Man Nature Orientation/ Relationship to Nature	Non-duality of humanity and cosmos and concern for harmony rather than conflict (Vachon 1983). *Tao* (the way), relates to fatalism/karma and harmony between man and nature.

An emphasis needs to be placed on the two facets of face (*mianzi* and *lien*). They are a well-researched notion within Chinese business ethics (Ang and Leong 2000), and a major principle in understanding Chinese consumption practices. If we focus on *lien* (the moral face), it builds on the notion that Chinese people have an 'oriental' worldview drawing on a collectivist orientation and deep concern for how others perceive their personal integrity and virtue as a member of this collectivist society (Ip 2003; Jenkins 2002; Piron 2006). The collectivist orientation of Chinese culture has been defined as consistent with support for corporate social responsibility activities (Ramaswamy and Yeung 2009; Tian et al. 2011) and the Chinese consumers' social sensitivity and 'other-orientation' (Bao et al. 2003; Li and Su 2007; Yau 1988) leads to a desire to avoid ethical conflicts (Gabrenya and Hwang 1996; Yau 1988). This is theorised to direct consumption behaviour and attitudes towards the environment such as the Cambridge sustainability research digest's (2007) assessment that found 83–86% of Chinese citizens are willing to take action/pay more or pay higher taxes to ensure the restoration of the environment. However, Yeung (1998) found that social sensitivity means the majority of Chinese are unwilling to take active roles in environmental protection where it conflicts with personal freedom, physical effort, expression of opinions or influencing others is involved. Similarly, others have suggested the material face (*mianzi*) counteracts this and supports a culture of CD piracy (Wan et al. 2009) or counterfeit goods consumption (Chan et al. 1998) and an appetite for luxury products and named brands regardless of other (potentially unsustainable) credentials (Tse 1996; Wong and Ahuvia 1998). Bao et al. (2003) go as far as to suggest that the array of traditional values limits the openness of Chinese consumers to new products, which invariably would include any attempts to launch sustainable brand variants of habitual consumption products.

Many early researchers attribute the low engagement with sustainable behaviour to be caused by a lack of education surrounding sustainable consumption (Martinsons et al. 1996; Yam-Tam and Chan 1998; Yeung 1998). On the other hand, more recent research supports the assertion that TCV might actually hinder the growth of sustainable consumption even in the event of high information availability (Wan et al. 2009; Wang and Lin 2009). Others even suggest that TCV are actually in decline in the face of the 'Westernisation' of China and are becoming less relevant (Li 2006; Wei and Pan 1999).

Even though values are relatively stable within contexts, several recent studies found that ethical perspectives of Mainland Chinese now reflect a mixed influence of Confucian values and an emerging market ethic (Erdener 1998; Redfern and Crawford 2004). Unlike the older generations of Chinese who were subjugated to the ideals of communism under the Marxist dictum 'from each according to his ability, to each according to his needs', the new generation has been allowed to embrace modernity (Durvasala and Lysonski 2010). Wang and Lin (2009) provide a seminal review of the changing nature of traditional values and we will not replicate that discussion here. However, we can point to a number of areas such as a growing tendency toward individualism (McEwen et al. 2006), materialism (Swanson 1995), and hedonistic consumption (Wang et al. 2000), which are starting to reshape the Traditional Confucian Values (TCV) to a new Modern Confucian Value (MCV) set.

Wang and Lin (2009) purport that Western influence has reshaped TCV, but they dispute that this is a Westernisation of Chinese culture. They suggest that there is clear demarcation between the young Chinese and their forbears, but that 'Chinese consumers express individualism (materialism and hedonism) in their own way' (Wang and Lin 2009). They may appear on the surface to be replicating a Western consumption pattern, but the roots for why they are doing so, what it means to them, and how it is enacted will be uniquely Chinese. In fact, Pan (1990) notes that, even when modern Chinese society feels the full impact of Western culture, many individuals still immerse themselves in their pride of national culture. Durvasala and Lysonski (2010) assert that Confucianism is viewed as a philosophy that can persist as a countervailing force to the social and ecological degradation and rampant materialism instilled in modern Chinese life. Understanding these Modern Confucian Values (MCV) and how they interrelate with consumers' views on sustainability and sustainable consumption is therefore the most important starting point in developing an understanding of the future for sustainable consumption in China. This MCV may go some way to explaining why existing research on sustainable consumption in China tends to over-estimate the reality of consumer behaviour towards sustainable consumption, but also points towards fruitful areas for its future development. This paper therefore aims to address the question of how, in the midst of rapid change, do young Chinese consumers relate to Confucian values and how it relates to the propensity to consume in a more conscious and sustainable fashion.

Methodology

Research within ethics (e.g. Fishbein and Ajzen 1975; Hunt and Vitell 1986; Chatzidaki et al. 2007; Carrigan and Attalla 2001) and specifically Chinese ethics (Chan et al. 1998; Chan 1999; Lee 2008; Yeung 1998) have mainly been quantitative, often reusing Western scales. The use of qualitative inquiry, which is neglected in Chinese consumer ethics research, is adopted within this study. It is suitable for new and exploratory research (Ghauri and Grønhaug 2002), and gaining descriptive accounts of individuals' attitudes, perceptions, beliefs, views and feelings, along with the meanings and interpretations from the participants' perspectives (Hakim 1994). When looking at ethical consumption, many have reported the evident attitude-behaviour gap/word-deed gap, such as De Pelsmacker et al. (2005), Boulstridge and Carrigan (2000), Shaw and Clarke (1999). This gap highlights precarious implications in developing managerial action based on a weak relationship between what consumers say and what they do. We have gone beyond recognising that this is evident;

what is needed is to look at the underlying causes of this phenomenon. Researchers need to dig deeper into the consumer's consciousness, assessing different aspects and philosophies rather than explicitly asking if they are ethical consumers, or whether they would pay more for an ethical product. The study adopts the Attitude Specificity principle (Hoyer and MacInnis 2001) that suggests the more specific the attitude is to a particular behaviour, the more likely the attitude is associated with the behaviour. This contributes to a more accurate picture of consumers' ethical behaviours and mitigates the attitude-behaviour dichotomy. Furthermore, due to the potentially sensitive nature of the role of ethics and values, interpretivism mitigates the predicament of social desirability (Devinney et al. 2010), which is prevalent in ethics research.

Taking into consideration China's past political and social ramifications that may impact consumption lifestyles, young (20–26 years old) Mainland Chinese consumers served as the sample. The participants were chosen in order to gain insight into consumer urbanites studying in the UK, suggesting the participants to be educated, relatively wealthy, and to be the future trendsetters in China. 43 interviews were conducted in tandem with the extensive literature review as part of an iterative, inductive and interactional process with simultaneous analysis, and emergent interpretation (Goulding 2005). In the interview guide, many sustainable practices and the purchasing of ethical products were considered, and open questions were asked thus allowing them to go into depth as to which category interested the participant the most. These were based loosely around the behaviour of their parents, in contrast to how they view their lifestyle, the changing nature of Chinese society, topics of recycling, buying from ethical sources, reusing, and reducing consumption. Tools borrowed from grounded theory (Glaser and Strauss 1967; Spiggle 1994) were used to explore and interpret the data. Phenomenological analysis through categorising and co-axial thematic coding (Dittmar and Drury 2000) provided a framework to guide the process of transcribing, coding and mapping, which brought out the following findings.

The Reshaping of Traditional Cultural Values

The purpose of the research was to explore young Chinese consumers' perspectives of the changing values and their perspective on sustainable consumption in China. Part of this process involves reconceptualising TCV in line with the modern changes that have been impacting young, affluent Chinese consumers. Many changes were discussed, values that were once integral to the Chinese lifestyle have been increasingly dismissed or interpretations of values have evolved to encapsulate more individualised life experiences fuelled by newfound opportunities. As seen in the data, young individuals in China are very aware and knowledgeable about traditional values, but suggest they do not play a part in daily lives of the younger generation.

From the data we see that Chinese values and society are perceived to have fundamentally shifted. The modern young Chinese consumers separate themselves both culturally and socially from their parents; a participant said 'Chinese people used to be honest but nowadays it's how to make money and how to make profits. The situation is not very good' (JY), and another participant spoke about the burgeoning differences of a collectivistic society and the changes to a more exciting life instilled with more individualistic values:

> We focus on what we like, focus on our own interests. We are braver than our parents. We know how to pursue our own dream. And for our parents, maybe they consider a lot of things. They neglected their own interest, their own dream. Maybe their life was stable but lacked excitement. They do not want to challenge a lot. (AG)

This speaks to the lack of a collectivist orientation and virtue as a member of this collectivist society (Ip 2003; Jenkins 2002; Piron 2006). In addition, shifts in being moderate, where saving money and being conservative with finances were a valued trait. This has shifted towards an appreciation of more risky behaviour:

> Chinese people are afraid of some complexity and seeing what could happen, so they tend to save the money in the bank. They do not like to invest and they like to have money in their hands. That is the feeling especially with the older generation like my parents and my parent's parents, they do not like to invest. (QL)

These points relating to the changes in values were made apparent by pointing out a myriad of fundamental shifts in consumer behaviour:

> In the older generation, they think that because something makes them feel full or makes them feel warm, it is enough. They don't care about the kind of clothes and they don't care about fashion. But now people just want to be more fashionable so they are buying products even though some of them do not work or they stop wearing them just because they think at that time it is fashionable, but about one month later, these clothes are not in fashion anymore and they just bin them. (KW)

> Some people are really rich and hold 80% of all the finance in the whole country and others are quite poor and they start to spend their money. In the last twenty years, people have changed a lot, like their daily lives. People have started buying things that they want and not what they need anymore. It is like they really have no sense in China. Especially rich people, they buy things as if they are crazy. (AZ)

The traditional values of frugality and saving are fundamentally undermined for young Chinese consumers. We see them being replaced with mass-consumerist materialism, evident in Western markets. In today's society, they witness Chinese consumers buying with their wants in mind, rather than needs, and aligning the consumption with fashion and status signalling to others.

In the interviews, the need to be filial along with desire to not waste money was shown, 'I would say I am a traditional girl, which is a girl who really respects her parents' opinion. I mean, when I have some views different from my parents, I would not argue with them. I will communicate with them and we will have a common understanding on a certain issue after communicating' (AG). Participants spoke about consumers maintaining a collectivistic attitude where the opinions of friends and family are most important, for instance 'a lot of customers are influenced by their friends and family. If they say a product is good and ask you to try, you will try. You believe your family or friends much more than a stranger' (SH). However, most of the interviews involved discussion about excess, overspending and unnecessary consumption and this would often be at the expense of the parents:

> Our parents always worked so hard. They were not afraid of very hard and difficult things, it has changed a lot. Our generation is not very responsible I think. My mother always thinks that I am not very responsible. The youth buy cars by borrowing money from the bank and it's my mother's generation that pays it off. They have credit now but they still want their parents to pay it off. (YY)

The rise of mass-consumerism and the development of a greater individualism in China have been attributed to the on-going consequences of the one-child policy. This is often termed 'China's little emperors syndrome', or '4-2-1 syndrome', denoting the amount of love the child receives, i.e. four grandparents and two parents for each child (Jun 2000). The dependence on the parents and the provision for the children within the family is also seen in the interview excerpts below:

> My parents would remind me, they would say, do not spend a lot of money, remind me to save money. They always remind me of that. But I just forget when I go shopping. Then as usual I go shopping, buy clothes and buy everything I want and my parents say, "Okay, if you like it, then buy it". (CZ)

> Now, I am already 23 and I do not have a job and my parents will pay for my living cost every month. They will give me money. I do not know whether your parents provide that but my German friend told me that when he was 18, his parents did not give him any money and he would go out to have one or two part-time jobs to earn money. But in China, if you do not have a job although you are 30 or 40, your parents will give you money. (AZ)

We find that despite family playing a pivotal role in influencing the type of consumption, it has little influence on the volume of consumption. We therefore find that young people in China sought to primarily satisfy their independent dreams, regardless of whether it contrasted with the views of family members.

Face, Moderation and Materialism

Both elements of face (*mianzi* and *lien*) are deemed important and remain integral in Chinese society. The participants illustrate the continuance of the notion of moderation in China in many aspects of daily life, but this does not refute the notions of rampant materialism. The distinction lies in the possibility of gaining *mianzi* through the conspicuous display of luxury purchases and lifestyle, whereas moderation lies in the mundane consumption, essentially the private consumption where there is less need to gain *mianzi*, and by avoiding overconsumption, *lien* is not lost.

> They [wealthier Chinese consumers] just buy nice cars and other luxury things to show off. They just care about that, just because they have money. (JY)

> If someone wants to find a boyfriend, the first thing she thinks about isn't if they love him or not, I think they will put this at the end. The first thing most girls will think about is whether they're rich or not, smart or not, his family, and so on. The last thing is about liking him or not. She isn't wrong sometimes, you do need some material, material first, then love. (SH)

> If someone is earning 1000 yuan a month, they will say they earn 2000 yuan. If they can't afford an iPhone, maybe they will borrow from friends and parents so they can show that they are better than you and they have a good life. (MQ)

Today *mianzi* is not bestowed upon them through what was traditionally seen as modest and reserved acts and behaviour, but prestige and success are brought to the consumer merely by having the latest consumer products. However, we see through the interviews that most participants consider materialistic desires (*mianzi*) e.g. buying nice cars, luxury goods etc. to be associated with being in contrast to one's moral standing (*lien*). There is therefore a line to tread for young Chinese between putting forward a good face through materialism (*mianzi*), and maintaining good moral standing through people's confidence in their integrity (*lien*).

Mianzi supports the development of materialism and materialism has provided physical manifestations of *mianzi*. This has in many ways replaced the traditional need for good ostentatious acts with ostentatious consumption. However, *lien* moderates the consumption, for instance in the conspicuous and luxury market so that drivers of *lien* such as frugality and moderation in private consumption can offset the costs of conspicuous consumption in public. There is therefore space for sustainable consumption in this interplay:

> If ethical products were developed as a status product, it would work. If you advertise ethical products as a sign of being well educated, I would want to say yes, I am well educated, I am a person who's different to others, I can realise something which other people can't. If you do some advertising to the whole society, people think yes, they will be better than others, different to lower class people, this can be a way to encourage ethical consumption. (RD)

In this way sustainable consumption can conform to both *mianzi* and *lien*, it is conspicuous yet morally reaffirming. However, once again this may be potentially imparting inappropriate Westernised views of virtuosity.

Modern Chinese Values and Sustainable Consumption

The participants do not speak of a Westernisation of Chinese consumption habits but an embracing of post-modernity with an underpinning of Chinese values. Our interest here is to see whether the values of today's young Chinese consumers provide opportunity for a growth in sustainable consumption. We find it is the interplay between face and filial piety alongside materialism and individuality where the success or failure of sustainable consumption is likely to play out.

For a start, the interpretation of what is sustainable is clearly very different in modern Chinese culture than we would potentially view it in the West. One of the most enlightening quotes was from 'LZ' where she stated:

> Yes, I read something that most clothing is made in the poor areas in China, I think about these poor conditions. Yes, so every time when I buy clothes, I will wash it before I wear it for the first time. (LZ)

In response to the media exposure of sweatshop labour we do not find revulsion but pragmatism regarding personal interaction with the product. This interpretation of labour rights was very clearly an area in which Chinese consumers simply do not see the main moral issue, as seen in the excerpts below:

> I heard about this, they have to do this, businesses cannot afford great working conditions, China is a developing country, people are still willing to work in these terrible conditions, it's better than having no job. (CA)

> China has a big, huge population. I heard a story of a Chinese software company. The workers work for 13 hours without sleeping. And I think the main reason is that China has a huge population. And may be 50% of people do not have a good education. They can only get some manufacturing job, go to the factories and to some, this kind of job is easy and they do not need you to think about it, they just need you to do it. (QA)

> Old clothes, I just throw them away. I don't like to give them to charity because if you give clothes to charity they would give clothes to the poor countries, which just ruins the industry there. If they do not give clothes to the poor countries, people there still have job opportunities to produce clothes by themselves. But if you give them free products and they do not have to produce them anymore, they will lose their jobs and everything gets worse. So I do not give them to charity. (SP)

> People may not pay extra for ethical goods, people will just laugh and think you're stupid, why did you pay more for that? (JY)

However, the interpretation of more environmentally sustainable initiatives were different yet again when the participants would suggest that Chinese consumers have habits that on the surface are deemed ethical, for instance, bringing reusable grocery bags, recycling, and reducing food waste. However, the reasoning behind these actions is more for monetary justifications:

> Everyone brings their own bags to go shopping, but it is because there's a one Yuan charge for a plastic bag. (LZ)

> I don't think my mum has got the same standard to protect the environment and recycle, it's just that she can earn money, she never throws empty bottles in the rubbish, because that is like throwing money away. (SA)

> People will recycle food or they don't waste food by eating the same meal again. Sometimes the vegetables are starting to mould, but they will still eat it . . . people don't think it's a way to protect the environment when they eat mouldy food, in China they don't think it's an ethical thing to do, it's just a habit. (ZI)

Chinese consumers may already have habits conducive to sustainable consumption, but it may not be on a moral or ethical basis, but rather based on pragmatic life reasoning. The area of recycling appears to create strong resonance with increased awareness for doing so; for instance one participant said 'I do think to recycle, sometimes other people consider recycling. We just know we should recycle.' (SH), and this is guided by conforming to more collectivistic attitudes and governmental guidance:

> More people are now recycling, actually the government is promoting ethical behaviours to Chinese people, the government want us to recycle, save more water, use less paper, through advertising. (SY)

> Health is one factor, but environmental too. My family thinks the environment is really important, they have a habit of recycling everything, papers, bottles, they like to buy natural things from the open market, sometimes they go to supermarket but they try to find organic produce. It starts because of personal reasons, like being cost conscious; now I know being a vegetarian will help the environment and protect the animals. The plants don't need a lot of artificial things like animals, it will be harmful to the animals, so it's not environmentally friendly. Animals are one of the members to the environment, we need to respect that. (YY)

Overall, along with more pragmatic and traditional approaches to consumption, we see sustainable consumption behaviour being aligned with personal as well as rationalisations of the harmonious man-nature orientation.

Discussion

It is evident that Chinese consumers now reflect a mixed influence of traditional Confucian values and an emerging market ethic as found by Redfern and Crawford (2004). During times of social and economic changes, Chinese cultural value systems have recently undergone phenomenal transformation (Shively and Shively 1972; Yau 1988). In the data, there was little evidence of the 'oriental world-view' (Chan and Lau 2000; Jenkins 2002; Ip 2003), highlighting the possible exaggerated influences that Confucian values bestow. Despite the changes, Yang's (1979) findings implicated that some of the traditional Chinese values were still held by young Chinese people (Yang 1979; Yau 1988) and a closer look at recent changes shows that these values e.g. filial piety, moderation, face, still permeate Chinese consumers' lifestyles. However, the prominence of materialism and individualism, influenced by the prevailing force of face suggests how convincing and dominant modern consumerist ideologies are; a few decades of economic reforms may be superseding 2000 years of Chinese moral doctrine.

There is evidence of rampant materialism amongst the middle-upper class of Chinese consumers, which is often seen to be at odds with sustainable consumption. However, Harrison et al. (2008) suggest that wealthier consumers can realise the desire to consume ethically once their primary needs have been met. Another point is that the value of individualism is seen to be increasing. This implies that these values will undergo more crucial changes, where the philosophies of ethics will be attained from many avenues that may possibly diverge from traditional values. With this in mind, the Chinese youth who readily embrace Western values would possibly be more attuned to comprehend values and ethics that are permeating the West that still have yet to reach mass concern in China, such as certain human rights issues, democracy, or in the context of consumption, issues of fair trade, sweatshop labour and eco-friendly products. In regards to the frugality/moderation value on more everyday consumption behaviour, the study sees consumers' actions resonating sustainable consumption, however this was largely attributed to having waste reduction and monetary justifications rather than justifications of sustainability. If ethical consumption is to be marketed in China, certain values aligning with face (*lien* and *mianzi*) could be considered further.

Conclusions for Sustainable Consumption in China

There are implications of growing individualism, and both elements of face (*mianzi* and *lien*) are deemed important and remain fundamental in Chinese society. There is a continuance of the notion of moderation in China in many aspects of daily life, but this does not refute the notions of rampant materialism in consumption concerning the public sphere. On that account, it seems that order and chaos are not contradictory, with each value holding a place, and fulfilling its purpose in consumers' life goals. Regardless of the seemingly contrasting values, there are managerial implications for those wanting to promote sustainable consumption in China. Since filial piety is strong, the younger generation are still looking upon their parents and elders for information. Sustainability marketers, practitioners and social policy makers cannot assume that the younger generation is the main and only target for new product information and promotions of behavioural change. This is due to the opportunity for transferring information and social behaviour from the older to the younger generations, which can still gain traction. On the other side, reverse socialisation, in which the younger generation teaches and pushes for change towards their elders can be harnessed due to the existing tight knit bond. The adoption of individualism is increasing and the philosophy of global ideals and ethics from other avenues cannot be undermined. Knowing this, it highlights the fundamental role that Western education has on the impact of setting the foundations of critical knowledge and education of sustainable consumption. Thus, Western education should hold a responsibility in supporting this knowledge transfer to increase the consideration of certain ethics. The concepts of face, both *mianzi* and *lien*, play critical roles in Chinese rationales of consumption. Marketers and policymakers should emphasise social consciousness and losing one's *mianzi* through unsustainable consumption behaviour. This can be utilised together with the provision of social avenues to conspicuously recycle or buy environmentally friendly products to develop their *lien*, especially in high visibility public areas. Conspicuous sustainable consumption could promote individual *lien* by advocating sustainable behaviour as indicators of wealth, education and of a righteous character.

By tapping into the frugality value, financial incentives in policies or social practice may result in immediate action and behaviour change amongst frugal consumers, eradicating the need for the slow process of nudging consumers to develop the appropriate ethical attitude and intentions. Through developing more systematic incentives for action, it can then build into habitual behaviour where they may later act ethically regardless of monetary enticement. Despite the maintenance of values concerning moderation and frugality, we see materialism in public arenas of consumption. The study recommends that marketers need to evoke appeals of being an ethical consumer by highlighting emotions of self-gratification and status, possibly promoted with unusual environmentally conscious products and conspicuous packaging. The overall association of ethical induced consumption behaviour should align with actions belonging to consumers amongst societies 'finest', the 'Chinese ethical self- actualisers' who are at the top of the achievement ladder; those who have achieved and acquired everything else that other people aspire towards.

This chapter addresses the gap of considering the renegotiations of traditional Confucian values taking place in modern China and how this affects the prospect of sustainable consumption. Its purpose is to fill a predominately-unexplored domain and cover the issues broadly, and thus the limitation lies in covering the breadth of the issue and may limit the comprehension of complex phenomena. Further research could delve into specific measures and variables addressing Chinese values and the perception of ethical consumption.

References

Arnould, E and Thompson, C. (2005). Consumer Culture Theory (CCT): Twenty Years of Research. *The Journal of Consumer Research*, 31(4),868–882.

Anderlini, J. (2010). China's growth model 'unsustainable' Financial Times, (accessed 11 June 2011), available at http://www.ft.com/cms/s/0/f38e08ce-0e84-11e0-b9f1-00144feabdc0. html#axzz1LExpbn6Y

Ang, S., & Leong, S. (2000). Out of the mouths of babes: Business ethics and youths in Asia. *Journal of Business Ethics*, 28(2), 129–144.

Auger, P., Burke, P., Devinney, T. M., and Louviere, J. J. (2003). What will consumers pay for social product features? *Journal of Business Ethics*, 42(3), 281–304.

Bartels, R. (1967). A Model for Ethics in Marketing. *Journal of Marketing* 31(1),20–26.

Bao, Y., K. Z. Zhou and C. Su (2003). Face Consciousness and Risk Aversion: Do They Affect Consumer Decision-Making? *Psychology & Marketing*, 20(8),733–755.

Belk, R. (1988) Possessions and the Extended Self. *Journal of Consumer Research*, 15(2),139–168.

Belk, R. W., Devinney, T. and Eckhardt, G. (2005). Consumer Ethics Across Culture. *Consumption Markets and Culture*, 8(3) 275–289.

Brinkmann, J., & Peattle, K. (2008). Consumer ethics research: reframing the debate about consumption for good. *Electronic Journal of Business Ethics and Organization Studies*, 13(1) 22–31.

Boulstridge, E. and M. Carrigan (2000). Do Consumers Really Care About Corporate Responsibility? Highlighting the Attitude-Behaviour Gap. *Journal of Communication Management*, 4(4),355–368.

Boyd, P. R. and Massey, W. (1972). *Marketing Management*, McGraw-Hill Education.

Cambridge Sustainability Research Digest (2007). (accessed December 2011), available at www.cpi. cam.ac.uk.

Carrigan, M. and Attalla, A. (2001). The Myth of the Ethical Consumer – Do Ethics Matter in Purchase Behaviour? *Journal of Consumer Marketing*, 18(7),560–577.

Chan, R.Y.K. and Lau, L.B.Y. (2000). Antecedents of green purchase: A survey in China. *Journal of Consumer Marketing*, 17(4),338–57.

Chan, A., S. Wong and P. Leung (1998). Ethical Beliefs of Chinese Consumers in Hong Kong. *Journal of Business Ethics*, 17, 1163–1170.

Chan, R. Y. K. (1999). Environmental attitudes and behavior of consumers in China: Survey findings and implications. *Journal of International Consumer Marketing*, 11, 25–52.

Chan, R., Wong, Y. and Leung, T. (2008). Applying Ethical Concepts to the Study of "Green" Consumer Behavior: An Analysis of Chinese Consumers Intentions to Bring their Own Shopping Bags. *Journal of Business Ethics*, 79, 469–481.

Cheng, C. Y. (2004). A Theory of Confucian Selfhood: Self- Cultivation and Free Will in Confucian Philosophy., in K. L. Shun and D. B. Wong (eds.), Confucian Ethics: A Comparative Study of Self, Autonomy, and Community (Cambridge University Press, UK), 124–147.

Creyer, E. and Ross, W. (1997). The Influence of Firm Behaviour on Purchase Intention: Do consumer Really Care about Business Ethics. Journal of Consumer Marketing, 14(6),421–432.

Crossley, G. and Yao, K. (2021) Reuters, (accessed 12 February 2021), available at https://www. reuters.com/article/china-economy-gdp/chinas-economy-picks-up-speed-in-fourth-quarter-ends-2020-in-solid-shape-after-covid-19-shock-idINKBN29N04C

Chatzidakis, A., Hibbert, S. and Smith, A. P. (2007). Why People Don't Take Their Concerns About Fair Trade to the Supermarket: The Role of Neutralisation. *Journal of Business Ethics*, 74, 89–100.

Christie, R. and Geis, F. (1970). Studies in Machiavellianism. New York: Academic Press.

Christie, P. M. J., Kwon, I. W. G., Stoeberl, P. A., & Baumhart, R. (2003). A cross-cultural comparison of ethical attitudes of business managers: India Korea and the United States. *Journal of Business Ethics*, 46(3), 263–287.

De Pelsmacker, P., Driesen, L. and Rayp. G. (2005). Do Consumers Care about Ethics? Willingness to Pay for Fair-Trade Coffee. *Journal of consumer affairs*, 39(2),363–385.

Deng, J., G. Walker, and G. Swinnerton. 2006. A comparison of environmental values and attitudes between Chinese in Canada and Anglo-Canadians. Environment and Behavior, 38 (1), 22–47.

Devinney, T. M., Auger. P., Eckhardt. G. M. (2010). *The Myth of the Ethical Consumer*. Cambridge University Press.

Dittmar, H. and Drury, J. (2000). Self-image-Is it the Bag? A qualitative comparison between "ordinary" and "excessive" consumers, *Journal of Economic Psychology*, 21(2),109–142.

Durvasula, S. and Steven Lysonski, S. (2010). Money, money, money – how do attitudes toward money impact vanity and materialism? – the case of young Chinese consumers. *Journal of Consumer Marketing*, 27(2) 169–179.

Erdener, C. B. (1998). Confucianism and Business Ethics in Contemporary China. *International Journal of Management*, 15(1),72–78.

Fan, Y. (2000). A classification of Chinese Culture. *Cross Cultural Management An International Journal*, 7(2), 3–10.

Fan, Y. (2002). Ganxi's consequences: Personal gains at social cost. *Journal of Business Ethics*, 38(4), 371–380.

Ferrell, O. C. and Gresham, L. G. (1985). A Contingency Framework for Understanding Ethical Decision Making in Marketing, *Journal of Marketing*, 49, 87–96.

Fishbein, M. and Ajzen, I. (1975). *Belief, Attitude, Intention, and Behaviour: An Introduction to Theory and Research*, Addison-Wesley: Reading.

Foxall, G. (1993). Situated Consumer Behaviour: a behavioural interpretation of purchase and consumption. *Research in Consumer Behaviour*, 6, 113–152.

Freestone, O. M. and McGoldrick, P. J. (2008). *Motivations of the Ethical Consumer. Journal of Business Ethics*,79, 445–467.

Fukukawa, K. (2003). A Theoretical Review of Business and Consumer Ethics Research: Normative and Descriptive Approaches, *The Marketing Review*, 3, 381–401.

Gabrenya, W.K. Jr. and Hwang, K.K. (1996). Chinese social interaction: Harmony and hierarchy on the good earth. In M. H. Bond (Ed.), *The handbook of Chinese Psychology* (pp. 309–321). Hong Kong: Oxford University Press.

Gamso, J. (2018). Is China Worsening the Developing World's Environmental Crisis, accessed on 17th November, 2020), available at https://theconversation.com/is-china-worsening-the-developing-worlds-environmental-crisis-100284.

Ghauri, P.N. and Grønhaug, K. (2002). *Research Methods in Business Studies: A Practical Guide*, 2nd ed, London, Financial Times Prentice-Hall.

Glaser, B. and Strauss, A. (1967). *The Discovery of Grounded Theory: Strategies for Qualitative Research*, Aldine, Chicago, IL.

Goulding, C. (2005). Grounded theory, ethnography and phenomenology: A comparative analysis of three qualitative strategies for marketing research, *European Journal of Marketing*, 39(3/4) 294–308.

Hakim, C. (1994), *Research Design: Strategies and Choices in the Design of Social Research*, London: Routledge.

Harrison R, Newholm T, Shaw D (2008). *The Ethical Consumer*, Sage: London.

Helm, A. (2004). Cynics and Skeptics: Consumer Dispositional Trust, *Advances in Consumer Research*, 31, 345–351.

Hendarwan, E. (2002). Seeing Green, *Global Cosmetic Industry*,170(5), 16–18

Ho, D. Y. (1976). On the concept of face. *American Journal of Sociology*, 81(4) 867–884.

Hofstede, G., Neuijen, B., Ohayv, D. and Sanders, G. (1990). Measuring organizational cultures: a qualitative and quantitative study across twenty cases, *Administrative Science Quarterly*, 35, 285–316.

Hoyer, W. D. and MacInnis, D. J. (2001). *Consumer Behaviour*, Boston: Houghton Mifflin Company.

Hu, H.C. (1944). The Chinese concept of face. *American Anthropologist, 46*. 45–64.

Hunt, S. and Vitell. S. (1986). A General Theory of Marketing Ethics', *Journal of Macromarketing*, 6, 5–16.

Hwang, D. B., Golemon, P. L., Chen, Y., Wang, T. S., & Hung, W. S. (2009). Guanxi and business ethics in Confucian society today: An empirical case study in Taiwan. *Journal of Business Ethics*, 89(2), 235–250.

Ip, Y. (2003). The marketability of eco-products in China's affluent cities A case study related to the use of insecticide: The marketability of eco-products. *Management of Environmental Quality: An International Journal*, 14(5), 577–589.

Ip, P. K. (2009). Is Confucianism good for business ethics in China? *Journal of Business Ethics*, 88(3), 463–476.

Jenkins, T. N. (2002). Chinese Traditional Thought and Practice: Lesson for an Ecological Economics Worldview. *Ecological Economics*, 40, 39–52.

Jiang, L., An, Y.,Shen, S. and Jin, W. (2009). The influence of money attitudes on young Chinese consumers' compulsive buying. *Young Consumers: Insight and Ideas for Responsible Marketers*, 10(2), 98–109.

Jun, J (2000). *Feeding China's Little Emperors: Food, Children and Social Change*, Stanford University Press, Stanford: California.

Kindle, I. (1982). A Partial Theory of Chinese Consumer Behaviour: Marketing Strategy Implications. *Hong Kong Journal of Business Management*, 1, 97–109.

Kozinets, R. V. (2002). The field behind the screen: using netnography for marketing research in online communities. *Journal of Marketing Research*, 39 (1), 61–72.

Lam, K. C. J. (2003). Confucian business ethics and the economy. *Journal of Business Ethics*, 43 (1–2), 153–162.

Lee, K. 2008. "Opportunities for green marketing: young consumers Opportunities for green marketing." Marketing Intelligence & Planning 26 (6): 573–586.

Leung, C. and Rice, J. (2002). Comparison of Chinese-Australian and Anglo-Australian environmental attitudes and behavior. *Social Behavior and Personality*, 30, 251–262.

Li, Q. (2006). PhD students say 'No' to Christmas. (China Daily, 21 December), available at http://www.chinadaily.com.cn/china/2006-12/21/content_764912.htm

Li, J. J. and C. Su (2007). How Face Influences Consumption: A Comparative Study of American and Chinese Consumers. *International Journal of Market Research*, 49(2),237–256.

Lin, L. H., & Ho, Y. L. (2009). Confucian dynamism, culture and ethical changes in Chinese societies–a comparative study of China, Taiwan, and Hong Kong. *The International Journal of Human Resource Management, 20*(11), 2402–2417.

Martinsons, M. G., Leung, A. K. Y., Loh, C. (1996). Technology transfer for sustainable development Environmentalism and entrepreneurship in Hong Kong, *International Journal of Social Economics*, 23(9), 69–96.

Martinsons, M.G., So, S, K., Tin, C. and Wong, D. (1997). Hong Kong and China: emerging markets for environmental products and technologies. *Long Range Planning*, 30(2), 277–290

McCracken, G. (1990). Culture and consumer behaviour: An anthropological perspective. *Journal of the Market research Society.*

Mok, C. and DeFranco, A. L. (2000). Chinese cultural values: Their implications for travel and tourism marketing. *Journal of Travel & Tourism Marketing*, 8(2), 99–114.

Mooij, M. D. (2003). Convergence and divergence in consumer behaviour: implications for global advertising. *International Journal of advertising*, 22(2), 183–202.

McEwen, W., Fang, X., Zhang, C., Burkholder, R. (2006). Inside the mind of the Chinese consumer, *Harvard Business Review*, 84 (3), 68–76.

Pan, J. (1990). The dual structure of Chinese culture and its influence on modern Chinese society. *International Sociology*, 5 (1),75–88.

Phau, I., & Kea, G. (2007). Attitudes of university students toward business ethics: a cross-national investigation of Australia, Singapore and Hong Kong. *Journal of Business Ethics*, 72(1), 61–75.

Piron, F. (2006). China's Changing Culture: Rural and Urban Consumers' Favorite Things. *Journal of Consumer Marketing*, 23(6),27–334.

Pitta, D., Fung, H. and Isberg, S. (1999). Ethical issues across cultures: managing the differing perspectives of China and the USA. *Journal of Consumer Marketing*, 16(3) 240–256.

Qian, W., Razzaque, M. A., & Keng, K. A. (2007). Chinese cultural values and gift-giving behavior. *Journal of Consumer Marketing*, 24(4), 214–228.

Ralston, D. A., Egri, C. P., Stewart, S., Terpstra, R. H., & Kaicheng, Y. (1999). Doing business in the 21st century with the new generation of Chinese managers: A study of generational shifts in work values in China, *Journal of International Business Studies*, 415–427.

Ramasamy, B (2009). Chinese Consumers' Perception of Corporate Social Responsibility (CSR). *Journal of Business Ethics*. 88, 119–132.

Ramasamy, B., & Yeung, M. (2009). Chinese consumers' perception of corporate social responsibility (CSR). *Journal of Business Ethics*, 88(1), 119–132.

Redfern, K. and Crawford, J. (2004). An Empirical Investigation of the Influence of Modernisation on the Moral Judgments of Managers in the People's Republic of China. *Cross Cultural Management*, 11(1), 48–61.

Romar, E. J. (2002). Virtue is Good Business: Confucianism as a Practical Business Ethic. *Journal of Business Ethics*, 38, 119–131.

Shaw, D., & Clarke, I. (1999). Belief formation in ethical consumer groups: an exploratory study. *Marketing Intelligence and Planning*, 17(2), 109–119.

Schaefer, A. and Crane, A. (2005). Addressing Sustainability and Consumption. *Journal of Macromarketing*, 25, 76–92.

Sen, S., & Bhattacharya, C. B. (2001). Does doing good always lead to doing better? Consumer reactions to corporate social responsibility. *Journal of marketing Research*, 38(2), 225–243.

Shively, A.M. and Shively, S. (1972), *"Value changes during a period of modernization – the case of Hong Kong"*, The Chinese University of Hong Kong, Social Research Centre, Hong Kong.

Singhapakdi, A. Marta, J.K., Rao, C. P and Cicic, M (2001). Is Cross-Cultural Similarity an Indicator of Similar Marketing Ethics? *Journal of Business Ethics*, 32(1), 55–68.

Spiggle, S. (1994) "Analysis and Interpretation of Qualitative Data in Consumer Research" *Journal of Consumer Research*, 21(3), 491–503.

Swanson, M. (1995). China puts on a new face, *China Business Review*, 22(5), 34–7.

Tian, Z., Wang, R., & Yang, W. (2011). Consumer responses to corporate social responsibility (CSR) in China. *Journal of business ethics*, 101(2), 197–212.

Triandis, H.C., Bontempo, R., Villareal, M.J., Asai, M. and Lucca, N. (1988). Individualism and collectivism: cross-cultural perspectives on self-ingroup relationships. *Journal of Personality and Social Psychology*, 54(2).

Triandis, H. C. 1989. The self and social behavior in differing cultural contexts. *Psychological Review*, 96(3), 506–520.

Tse, D. K. (1996). Understanding Chinese People as Consumers: Past Findings and Future Propositions', in M. H. Bond (ed.) *The Handbook of Chinese Psychology*, Oxford University Press: Hong Kong, 352–363.

Tu, W. M. (1998). *Humanity and Self-Cultivation: Essays in Confucian Thought*, Cheng & Tsui: Boston.

Vachon, K., (1983). Relations de l'Homme a` la Nature dans les Sagesses Orientales Traditionelles. *Ecologie et Environnement (Cahiers de Recherche e´thique)*, Montreal, 9.

Wan, W., Chung-Leung Luk, C., Yau, O., Tse, A., Leo Y. M. Sin, K. Kwong, K. and Chow, R. (2009). Do Traditional Chinese Cultural Values Nourish a Market for Pirated CDs? *Journal of Business Ethics*. 88(1),185–196.

Wang, C.L., Chen, Z.X., Chan, A.K.K. and Zheng, Z.C. (2000). The influence of hedonic values on consumer behaviors: an empirical investigation in China. *Journal of Global Marketing*, 14(1/2), 169–86.

Wang, Y. and Duce, J. (2010). China May Spend $738 Billion on Clean Energy Projects. Bloomberg, (accessed on 23 May 2011), available at http://www.businessweek.com/news/2010-07-20/china-may-spend-738-billion-on-clean-energy-projects.htmlasat23-04-11.

Wang, C. and Lin, X. (2009). Migration of Chinese Consumption Values: Traditions, Modernization, and Cultural Renaissance. *Journal of Business Ethics*, 88, 399–409.

Wei, R. and Pan, Z. (1999). Mass media and consumerist values in the People's Republic of China. *International Journal of Public Opinion Research*, 11(1),76–97.

Winfield, B. (2000). Confucianism, collectivism and constitutions: press systems in China and Japan. *Communication Law and Policy* 5(3),323–348.

Woods, L. and Lamond, D. A. (2011). What Would Confucius Do? – Confucian Ethics and Self-Regulation. *Management Journal of Business Ethics*, 102, 669–683.

Wong, N. and Ahuvia, A. C. (1998). Personal Taste and Family Face: Luxury Consumption in Confucian and Western Societies. *Psychology and Marketing*, 15, 423–441.

Wrightsman, L. (1992). Assumptions about Human Nature. Newbury Park, CA: Sage Publications.

Yam-Tang, E. P. Y. and Chan, R. Y. K (1998). Purchasing Behaviours and Perceptions of Environmentally Harmful Products. *Marketing Intelligence and Planning*, 16(6), 356–362.

Yang, K.S. (1979). Research on Chinese National Character in Modern Psychology, in Wen, C.I. S. et al. (Eds.), *Moderation and Change of Value, Thought and Word Association*. Taipei.

Yau, O. (1988) Chinese Cultural Values: Their Dimensions and Marketing Implications. *European Journal of Marketing*, 22(5) 44–57.

Yau, O.H.M., Chan, T.S. and Lau, K.F. (1999). Influence of Chinese cultural values on consumer behavior: A proposed model of gift-purchasing behavior in Hong Kong. *Journal of International Consumer Marketing*, 11, 97–116.

Yeung, S. P. (1998). Environmental Consciousness among Students in Senior Secondary Schools: the case of Hong Kong. *Environmental Education Research*, 4(3),251–268.

Yao, X. Z. (2000). An Introduction to Confucianism, Cambridge University Press, Cambridge.

Zhang, W. B. (2000). *Adam Smith and Confucius: The Theory of Sentiments and the Analects*, Nova Science Publishers: New York.

Zhao, B. and Xu, S. (2013). Does Consumer Unethical Behavior Relate to Birthplace? Evidence from China Confucian dynamism, culture and ethical changes in Chinese societies· comparative study of China, Taiwan, and Hong Kong. *Journal of Business Ethics*, 113, 475–488.

Maedeh Ghorbanian Zolbin, Amir Faridhashemi
and Carolyn Strong

12 The Passing of Time and Consumption Behavior of the Elderly in Three Countries: Differences and Similarities

Introduction

Due to the rapid growth of elderly people, health promotion and providing appropriate care for the elderly are of importance and defining the key factors in having a healthy society (Bahrami, Mirzaei, and Salehi-Abargouei. 2016). Nearly most countries are experiencing growth in both the absolute number and relative percentage of consumers aged 60 years and older. Between 2015 and 2030, it is expected that the number of older consumers to grow by 56 percent worldwide to 1.5 billion consumers, a figure that is projected to more than double by 2050 (United Nations 2019, p. 7). Studies also showed that Iran's population is aging like the rest of the world and we will face an enormous increase in the number of elders in Iran (Bahrami, Mirzaei, and Salehi-Abargouei. 2016). This acceleration in the growth of an aging population has effected most industries and markets. Additionally, Consumption habits change with age, since people have different needs and desires at their life cycle (Hurd and Rohwedder 2010). The most important changes in the behavior of people are related to their need for health services. As there is a negative relationship between health and age (Tse et al. 2014), thus, older adults have worse health status than younger adults. Health promotion has recently been considered an essential strategy to decline inequalities in health and providing high-quality primary care. Therefore, products and stuff that aged people consume disproportionately (e.g., health care) will profit from this worldwide demographic shift rapidly. While, other products (e.g., clothing) will not (Drolet et al. 2018).

Aged consumers are now the most economically powerful and fruitful section of all age groups (Drolet et al. 2018). As the way, people make their decisions change in their later life, a better understanding of this shift beneficial for all industry owners. Older consumers (60 years) are now commanding greater academic and practitioner attention, with businesses and researchers identifying that this age group owns the key characteristics to justify targeted selection in the marketplace (Chaston 2011). 'Older consumer' researches inform the empirical development of a new scale, which is subsequently used to satisfy the requirement for an age-based typology, namely for older shoppers (Sudbury and Simcock 2009). Accordingly, investigations of age-related

https://doi.org/10.1515/9783110659566-012

changes in decision-making processes employed across a variety of consumption do-
mains constitute a vital area of study. Despite the clear importance of such studies for
understanding the aging process and developing better ways to serve older consumers,
research on aging and consumer decision making has been relatively limited (Carpenter and Yoon 2015a).

There has been little systematic research done concerning the most basic questions
related to changes in behavioral consumption in the elderly, over time, especially in
less developed countries. Thus, this study aims to fulfill this gap and investigate the
consumption behavior of elderly people deeply.

Literature Review

Consumption Behavior

According to Zukin and Maguire (2004, p. 173), consumption is a cultural and socioeconomic process of picking goods. It enables people to specify their identity. 'Consumer
behavior is a process when people select, purchase, use or dispose of products, services, ideas or experiences to satisfy their needs and desires' Consumer behavior 'includes mental, physical and emotional activities which people do when they want to
select, purchase, use or throw away the product or the service that fulfills their needs
and demands' (Eshra and Beshir 2017). While, Main factors of consumer behavior, such
as mental, physical, and emotional activities that may involve them in the selection,
purchasing, and usage of products to fulfill their needs and demands (Pariest, Carter
and Statt 2013). These factors might affect their choices, such as what to buy, why to
buy when to buy, where to buy and how to use a product may be some critical points
of view in the mind of older consumers. Further, Furaiji., Latuszynska, and Wawrzyniak (2012, p. 77) have expressed that 'consumer buying behavior is a series of actions
in which consumers initially recognize their needs, seeking sources to solve these
needs, making the decision to purchase something to satisfy these needs, analyze
available information, set plan and finally try to implement this plan'.

Some personal characteristics can influence the buying patterns of people, as
all people are unique in these features. The important personal features are age, occupation, socioeconomic conditions, lifestyle, personality, and self-concept. Yakup
and Jablonsk (2012, p. 61) supported this idea. They have supposed this conception
that personal characteristics such as; age, occupation, economic situations, lifestyle, personality, and self-concept have an extensive influence on the buying behavior of consumers. All in all, it is obvious that Age is known as a crucial element
in marketing strategies as this item makes differences among consumers' consumption patterns and choices and the hobbies and choices of consumers may change
with time. Age is the key factor in buying decisions as the wants and preferences of

consumers change over time. Yakup and Jablonsk (2012) have also anticipated this conception that the passing of time can change the consumption behavior of people. For example, at the upper age level, consumers like to use more health-related products.

Definition of the Elderly Consumers

The term 'elderly consumer' has many synonyms such as senior, aged, old, mature, or silver shopper. However, the definition of an elderly is quite unclear since this group consists of different kinds of consumers with different socioeconomic characteristics and shopping preferences. Lifestyle and psychological age are more important than the biological age in terms of consumption patterns. The chronological age is a clear and most frequently used method of classifying the elderly but there is no clear consensus on the age brackets (Ahmad 2002). In several studies, the elderly is considered consumers who are 65 years and older (e.g., Whelan et al. 2002) but in some studies, the elderly or older consumers have included consumers at the age of 55 or 60 and older (Meneely, Strugnell, and Burns 2009, p. 458). In this paper, the word elderly refers to consumers who are 60 and older because this is the classification used in many Iranian official statistics.

Elderly Consumption Behavior

The main factor of the aging process is physiological changes that noticeably change older people's lifestyles (Yoon and Cole 2009). Physical disabilities, such as visual impairments decrease the ability of elder people to obtain written information from any sources. Additionally, their auditory capacity is reduced, putting them in difficulties in understanding speech. Aside from these, declination in cognitive abilities, may cause them deficits in short memory and limit their information literacy ability. Also, stressful and unexpected events, such as retirement, illnesses, and loss of one's spouse can significantly change their interpersonal life. All the above-mentioned changes may have relevant repercussions on older consumers' buying habits and can be expected, in particular, to alter their purchase decision-making process (Guido 2014). Wilkie (1994) express that, the process of the elderly consumption pattern includes five basic stages, including i) the acknowledgment of a certain need; ii) the search for information about the products/services suitable to satisfy such a need; iii) the comparison of the diverse products/services the industry offers to satisfy the need in discussion; iv) the selection of the product/service reputed able to efficaciously and effectively satisfy the need at issue, and v) the usage of the selected product/service.

Older consumers are surrounded by many sophisticated choices around health equipment. Various items determine these choices, such as lots of information, high risk, recent innovations, uncertainty, and essential outcomes. Previous researches on old people and health-related decisions have commonly suggested that older adults are vulnerable consumers and decision-makers because of cognitive, and socioeconomic concerns that compromise their information literacy skills. However, extant research on health and medical decision making has also identified a more proactive and agented view of aging consumers (Carpenter and Yoon 2011b).

Healthcare services consumers' behavior demonstrates a multidimensional concept that implies the cumulative effects of various items. In the case of healthcare services, the process of consumption is very different and complex due to the two reasons the nature of the needs and consumption motivations and complexity of the services. Health care products consumers face some basic choices. For example, a function of their preferences, the prices of goods, and those goods' attributes. However, in the case of facing many options, consumers struggle to make better decisions and they might be less satisfied than if they had fewer options. Furthermore, consumers tend to stick with the status quo or the default, when they are not going to make decisions (Erin Audrey et al. 2016).

Einav et al. (2013) stated that consumers might choose between the ranges of potential sensitivity to cost-sharing, which the authors refer to like the selection of moral hazard. However, price is the most effective factor, consumers are also sensitive to providers included in the network (Tumlinson et al. 1997; Nichols et al. 2004), benefit (Tumlinson et al. 1997; Politi et al. 2013), design (Polsky et al. 2005), and perceived quality (van den Berg et al. 2008, p. 2448). Aside from this, consumer characteristics influence preferences. Naessens et al. (2008) found that 'consumers with worse health status are likely to choose costlier plans than those with better health status choices'. Mikels, Reed, and Simon (2009) found that having more options is not a priority for older adults in the case of health-related products, which is very important for younger adults. Authors have described a model of consumers to understand their interaction stimuli, characteristics, decision process. (Furaiji., Latuszynska, and Wawrzyniak 2012). The mechanism of marketing stimuli is settled by businesses and the environmental stimuli are due to social factors like economic, political, technology, and cultural situations of a locality. This is a famous model of consumer behavior, explaining the consumers' perceived exposure toward marketing stimuli and their actual purchase decision. It has assumed that consumers will respond in a specific way to various stimuli at different stages in their minds.

Although most researches do not place a premium on age due to wide variations in abilities across individuals of the same period (Birren and Cunningham 1985), it plays a vital role in socialization models (Moschis, Lee, & Mathur 1997). Despite extensive variability in aging, the ability to respond to, and preferences for, physiological and psychological aging can effect specified marketing stimuli. For example, aging is linked to a declining health condition, and ailments are most common among older adults and are likely to create needs for products most likely to be purchased by older people. Also, age is expected to affect the criterion measure via socialization processes indirectly. Previous studies express that physiological reasons and social causes constrictions of the older person's social environment (Atchley 1987), leading to social isolation as suggested by disengagement theory. Therefore, age is more likely to be related to interaction with personal sources of information closely. If consumers' decisions depend on deliberation, the robust age-related declines in executive functioning and numeracy suggest that the quality of judgments and decisions will inevitably suffer as people age. Several studies have identified biases in judgment processes that increased with age and are linked with deliberative processes such as working memory. Mutter (2000) found that older adults' judgments were more influenced by prior expectancies than were those of younger adults. Older adults, however, are faced with more decisions about critical health, financial, and other personal issues.

According to Keller and Kotler (2006), four major items (each of these factors also have sub-categories) influence consumer behavior in each age group. These factors are marketing stimuli (price, promotion, distribution, and communication), other influences (economic, diplomatic, political and cultural conditions of the country), psychological factors (motivating factors, perception, learning, and memory) and personality factors (culture, social factors, and personal factors). Since this study intends to examine the high volume of the sample in different communities, it prefers to use a comprehensive model of consumer behavior. The Keller and Kotler model (2006) is the model used in this study.

Methodology

The domain of study embraces health care and health products including adult diapers, crutches, walkers and wheelchair, blood glucose meter, and sphygmomanometer. The reason for choosing these products is the lack of attention they receive in consumer research whilst they are essential marketplace items. This study has two-phase. The first phase of the study was conducted amongst the Iranian elderly; the second phase amongst Iran, Turkish, and Azerbaijani elderly. The statistical population for the first phase was all Iranian elderly, but the statistical community for the second phase in Iran included the elderly who had previously participated in the study and expressed their willingness to participate in the second phase. There were no specific geographic restrictions in the data collection. All towns were considered in Iran, Turkey, and the Republic Azerbaijan. The questionnaire used the Likert scale and the model of the Consumer Behavioral Model proposed by Kotler and Keller (2006). Demographic features, including age, gender, education, and income were measured using fifteen items of consumption behavior.

Cronbach's Alpha was adopted to measure reliability. The alpha for marketing stimuli is 0.755, the alpha for other stimuli is 0.984, the alpha for the consumer psychology dimension is 0.833, and the alpha for the consumer character is 0.866. The alpha number for all variables is higher than 0.5, indicating that the questionnaire has the required reliability. The related questions were reviewed and approved after peer assessment and pointing. The data collected at each stage are analyzed by the SPSS software and to respond to the assumptions the one-way ANOVA test is used. The initial sample consisted of 432 subjects. 211 of these respondents from across Iran (Tehran, Tabriz, Mashhad, Shiraz, Esfahan, Karaj, Uremia, Qom, and other cities) agreed to be part of phase two of the study. The same questionnaire was repeated with this sample two years later, and the results of both studies compared.

Table 12.1: Demographic factor in Iranian respondents.

Demographic factors		2018(Iran)	2016(Iran)
Gender	men	59%	59%
	women	41%	41%
Age	60–70	32%	53%
	71–80	44%	30%
	upper than 80	26%	17%
Education	school education	42%	42%
	college education	58%	58%
Income	low	31%	31%
	medium	54%	54%
	high	15%	15%

Four hypotheses are developed in phase one: relating to the comparison of four measures (marketing stimuli, other stimuli, personality factors, and psychological factors) of the consumption behavior of Iranian elderly over two years. In this phase of the research.

Data was analyzed using SPSS, and the one-way ANOVA employed to categorize the groups.

Table 12.2: One way ANOVA test between 2 years in Iran (2016 and 2018).

Variable	F	Sig.
Marketing	9.394	0.002
Other	9.166	0.003
Personality	0.950	0.330
Psychology	17.343	0.000

Hypothesis

H_1: *There is a significant difference between the consumption behaviors of the elderly in terms of marketing stimuli between the two stage studies.*

According to one-way ANOVA test, which indicates a significance of 0.02 < 0.05 for marketing stimuli, there is a significant difference between the consumption behavior of the elderly in Iran, concerning the consumption of medical products from the perspective marketing stimuli. Over the phases, this factor has been able to gain a better position.

H_2: *there is a significant difference between the consumption behaviors of the elderly in terms of other stimuli over the two stages.*

According to one-way ANOVA test, which indicates a significance of 0.03 < 0.05, for the variable of other stimuli, there is a significant difference between consumption behaviors of the elderly in Iran between the two stages of the study. Concerning the consumption of medical products from the perspective of other stimuli. Over the years, this factor has been able to gain a better position.

H_3: *There is a significant difference between the consumption behavior of the elderly in terms of personality factors in 2016 and 2018.*

According to one-way ANOVA test, which indicates a significance of 0.330 > 0.05 for the variable of personality factors, there is no significant difference between the consumption behaviors of the elderly in Iran when consuming medical supplies from the perspective of the personality factors. Over the second stage, the status of this factor has failed to improve.

H_4: *There is a significant difference between the consumption behaviors of older people in terms of psychological factors between the two stages.*

According to the one-way ANOVA test, which indicates a significance of 0.000 < 0.05 for the variable of psychological factor, there is no significant difference between the consumption behaviors of the Iranian elderly over time from the perspective of psychological factors. Psychological factors regarding the use of these products have seen a dramatic change over the time period of the two studies.

The Comparison Study

The second phase of the study draws a comparison between the behavior of the elderly consumers in three countries of Azerbaijan, Turkey, and Iran: a questionnaire was distributed among 200 elderly people in Turkey and Azerbaijan. 83 useable questionnaires from Turkey and 87 questionnaires from Azerbaijan were collected which can be ana-lyzed. To create an equal sample, four questionnaires from Azerbaijan were randomly deleted. Among the questionnaires completed by Iranian elderly 83 questionnaires were randomly selected. A limitation of this study, not perceived to be an issue until data col-lection, is that in some cases, the elderly were not able to answer the questionnaire. These responses were solicited from a child or relative who assisted in completion of the questionnaire. If the older person was alone, the researcher completed their question-naire based on the subject's answers.[1]

Table 12.3: Demographic factor in three countries in stage two.

Demographic variables		Iran	Turkey	Azerbaijan
Gender	men	65%	39%	43%
	women	25%	61%	57%
Age	60–70	16%	48%	60%
	71–80	44%	31%	26%
	upper than 80	40%	21%	14%
Education	school education	46%	69%	78%
	academic education	54%	21%	22%
Income	low	46%	61%	55%
	medium	33%	19%	31%
	high	18%	20%	14%

In this stage of research, four hypotheses are presented, relating to the comparison of four factors (marketing stimuli, other stimuli, personality factors, and psycholog-ical factors) in the consumption behavior of the elderly among the three countries. The data were analyzed using SPSS software, and the one-way ANOVA test was em-ployed to categorize the groups. The results are presented in Table 12.4.

---

1 The researchers were fluent in Turkish and Azeri.

Table 12.4: ANOVA test in the three countries.

Variable	F	Sig
Marketing factor	1.728	0.056
Another factor	1.057	0.398
Psychology factor	1.779	0.047
Characteristic factor	1.803	0.054

Testing of the Second Stage Assumptions

H_5: *There is a significant difference between the three groups in terms of marketing factors*

According to the one-way ANOVA test, which indicates a significance of 0.056 > 0.05, for the variable of marketing stimuli, there was no significant difference between the consumption of medical supplies between the elderly in the three countries from the perspective of the variable of marketing stimuli. In this regard, all three groups demonstrated identical behavior.

H_6: *There is a significant difference between the three groups in terms of other stimuli.*

According to one-way ANOVA test, which shows a significance of 0.398 > 0.05 for the variable of other stimuli, there is no significant difference between the consumption behavior of the elderly in the three countries with regard to the consumption of medical materials from the view of other stimuli, and all three groups display identical behavior in this regard.

H_7: *There is a significant difference between the three collections in terms of Individual feature.*

According to one-way ANOVA test, which shows a significance of 0.054 > 0.05 for Characteristic factors, there is no significant difference between the consumption behavior of the aging in the three countries about the consumption of medical supplies from the perspective of characteristic stimuli, and all three groups display identical behavior in this regard.

H_8: *There is a significant difference between the three groups in terms of psychological factors.*

According to one-way ANOVA test, which shows a significance of 0.047 < 0.05 for the variable of psychological factors, there is a significant difference between the consumption behaviors of the elderly in these three countries with regard to the use of medical supplies from the perspective of psychological factors, and all three groups demonstrated different behaviors in relation to this factor.

The Research Model

To extract the research model, Amos software was utilized, and the data for all three countries developed in the extraction of the model. Based on the data from the three countries, a model for the elderly shopping behavior for products related to aging needs has been developed. Developing the Amos (date) model of output, the relationships between the elements of marketing stimuli, other stimuli, personality factors, and psychological factors to purchase products associated with aging are evident in Figure 12.1.

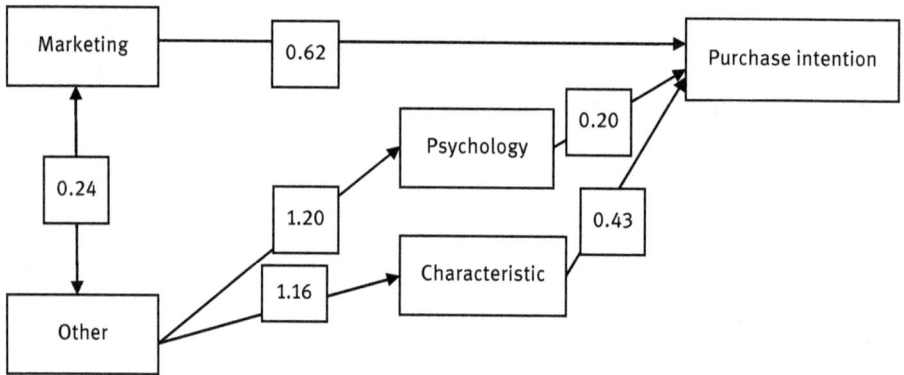

Figure 12.1: A model of elderly shopping behavior.

Analysis Model Fit

Based on software output analysis the model has a suitable fit, see Table 12.5. The acceptable level of CMIN/DF is less than 3, which is 2.549 for this model. The adequate level for RMSEA is below 0.08, which is 0.080 in this model; the acceptable standard for IFI is more significant than 0.9, which is 0.903 in this model.

Based on the output obtained from the software, it can be acknowledged that there are relationships between the variables of the research:

According to the model derived from the data collected, there is a clear relationship between marketing factors and other factors (with a coefficient of 0.24). Marketing, physiology, and personality factors have a direct impact on buying intent. The effects of marketing factors on the purchase intention of elderly people across

Table 12.5: Model fit.

Item	Value	Result
RMSEA	0.080	accepted
IFI	0.903	accepted
CMIN/DF	2.549	accepted

the three countries was higher than other factors (with a coefficient of 0.62). Factors such as product and service, price, distribution, and communication have the most impact on the purchase of these products. Individual factors, such as culture, social and personal factors are essential in the second stage (with a coefficient of 0.43). The psychological use of these products, including motivation, perception, learning, and memory is ranked third for elderly consumers (a coefficient of 0.20). However, the influences of other stimuli were not directly related to the purchase of these items: the personality and physiological factors act as mediator variables.

Discussion and Conclusion

There is an increasing concern about the health and well-being of the global elderly population and their growing consumer trends. Research into this target market in Iran and her neighboring countries is based on the behavior of the elderly related to the aspects of lifestyle and links to topics such as nutrition, medical, therapeutic issues such as medicine, and medical care (for example, the work of the Johari et al.). This research pays attention to the need of the elderly community for products including adult diapers, crutches, blood glucose measurement, and barometric measurement tool, to date little attention has been paid to such products by academic researchers who ought to look at the elderly and they are significant as marketing community The results of this study show a shift in emphasis of the importance of the elderly consumer target market; there have been many changes in the marketing of these products over the recent years in Iran (which are beyond the scope of this research). There is also a change in the focus of the marketing of these products, such as technological development, society, political and economic conditions, and the community had shown positive reactions to the adoption of these products. Another factor that has changed in the last three years is the physiological factor; this factor examines the effects of perception, motivation, learning, and memory, and according to the results obtained. It is found that the elderly has been able to orient their perceptions and self-provoking issues regarding these products, toward an increasing acknowledgment of the need and trend for these products. However, an interesting and notable point is the lack of change in personality factors, and due to their age, these changes in personality factors have not been observed.

Considering that all three countries studied in this study are adjoining and neighboring and that all three countries have a rising elderly population rate, they have the same economic, cultural, and educational conditions. The marketing factors are the same in all three countries, and this result is an essential finding for the industry market leaders associated with these products; they can adopt the same strategic marketing approach to all three countries.

Personality factors among elderly people in all three countries do not differentiate, these factors are related to the neighborhood, proximity of culture, and lifestyle across the three cultures. The interesting of comparison between these three countries is the difference between the psychological factors; the factors affecting a person's perception and memory, the sense of need and an understanding of the demand for these products vary between these three countries, and the perceived stimuli of the three states are different.

Based on the analysis of the data collected, we concluded that in Iran, in terms of marketing incentives (price, product, distribution, and communication), and other incentives (economic, technological, political and cultural conditions), over the last three years, the behavior of older consumers has not changed. These factors did not change over the three years and did not change the behavior of older consumers. However, psychological factors (motivation, perception, learning, memory) and personality factors (cultural, social, and personal) changed over these three years and led to changes in consumer behavior. In general, psychological and personality factors have changed over these years toward an improvement in the attitude and usage of older people from medical products and have led to improved acceptance.

Comparison of data from three countries the data analysis showed that the marketing factors and other triggers are similar between the three countries and all of them, considering neighboring and adjacent, have close economic and political conditions. Also, all three countries have shown typical behavior in terms of the action of the elderly for medical products. There are differences between the three countries regarding the behavior of the elderly for medicinal products in terms of personality and psychological factors. In Iran, the personality factor is more effective in dealing with the action of older people than in the two countries, Turkey and Azerbaijan, and in this respect, it differs from the above two states.

In Azerbaijan, the psychological influence on the behavior of the elderly is less influential than Turkey and Iran. The elderly in Iran and Turkey show similar behavior in terms of the impact of psychological factors.

Implications

Medical equipment including blood pressure gauge and blood glucose meter and heart rate monitor are some of the vital consumer products for the elderly, other materials such as walkers, wheelchairs, and clothing are essential yet auxiliary products, however, the majority of this demographic group cannot afford to buy these products due to the economic restrictions. The growing population of this age group in these three countries (although this growth in Azerbaijan is less than Turkey and Iran) is rapid, this research suggests that social support is needed to provide these items and that marketers can contribute to this need through sponsor hop, lower pricing strategies, and the acknowledgment that these products are essential items, not cash cows.

To encourage the acknowledge of the need and usage of these products, this paper suggests that information communications campaigns are developed for communication on official networks of each country or cities in collaboration with government municipality (use of billboards in supermarket centers) to encourage the acceptance, use and improved public attitude towards these essential products.

References

Abdel-Ghany, M., Sharpe, D.L., (1997). Consumption patterns among the young-old and old-old. The Journal of Consumer Affairs. 31 (1), 90–112.

Atchley, R. C. (1987). Aging: continuity and change. 2nd ed. Belmont, Calif.: Wadsworth Pub. Co.

Ahmad, R., (2002). The older or ageing consumers in the UK: are they really that different?. International Journal of Market Research. 44 (3), 337–360.

Bahrami, D., Mirzaei, Masoud., Salehi-Abargouei1, Amin., (2016). Dietary Behaviors of Elderly People Residing in Central Iran: A Preliminary Report of Yazd Health Study. Elderly Health Journal. 2(1),6–13.

Birren, F., and Cunningham, R., (1985). Research on the psychology of aging: Principles, concepts and theory. In J. E. Birren and K. W. Schaie (Eds.) The handbooks of aging. Handbook of the psychology of aging. Van Nostrand Reinhold Co. pp. 3–34.

Carpenter, S. M., & Yoon, C. (2011b). Aging and consumer decision making. Annals of the New York Academy of Sciences, 1235(1),E1–E12.

Chaston, I., (2011). Older consumer opportunities: small firm response in a selected group of UK service sector markets. Service Industries Journal. 31(3),371–384.

Carpenter, S. M., & Yoon, C. (2015a). Aging and Consumer Decision Making. Aging and Decision Making, 351–370.

Cole, C. A., Lee, M. P., & Yoon, C. (2009). An integration of perspectives on aging and consumer decision making. Journal of Consumer Psychology, 19(1),35–37.

Dehghankar, L., Shahrokhi, A., Qolizadeh, A., Mohammadi, F., & Nasiri, E., (2018). Health Promoting Behaviors and General Health among the Elderly in Qazvin: A Cross Sectional Study. Elderly Health Journal. 4(1),18–22.

Drolet, A., Jiang, L., Pour Mohammad, A., & Davis, C. (2018). The influence of aging on consumer decision-making. Consumer Psychology Review. 2(1),3–16.

Einav, L., Finkelstein, A., Ryan, S.P., Schrimpf, P., and Cullen, M., (2013). Selection on Moral Hazard in Health Insurance. American Economic Review. 103(1),178–219.

Eshra. N., Beshir. N., (2017). Impact of Corporate Social Responsibility on Consumer Buying Behavior in Egypt. World Review of Business Research. 7(1) 32–44.

Furaiji, F. Latuszynska, M. Wawrzyniak., A. (2012). An Empirical Study of Factors Influencing Consumer Behavior in Electric Appliances Market. Contemporary Economics. 6(3),76–86.

Guido, G., Amatulli, C., Peluso, A. M., & Yoon, C., (2014). Aging and Product Choice: The Effects of Feel-Age and Social Context. Advances in consumer research. Association for Consumer Research (U.S.) 42,106–112.

Hurd, M. D., and Rohwedder, S. (2010). Spending patterns in the older population. In Drolet, A., Schwarz, N., Yoon, C., (Eds.), The aging consumer: Perspectives from psychology and economics. New York, NY: Routledge. pp. 25–50.

Kotler, P., and Keller, K., (2006). Marketing management. 12th ed. New Jersey, USA, Pearson Prentice Hall.

Mikels, J. A., Reed, A. E., & Simon, K. I. (2009). Older Adults Place Lower Value on Choice Relative to Young Adults. The Journals of Gerontology Series B: Psychological Sciences and Social Sciences, 64B(4), 443–446.

Moschis, G.P, Lee, E., & Mathur, A., (1997). Targeting the mature market: opportunities and challenges. Journal of Consumer Marketing 14 (4), 282–293.

Meneely, L., Strugnell, C., Burns, A., (2009). Elderly consumers and their food store experiences. Journal of Retailing and Consumer Services. 16 (6), 458–465.

Mutter, S. A., (2000). Illusory correlation and group impression formation in young and older adults. Journal of Gerontology. Psychological Sciences, 55B, 224–237.

Naessens, J. M., Khan, M., Shah, N. D., Wagie, A., Pautz, R. A., & Campbell, C. R. (2008). Effect of Premium, Copayments, and Health Status on the Choice of Health Plans. Medical Care, 46(10), 1033–1040.

Nichols, L. M., Ginsburg, P. B., Berenson, R. A., Christianson, J., & Hurley, R. E. (2004). Are Market Forces Strong Enough To Deliver Efficient Health Care Systems? Confidence Is Waning. Health Affairs, 23(2),8–21.

Politi, M. C., Kaphingst, K. A., Kreuter, M., Shacham, E., Lovell, M. C., & McBride, T. (2013). Knowledge of Health Insurance Terminology and Details Among the Uninsured. Medical Care Research and Review, 71(1),85–98.

Polsky, D., Stein, R., Nicholson, S., & Bundorf, M. K. (2005). Employer Health Insurance Offerings and Employee Enrollment Decisions. Health Services Research, 40(5p1), 1259–1278.

Pariest, J. Carter, S. & Statt, D. (2013). Consumer behavior. Third edition. England. Edinburg Business School.

Erin Audrey, T., Grace, Carman, K., Lopez, A., Muchow, A. N., Parisa, R., & Eibner, Ch. (2016). Consumer Decision making in the Health Care Marketplace. Santa Monica.

Sudbury, L., & Simcock, P. (2009). A multivariate segmentation model of senior consumers. Journal of Consumer Marketing 26 (4), 251–262.

Tse, M., Chan, K. L., Wong, A., Tam, E., Fan, E., & Yip, G. (2014). Health Supplement Consumption Behavior in the Older Adult Population: An Exploratory Study. Frontiers in Public Health, 2(5), 10.

Tumlinson, A., Bottigheimer, H., Mahoney, P., Stone, E. M., & Hendricks, A. (1997). Choosing A Health Plan: What Information Will Consumers Use? Health Affairs, 16(3),229–238.

United nation. (2019). World population aging. Department of Economic and Social affairs.

Van den Berg, B., Van Dommelen, P., Stam, P., Laske-Aldershof, T., Buchmueller, T., & Schut, F. T. (2008). Preferences and choices for care and health insurance. Social Science & Medicine, 66(12),2448–2459.

Wilkie, W. L., (1994) Consumer Behavior, Third edition New York: Wiley.

Whelan, A., Wrigley, N., Warm, D., & Cannings, E. (2002). Life in a "Food Desert." Urban Studies, 39(11),2083–2100.

Yakup, D., & Jablonski, S., (2012). Integrated Approach to Factors Affecting Consumers Purchase Behavior in Poland and an Empirical Study. Global Journal of Management and Business Research. 12(15), 61–87.

Zukin, S., & Maguire, J. S. (2004). Consumers and Consumption. Annual Review of Sociology, 30(1), 173–197.

Concluding Comment

As we all come to terms with the unpredictability of the pandemic and what the future holds, I am hoping that after reading this text you are in agreement that if we can do anything, we can be considerate, kind and look to how we can positively contribute to society. This book reframes marketing's positive contributions to society and offers an inspirational approach to how we can achieve social and ethical improvement.

As we move towards more certain times we can grow and learn from the volatile situation we have been living in whilst preparing this book. There is now an even greater need for every effort to be made to overcome barriers to change, we are all responsible citizens and sustainable contributors to society. The challenge we now face is the longevity of our convictions and actions. I hope this book has inspired many readers and demonstrates that when it comes to protecting society there is an extraordinary amount marketing academics can do.

Thank you to everyone involved in the inspirational text, a special thank you to Steven Hardman and Maximilian Gessl at De Gruyter who made this book a reality.

https://doi.org/10.1515/9783110659566-013

About the Contributors

Amani Alsalem is a specialist in health marketing with a focus on improving the organ donation system in the Kingdom of Saudi Arabia. While she is the first recognised researcher in the Middle East to have produced tangible results in addressing organ shortage crisis, she is now seeking to expand the scope of her research to instigate real change in influencing donor choice and enhancing organ donation systems. In doing so, the key of her plan is to enhance the quality of life for the Saudi citizen, which comes in line with the aspirations of the Kingdom's 2030 vision.

Linda Brennan is a Professor at the School of Media and Communication at RMIT University. Her research interests are social and government marketing and especially the influence of marketing communications and advertising on behaviour.

Timo Dietrich is the Engagement Director and a Senior Lecturer at Griffith University. He is a behavioural architect who builds engaging marketing solutions that deliver results. Drawing on marketing fundamentals, behavioural theories, and gamification, he co-creates marketing solutions that engage and move users from awareness to action, loyalty and ultimately advocacy. Timo Dietrich has helped small and larger organisations from the environment, health, technology and finance sector to get insights and results that increase Return on Investment. For example, his work has positively impacted thousands of lives across change projects such as Blurred Minds, O-it, 5 a day, and REMI and he has trained thousands of professionals and students through his keynotes, masterclasses, and training workshops. He has attracted more than $AUD 3 million in research and consultancy income and has published more than 100+ peer-reviewed papers. Timo Dietrich's research produces impact and drives change for the better.

Amir Faridhashmi is a translator, who was awarded a bachelor's degree at the Azad University of Tabriz in the English Language, he is interested in international marketing with a focus on Digital Marketing. His interest in Marketing began during the practical experiments when he had the opportunity to work as a marketing manager in her family business. He learned about the strategies affecting markets, experienced the marketer's culture, and became proficient in B2B marketing. Inspired by this practical experience, Amir Faridhashmi starts his self-studying in marketing books and articles in International marketing, conducting research on consumer behavior in middle-east. He aspires to pursue a get some degrees in international marketing and have a career in this area. When he is not busy reading about new marketing strategies in Europe, Amir Faridhashmi enjoys watching new brands' advertisements and follows inspirational characters on social media.

Giuseppe Fattori is anesthesiologist by training with residencies in nutrition science, biotechnology, hygiene epidemiology and public health. From 2000 to 2017 was the director of Communication and Social Marketing department at the national health system in Modena – Emilia Romagna (Italy), leading the Program for Health Promotion. During this period, he coordinated the "Map of Health Opportunities" and "Help-AIDS" projects for the region. Since 2006 he has been adjunct professor at the department of Political science, University of Bologna (Italy), titular of a series of lectures on Social Marketing at the master program. Dr Fattori's current interests lie in the promotion of health, social marketing and social media. He has peer-reviewed publications in several areas of medical science and social marketing.

Maedeh Ghorbanian Zolbin finished her Master's studies at Zanjan University in Iran where she had a final thesis in Consumer Behavior. Although she has yet to declare her interest to continue

https://doi.org/10.1515/9783110659566-014

her studies, she's considering getting a PhD in marketing. In Bachelor degree, Maedeh studied management with a focus on Customs and was fascinated by this major by working as a marketer in a company in Iran. From this experience, she learned the value of hard work, efficiency, and communication. In the future, she hopes to continue her studies and get a PhD in this major. Maedeh spends her spare time watching movies and reading marketing books.

Louise Hassan is a Professor in Consumer Psychology at Bangor Business School. Her research interests are international in nature with a focus on transformative consumer research and social marketing. In particular, she is interested in understanding psychological processes underlying consumption decisions. She is a co-investigator for the International Tobacco Control Evaluation project (ITC). Professor Hassan's work has appeared in journals such as the *Journal of Advertising, Journal of Business Research, Journal of Consumer Affairs, Psychology and Marketing, International Marketing Review, Journal of International Marketing, European Journal of Marketing, Alcohol and Alcoholism, British Journal of Management* and the *Journal of Social Marketing*.

Erin Hurley is a Research Fellow at Social Marketing at Griffith University. Her research interests are predominantly in the areas of social marketing, co-design and health behaviour. She strives to drive positive change in local communities, with extensive experience in the co-creation, implementation and evaluation of social marketing programs. Her research is currently focused on integrating behaviour change theory into the co-design process with the aim of helping to close the gap between theory and practice. Erin Hurley's work has been published in high-quality journals, book chapters, international conferences and industry partner reports.

Michael Marinetto is an academic at Cardiff University Business School where he teaches on business ethics and the management of organised crime. As well as writing about business ethics, his current research interest concerns the role of the public intellectual in the modern academy. He has also written for a number of journalistic outlets, including the *Times Higher Education, Chronicle of Higher Education, Campus Review, The Conversation* and the *New Statesman*. Michael Marinetto is currently trying to write a book-length expose of the modern research-publishing complex in universities.

Luu Nguyen is a PhD candidate at the School of Economics, Finance, and Marketing, RMIT University. Her research focuses on the marketing dynamics of sustainable markets and social enterprises.

P.K. Nousha is a PhD candidate at the School of Management Studies at Cochin University of Science and Technology, Kochi, Kerala, India. His research focuses on Corporate Social Responsibility, and the communication of CSR. He is currently working on the effectiveness of the Corporate Social Responsibility communication efforts of various organisations over social media platforms.

Justin Paul serves as Editor-in-chief of International Journal of Consumer studies, and as an Associate Editor of Journal of Business Research (A Ranked journals in Australian Business Deans' council). A former faculty member with the University of Washington, he is a full professor of PhD & MBA programs, University of Puerto Rico, USA. He holds three honorary titles as 'Distinguished Vis Professor' with three reputed universities including- Indian Institute of Management (IIM-K). He is known as an author/co-author of best selling books such as *Business Environment* (4th ed), *International Marketing, Services Marketing, Export-Import Management* (2nd edition), *Management of Banking & Financial Services* by McGraw-Hill, Oxford University Press & Pearson respectively. Dr Paul has served as Lead Guest Editor with the *International Business Review*, *Journal of Business research, Journal of Retailing & Consumer services, Asia Pacific Business Review* and *European Business Review*. He serves as Associate Editor with *European Management Journal* and *Journal of Strategic Marketing*. Dr Paul introduced the Masstige model and measure for brand management, CPP Model for internationalization, SCOPE framework for Small firms and 7-P Framework for International Marketing. His articles have been downloaded over 700,000 times during the last six years. He has published over 75 research papers in SSCI journals and 100+ in Scopus. Over 50 papers are in A or A star journals. He has also served as a faculty member of Nagoya University, Japan and IIM. In addition, he has taught full courses at Aarhus University (Denmark), Grenoble Ecole de Management and University of Versailles (France), University-Lithuania, Warsaw (Poland) and has conducted research development workshops in countries such as Austria, USA, Spain, Croatia, China. He has been an invited speaker at several institutions such as University of Chicago, Vienna University (Austria), Fudan & UIBE-China, Barcelona and Madrid and has published three best selling case studies with Ivey & Harvard.

Ken Peattie a Professor in Marketing Strategy, Head of the Marketing and Strategy Section at Cardiff Business School and Co-Director of Cardiff University's Sustainable Places Research Institute. He also spent 12 years as Director of the ESRC funded BRASS Research Centre based at Cardiff, which specialised in research into business sustainability and corporate social responsibility. Before working as an academic he worked in marketing and strategic planning in an American paper multinational and a UK electronics company. His research interests focus on the impact of sustainability on marketing and corporate strategy making; social marketing for healthy and sustainable lifestyles; social enterprise and CSR. He has published three books and numerous book chapters on these topics, and has published in journals including *Journal of World Business, California Management Review, Journal of Business Research, Journal of Marketing Management, Public Policy & Marketing*, and *Business Strategy & the Environment*. His book with Frank-Martin Belz, *"Sustainability Marketing: A Global Perspective"*, was named *Business Book of the Year 2010* by the German Business Research Association.

Miriam McGowan is a lecturer in Marketing at the University of Birmingham. Her research draws on a consumer psychology perspective to understand consumer decision making and the role of emotions. She is interested in how peoples' behaviours can be changed for good, such as by encouraging pro-social and pro-environmental choices. Much of her research focuses on understanding how identity and social influences impact consumers' information processing and decision making. Miriam McGowan has published in the *European Journal of Marketing* and the *Journal of Consumer Behavior*.

Nhat Tram Phan-Le's research focus is on social marketing, behaviour change, sustainability, and mindfulness. She has undertaken qualitative research through observation and in-depth interviews. Nhat Tram Phan-Le earned a distinction master's degree in marketing communications at the University of Birmingham. She also worked in corporate social responsibility for five years.

Lukas Parker is a Senior Lecturer at the School of Media and Communication at RMIT University, Melbourbe Australia. He has published widely, and his research interests are in social marketing, behaviour change and digital advertising.

Sharyn Rundle-Thiele the founding Professor of Social Marketing at Griffith University, which is the largest university based group of social marketers in the world. She is Founding Co-Editor of the *Journal of Social Marketing*. Sharyn Rundle-Thiele has attracted $12 million to fund her research program. She has led projects that have changed behaviours for 10,000's of people in areas including health, the environment and for complex social issues. Awards and appointments including The Philip Kotler Social Marketing Distinguished Service Award and the Australian New Zealand Marketing Academy Fellow acknowledge her innovative, high-quality practice and science and her leadership.

Anthony Samuel has a PhD from Cardiff University Business School and his multidisciplinary research navigates the complex interfaces between place management/ marketing, social enterprises, sustainable business practices and ethical consumption. Dr Samuel sits on the Editorial Board of The Journal of Macromarketing and his work has been published in a number of leading journals including, *The Journal of Business Ethics*, *The European Journal of Marketing*, *Tourism Management*, *The Journal of Consumer Behaviour*, *Local Economy* and the *Journal of Macromarketing*.

S. Sreejesh is an Assistant Professor of Marketing at the Indian Institute of Management Kozhikode, India. His research is published in prominent outlets such as *Industrial Marketing Management, European Journal of Marketing, Journal of Advertising Research, Computers in Human Behaviour, Journal of Brand Management, Journal of Product and Brand Management, Journal of Service Theory and Practice,* and many others. He serves on the editorial board of *International Journal of Consumer Studies* and has authored books with Pearson and Springer International.

Chin Shinyi is a doctoral candidate at the School of Media and Communication at RMIT University. Her research interests are digital marketing and social marketing with a focus on promoting and encouraging positive behaviour change by furthering our understanding of how and why people use digital technologies.

Carolyn Strong is a Reader in Marketing at Cardiff Business School. She has been an active learning and teaching scholar for over 30 years. She has published in the *Services Industries Journal, Journal of Strategic Marketing, Journal of Business Research, European Journal of Marketing*. More recently she has published in *Journal of Business Research, International Journal of Information, International Journal of Consumer Studies, Marketing Letters* and the *European Journal of Marketing*. She is Editor in Chief of the *Journal of Strategic Marketing*. She currently researches and consults in social, ethical and environmental research, the key theme of this work examines how marketing can contribute positively to society.

Park Thaichon is the Cluster Leader of the Relationship Marketing for Impact research cluster, Griffith Business School. He is an Associate Editor of *Australasian Marketing Journal* and *Journal of Strategic Marketing*. He is a member of Griffith Institute for Tourism and Griffith Asia Institute. His research, teaching and consulting focus is around relationship marketing, digital marketing, technology, and consumer behaviour. He is open for research collaboration, consulting projects and commercial research with industry.

Ekant Veer is a Professor of Marketing and the Director of the Christchurch Knowledge Commons at the University of Canterbury, Christchurch, New Zealand. He is a multi-award winning teacher and researcher having been named in the Top 40 under 40 Business School Professors worldwide; an Ako Aotearoa Tertriary Teaching Excellence Award winner; UC's Teaching Medal awardee in 2017 and five times winner of the UCSA's lecturer of the year award. His work looks at the role that marketing can play in both driving social change and community wellbeing as well as what impact digital technology plays in consumer interactions and their sense of identity. His research has been published in numerous international journals, such as the *Journal of Marketing Management*, *The European Journal of Marketing*, and *The Journal of Public Policy and Marketing*. Professor Veer has recently taken on the role as Director of the Christchurch Knowledge Commons which looks to support the University of Canterbury's commitment to kotahitanga [partnerships] and engagement between tertiary sector and businesses, community and the public sector.

Sy Nurleyana Wafa is a PhD candidate at the School of Media and Communication at RMIT University. Her research focuses on the use of augmented reality in marketing communications, specifically aimed at understanding how the industry perceives the use of this technology. Her research interests include immersive technologies, advertising, and consumer behaviour.

Scott Weaven is a Professor and Head of the Department of Marketing at Griffith University. His recent research has focused on examining digital, relational and hybridized methods of international market entry, e-commerce and encroachment issues in franchise systems, hybrid sales structures and consumer sentiment analysis and market segmentation in a variety of business contexts. Scott serves as an assessor for the Netherlands Organisation for Scientific Research (NOW) for joint European research projects in the social sciences and the Australian Research Council, and is regularly consulted by government on policy issues (e.g. Parliamentary Joint Committee on Corporations and Financial Services Inquiry into the Franchise Code of Conduct 2010, 2019). He been successful in securing A$ 2m in research funding from the Australian Research Council (with the Australian Competition and Consumer Commission, Franchising Council of Australia) and has conducted a number of consultancy projects for the private and public sectors (e.g., the Department of Industry Innovation and Science, Franchise Council of Australia, CFLD International, CPA Australia).

Amy Yau is a lecturer in the Marketing and Strategy section at Cardiff University. She received her PhD titled "People, Places and Spaces: Theorising Consumer Re-enculturation" from University of Bath in 2016. Her research involves exploring various aspects of consumer research and socio-cultural marketing through the use of qualitative methods. Dr Yau's research areas include consumer acculturation and global mobility, sustainable and ethical consumption, social media, creative small businesses and entrepreneurship.

Kseniia Zahrai's research looks at the ethical and appropriate use of social media and digital technologies by consumers. Her PhD, from the University of Canterbury, specifically looked at the role that self-control and other constructs play mediating the ill-effects of social media on mental well-being among users. Her work has been published in the Journal of Marketing Management as well as being instrumental in the development of practices to promote well-being in young consumers in New Zealand. She is currently a research associate at the University of Canterbury.

Index

https://doi.org/10.1515/9783110659566-015

www.ingramcontent.com/pod-product-compliance
Lightning Source LLC
Chambersburg PA
CBHW051116200326
41518CB00016B/2525